GENE KILGORE
RANCH
VACATIONS
2016

UNITED STATES
CANADA
MEXICO
ARGENTINA

ABOUT GENE KILGORE

In 1960, at the age of seven, Gene Kilgore visited his first dude ranch in Jackson Hole, Wyoming. Trail Creek Ranch left an indelible memory, and one that you might say resulted in this guide. It was Gene's dream to become a doctor, and he followed this pursuit to medical school. It was there that he realized his heart and soul were meant to be outdoors where the buffalo roam. In 1980, he left to follow his heart, with a vision of being involved in guest ranching. And what a journey it has been. In 1980 he created the Kilgore Ranch Company. Today, Gene Kilgore's name is synonymous with one of the world's great traditions. He has travelled thousands of miles exploring ranches in the United States, Canada, and South America, bringing ranch country to millions of people worldwide. As a best selling author, Kilgore has appeared on radio programs and numerous TV networks including CNN, ABC's Regis and Kathy Lee, CBS, and has been featured in the New York Times, People Magazine, National Geographic Traveler, and Sunset. He is one of the first lifetime members of the Dude Ranchers' Association. As Gene says, "It is my hope that my guide and RanchWeb will help travelers discover, like I did 55 years ago, the magic and beauty of these beautiful ranches and the wonderful men and women who run them."

ACKNOWLEDGMENTS

Special thanks to Sarah Paynter and Sheri Elkins for typing and editing the ninth edition, to Stephanie Long, production coordinator and graphic designer for all her great work, to my son for sharing his thoughts in his beautiful foreward, and to all the ranchers who have shared their homes and lives with me all these years.

SADDLE UP   3 6109 00515 7471

We are always working to make each guide better than the last, and welcome your ideas, suggestions, and thoughts. Your comments are very important. Please contact us at: suggestions@RanchWeb.com

"The book you're about to read is more than a guide to the best vacations on earth. This is a book about dreams–the kind of ranches you just didn't know existed until Gene's book showed us the way. And what a way it is! It's a map to shining places in the heart of America, and a reminder of a truth as fresh and timeless as the scent of wild sage."

— Merv Griffin

Dude Ranch Testimonials

"Like all classics, you have to start with the original. Gene Kilgore has dedicated his life's work to our industry and has set the foundation for others to follow. We have benefitted from his commitment. He is the leader in the field, and we are very grateful."

—G.C., Wyoming

"I want to express my overwhelming appreciation for all your efforts. Keep up the good work. You are the authority in this field."

— K.J., Colorado

"We stand in awe! You're like having all the railroads rolled into one and then accomplishing even more. You have worked marvels. Your book is done with such care, such insight, and with the knack of leading potential guests to the ranch that will be right. It's as if a friend were advising each person as to the place that would suit him best. We appreciate you very, very much."

— J.M., Arizona

"The dude ranch is a wonderful thing for America and the world. You surely have done more than anyone to foster the idea.

— B.F., Wyoming

Foreword

There is nothing like being on a ranch. From your arrival down a dusty drive-way, ranch country beckons: the gentle rocking of your truck over well-worn potholes; the sweet smell of sage wafting through the open windows; a distant horse's neigh. And in the morning, when you put your cowboy boots and tuck them into your extra-long blue jeans, you join an historic culture, one that brings real adventure just outside your cabin door. When you're on a ranch, you're ready to ride.

I've grown up visiting ranches and though each is different, there's something special that makes a ranch a ranch. Each boasts captivating outdoors and views punctuated by vivid sunsets; rushing sounds of mountain rivers and melodic bird songs; sweet, wild smells of evergreens and horses. After invigorating days on horse-back, or fishing in crystal-clear streams, guests will find a perfect place to relax, whether in a cozy lodge or on the deck of a rustic cabin. One of the most special of ranch ingredients is that they bring out the best in people. When you get together with ranch hands and other guests, you're a part of the family. And over the course of a few days or a few weeks, you'll grow to miss the friends you made on your ranch vacation. Not to mention the food! From cowboy cornbread to culinary delicacies, after a long day of ranch life the food is fantastic.

Our 21st Century life-style often barrages us with information from all directions. There is so much to do, it's hard to find just a few, good things in the noise. The beauty of the west is that it takes you away from that, from the overwhelming routine of city life—it gives you a chance to escape technology and enjoy the great outdoors without distraction. For at least one evening on the ranch, stay up late, look at the sky, and experience the stunning and silent fullness of a starry, western night. Once you feel the breath-taking grandeur of the Milky Way, you'll know what it's like to be connected.

People love asking me about my favorite ranch, and the truth is, I don't have one. Each ranch is unique and provides a wholly different experience for every guest. With so many excellent options, choosing the right ranch can be overwhelming. The key to ranch country is in a book – this book. It will act as a guide, and, I hope, as a friend. Sitting in a comfortable chair by the fire and flipping through its pages is a great way to dive into the many opportunities to find a customized, one-of-a-kind vacation with memories to last a lifetime.

I've been lucky enough to call Gene Kilgore—the man who put it all together—my dad, and I know he truly loves to share what he does. We hope you enjoy this book and the promise of ranch country that comes with it – we know we sure have.

Happy Trails,

W. Francisco Kilgore

Greetings, Travelers!

Welcome to the 2016 edition of Ranch Vacations. It is hard to believe that I am celebrating thirty-six years in Dude Ranching. It is even harder to believe that I have written nine editions over the past thirty-six years. Time really does fly!

Today the world of ranching offers so much more that it did when I began. And yet, the essential authentic qualities that make this so special have remained constant - hospitality second to none, the great outdoors, and nature. Horses are still a vital aspect, but today only part of the story. Many years ago, I said on CNN: "Take a child to a beach and ask them ten years later to name the beach, and they will have forgotten. Take them to a ranch, and they will remember its name, and their horse's name for the rest of their lives." And that is really true. Today I like to say about ranching, that it is all about "Good people, good horses, beautiful places and darn good food."

Ranch life, as far as I can see, remains one of the last authentic traditions in a landscape of technology where everything is instantaneous and up in the air. Ranching is a down to earth thing that helps us to reconnect with the natural rhythm of the earth, not the frantic ways of modern day life. Its goodness is so soothing and centering. The only real challenge is to get the time off to ride from your city to wherever you decide in the United States, Canada, Mexico, or Argentina.

I said earlier, ranch vacations today offer much more than just horseback riding. In fact, you don't even have to like horses or horseback riding to enjoy the properties described in this guide. Some ranches today offer fly-fishing, gourmet dining, tennis, swimming, white-water rafting, natural history guides, massage, spa treatments, yoga, and more. Quite simply, what makes these vacations so special are their wholesome and unforgettable adventures in nature. Everyone—grandparents, children, singles, and families—can find a ranch vacation to suit them. Ranches also offer facilities to professional groups, corporations, schools, and churches for seminars, retreats, and workshops. They also offer wonderful opportunities for family reunions, weddings, and honeymoons. Ranch vacations offer one of the greatest vacation opportunities in the world today.

More than ever, people are seeking relief from the ever-increasing stresses of our fast-paced world. There is no better way for families and individuals to unwind, recharge batteries, gain perspective, reconfirm values, spend time with family members, meet interesting people from around the world, and most of all, experience the natural beauty and tranquility of the outdoors, than on a ranch vacation. As we go faster and faster in our everyday personal and business lives, I believe we will listen more and more to the call of the wild of getting back to nature and Mother Earth. Indeed, the more advanced we become technologically, the more we will crave the simpler pleasures of life: Nature, home-cooked meals, kindness, and sincere hospitality.

This guide will put you in touch with a wonderful, unique group of ranches and people who offer an incredible life-enhancing experience; a way of life; a vacation to be enjoyed by both the young and the young at heart.

WANTED
Guests from around the world

You're about to begin one of your most exciting adventures: selecting the right ranch for you, your family, your friends, your company, or your clients. So sit back and relax, maybe prop your feet up on your desk or settle into your favorite chair in front of a blazing fire. My goal is to help you discover the right ranch for you. Unlike any other holiday experience that I know of, the secret to this one is chemistry. And just like a marriage, if the chemistry is good, the experience is golden. If not, as an old cowboy once told me, "Better saddle up and ride on."

As you turn the pages, you'll begin to explore this wholesome, real and authentic vacation that is guaranteed to touch your heart and soul. Be sure to visit www.Ranchweb.com for more information. And just in case you need a little more help, you are welcome to give our office a call. We are always delighted to help — 707-217-5205.

Finally, and maybe most important of all, when contacting ranches be sure to ask for guest references - folks who have been to the ranch or visit TripAdvisor.com, many ranches are profiled and reviewed there. This will help you confirm which property fits your needs and desires. We also highly recommend that you call ranches you are interested in and talk with them personally. They always appreciate a phone call, and you will learn so much!

What Readers are saying

"Thanks to your fantastic guide, we have visited six ranches over the years!" — H.T., Connecticut

"I love your book! I am so glad you've taken the time to write about what I love so much dude ranches!" — H.W., California

"An excellent publication." — M.B., Australia

"If you are a fan of ranch life, Gene Kilgore's woven tapestries of discerning descriptions and available services form an indispensable guide book on this thrilling subject of Americana." — J.N., California

"Ranch Vacations arrived today. It's just terrific! I love the forward and find its organization so helpful. Congratulations on a great job."
— D.O., California

"I recently purchased your book on ranch vacations and have read a cover to cover. Excellent!!"–D.S., New Jersey

"I have enjoyed your publication and only wish that more families would experience the pleasures of guest ranching." — R.G., Georgia

"I was asked to choose a location for a small working meeting (50-60 participants) …a friend gave me your guest ranch guide, and it was indeed a boon! We are now in process of making a final decision, and I wanted to write a thank you for the help you're guide provided."
— L.D., California

Dedication

To all the ranchers who reconnect us with the natural rhythm of the earth and share their wonderful and needed way of life.

To Regina, my loving wife, who is the wind beneath my wings. To our son Francisco — you are my inspiration.

Favorite Quotes

"Kindness transforms the world... travel unites it."

"We have gentle horses for gentle people,
Spirited horses for spirited people,
And for people who don't like to ride,
We have horses that don't like to be ridden."
—Colorado rancher

"There is something about the outside of a horse that is good
for the inside of a man."
—Winston Churchill

"You can get in a car to see what man has created, but you have to get
on a horse to see what God has created"
—C.M. Russell

"Thousands of tired, nerve-shaken, over-civilized people are beginning
to find out that going to the mountains is going home; the wilderness is a
necessity; and that mountain parks and reservations are useful not only as
fountains of lumber and irrigation routers, but as fountains of life."
—John Muir

"From the forest and the wilderness
come the tonics and barks which brace mankind."
—Henry David Thoreau

"All America lies in the end of the wilderness road, and our past is not a
dead past, but still lives in us. Our forefathers had a civilization inside
themselves, the wild outside. We live in the civilization they created, but
within us the wilderness still lingers. What they dreamed, we live, and what
they lived, we dream."
—T.K. Whipple

"Our world in steel and speed is sometimes a trap in which we become en-
slaved as we chase after the materialism of life. Thus, we have a tendency
to forget that which we too often take for granted:
Nature's wondrous beauty."
—Bruce Harvey, Queenstown, New Zealand

"Of all the teachings we receive this is one of the most important: Nothing
belongs to you. Of what there is, of what you take, you must share."
—Sioux Teaching

"There are precious moments when the mind is quiet and I enjoy
my senses with no interference."
—Brian Tedrick

"The Earth does not belong to man, man belongs to the Earth. All things
are connected like blood which unites us all. Man did not weave the web of
life, he is merely a strand in it. Whatever he does to the web,
he does to himself."
—Chief Sealth (Seattle), Suquamish Indian Tribe

Ranchweb.com

The leading online travel guide to the very best ranch vacations in the world.

In 1995, Ranchweb was created to bring the world the very best ranch vacations! Today, it is recognized as the leading internet site bringing travelers the very best of ranch country.

We hope you will use Ranchweb.com in collaboration with the guide you are holding in your hands to book your next memorable ranch vacation.

Wishing you and yours many more happy trails as you ride into ranch country.

Table of Contents

Appendix

17

A Brief History of Dude Ranching

Ranching began centuries ago in central and south America and over time headed north to the Americas and Canada. Long before there were big cities, trains, planes and fast cars, men and women made their living raising cattle and living off the land. Today, whether in North or South America, while many things have changed in ranching, the core values of camarderie, love of the land and livestock remain. The very essence of ranching continues to be something that, you might say, helps us all to be connected with the land and offers so many valuable lessons about life, animals and nature.

The beginning of ranch vacations started in South America, where gauchos and estancias with thousands of acres welcomed guests to savor the rich traditions that still exist today. Similarly, in the early 1900's, ranches in the United States and Canada began to welcome guests. The ranch vacation industry was born, and became known to all as Dude Ranching. This caught on, and over the years has evolved into a sizeable industry, hosting collectively thousands of families, couples, and singles seeking relief from the pressures of big city life.

American ranch vacations can be traced to the days of Theodore Roosevelt's Rough Riders in the late 19th century. As the story goes, the Eaton Brothers—Howard, Willis, and Alden—established a hay and horse ranch near Medora, North Dakota, in 1879. Soon, friends from the East headed west by train to be a part of the Eatons' new and exciting life. Before they knew it, the Eatons were baby-sitting these big-city dudes, taking them out to help with the chores and cattle. The more the dudes did and the dirtier they became, the happier they were.

Word spread, and soon more of these early-day city slickers came out and fell in love with the rugged simplicity of the West and all it gave them. In those days, visitors came by train—not for a week, but for months at a time. One guest was so at home on the range that he asked Howard Eaton if he could pay room and board in order to stay on. This exchange of money gave birth to an industry.

In 1926, The Dude Ranchers' Association held its first meeting. This association is more active today than ever. It is dedicated to preserving and maintaining high standards in the west.

In general, the underlying theme of today's ranch vacation, wherever the ranch may be in the world, is the horse. Most of the properties included in this guide provide a variety of riding opportunities—for beginner, intermediate, and advanced riders. Every ranch is different, expressing the personality of the terrain as well as that of the host or owner.

Today, while most of the properties are preserving ranch life, many also are keeping up with the present by providing modern amenities and services. Besides horseback riding programs, many offer swimming, mountain biking, fishing, hiking, rodeos, tennis, skeet shooting, hayrides, massage, naturalist talks, art, and photography workshops.

Ranch vacations enable parents to vacation with their children in a setting where both learn an appreciation for animals and nature. In addition, on a ranch vacation, people of all ages, from all walks of life, can interact socially, intellectually, and artistically in a marvelously wholesome, intimate, and unique atmosphere. Accommodations range from very rustic cabins (even sleeping under the stars) to luxury suites. Some have natural hot-spring pools, golf, and tennis; others feature whirlpool spas, saunas, exercise equipment, and even massage. Ranches that take guests include guest ranches, resort ranches, working cattle ranches, fly-fishing ranches, pack-trip ranches, and cross-country skiing ranches. They can be found throughout the United States, Canada, Mexico, and South America. Native ranch customs, architecture, equipment, and clothing vary, too. If you want to see adobe buildings and mesquite and enjoy arid, warm temperatures, there is a property in this guide for you. If the saw-toothed Rocky Mountains are more to your liking, you can experience that, too. Each region offers different attractions and activities. Finally, ranches have different weather and landscapes depending where they are located. While the location and climate vary, one thing usually remains the same: Down-home hospitality.

On Being a Good Dude

The perfect dude takes it easy the first two days at the ranch and works into the program slowly. "Relax, unwind, don't push too hard too fast," said one rancher to a young Wall Street broker. He added, "Remember, you'll be able to come back year after year for the rest of your life." Most of all, the ability to relax and have fun is essential to being the perfect dude.

Selecting a Ranch

The ranches included in this guide offer a wide range of choices. The most challenging part of your vacation will be selecting where you want to go. As rates are in constant fluctuation, we have chosen to use the following rate codes:

$ = $0-100 per person per day
$$ = $100-150
$$$ = $150-250
$$$$ = $250-300
$$$$$ = $300-400
$$$$$$ = $400 and up

For the most part, rates listed are for American Plans with meals, lodging, and activities included. When you're confirming your reservation, we recommend you verify the rates and exactly what they include.

We suggest you telephone and speak personally with the owners or managers; you can get a pretty good feel for things by phone. Ask for a brochure and the names of several past guests you might contact. Call them and ask what sort of time they had, if they have children, too, and if they had any special considerations like yours. Perhaps the most important thing of all in ranch travel is chemistry between the owner/manager/staff and you, their guest.The following are some questions you might ask when you call a ranch.

Questions to Ask

Highly Recommended: It is strongly suggested that individual properties are contacted directly to confirm information presented.

Also, we recommend that you ask ranches for references, and or visit TripAdvisor.com.

Rates

• What are your rates?
• What is the tipping/gratuity policy? (Rates don't always include gratuities or all activities.)
• Are there special rates for families, children, seniors, or corporations?
• Do you have a non-riding rate?
• Are there off-season rates?
• Is there a minimum length of stay?
• Besides state and local taxes, what do your rates not include?

Vacationing with Children

- Is this a child-oriented ranch?
- Does the ranch have a children's program? What does it include?
- What age must children be to ride? (Today's insurance regulations may not allow very young children to ride.)
- Is child care provided, and to what extent?
- Are parents welcome in children's activities?
- Can children ride with parents?
- Can parents ride with children?
- Do children eat separately?
- Can children eat together?

Horses and Riding

- What kind of riding program does the ranch have?
- What kind of rides are there: Morning, afternoon, all-day, side-by-side, slow to fast?
- Is it open-meadow riding, or mountain-trail riding?
- How long are typical rides?
- Are riding lessons available?
- What style of horsemanship do you use or teach?
- Is the program best suited to beginners, or are there opportunities for intermediate and advanced riders, too?
- If I'm an intermediate or advanced rider, can I trot or lope?
- Do the owners/managers take part in the riding program?
- How many wranglers and guests go out on rides at a time?
- Do I get the same horse all week?
- Can I brush and saddle my own horse?
- Are riding helmets required? Are they provided? Can I bring my own helmet?
- Do I need my own cowboy boots, or is there a boot rental program?
- Can I bring my own saddle?
- Can I bring my own horse?
- Are there non-riding days? Do I ride all days of the week?
- Will I need to sign an assumption of risk or waiver form before riding?

Cattle Work

- How many cattle do you run?
- Do guests participate in all cattle activities?
- Can guests brand with the cowboys?
- Do you teach roping?
- Do you teach cattle or team penning?

Miscellaneous

- Is there a staff naturalist?
- Are there enough activities at the ranch for non-riding or non-fishing members of a family?
- Will the ranch cater to special diets? (Some have vegetarian, low-salt, and low-cholesterol menus.)
- Will the ranch provide guest references?
- Are there special clothing requirements?
- Will the ranch provide a clothing/equipment list? (Usually standard procedure.)
- What equipment does the ranch provide? (Fishing rods, tennis rackets, etc.)
- Do I need a license to fish? Should I buy one before I arrive?
- What will the weather be like?
- Can we buy sundry items at the ranch? (Not all ranches have stores on premises.)
- Do you provide airport, train, or bus pickup? (Many ranches are happy to pick you up. There is often a nominal charge.)
- Do you recommend rental cars? (In most instances, once you arrive, you'll not want to leave the ranch. However, you may opt for flexibility and independence.)
- Are laundry facilities available? (Many ranches have laundry facilities; some will even do your laundry.)
- What is your liquor policy? (Many ranches ask that you bring your own wine or liquor. If desired, you can pick these up on your way, or the ranch will get them for you, with advance notice. Some ranches offer wine and Beer, and a number have fully licensed bars and extensive wine lists.)
- Are any foreign languages spoken?
- Are pets allowed?
- What is the elevation of the ranch?
- Are there wheelchair facilities?
- What is your smoking policy?
- Are there nonsmoking rooms?
- Do you provide internet access?
- Do you allow cellular telephones?
- Do you have Wi-Fi?

Getting There

Whatever method of transportation you choose, it's a good idea to check with the ranch or lodge before you make travel plans. Your hosts will advise you about roads, major commercial airports, and private airstrips. They'll also tell you whether they are able to pick you up.

What to Wear

Clothing is an essential part of the ranch vacation experience. It's important to pack correctly, and bring clothes that will enable you to enjoy your Western experience—a pair of boots, several pairs of jeans, a good cowboy belt with a buckle, a cowboy hat, several shirts, and a warm jacket are about all you'll really need. Over the years, after hundreds of miles on horseback and thousands of miles in automobiles and airplanes, I know quality clothing is better than quantity. (Well, I guess that goes for most everything in life.)

Here are a few Gene Kilgore clothing tips: Along with quality, think comfort.

1. Invest in a good pair of boots and a cowboy hat. Make sure your boots are well-worn before you arrive—you don't want blisters.

2. Buy at least three pairs of extra long jeans and wash them at least four times, using softener. They'll be much more comfortable and will have faded a bit.

3. Take along a warm jacket, a sweater, and even a vest. Early mornings and evenings can be cool.

Finally, when making your reservation, ask the ranch or lodge to send you a clothing list to help with your packing. The ranch or lodge you've selected will be more than happy to give you all the advice you require. And pardner, one last thing: Don't forget a flashlight, some lip protection, mosquito repellent, and sunblock.

Essential Quick Check List

Boots (Riding and hiking)
Socks
Jeans (Three pairs, washed and longer than normal length)
Long sleeved shirts and T-shirts
Cowboy hat, and a cap with a visor
Warm jacket and vest
Sport bras
Rain gear
Comfortable sleepwear
Gloves
Bathing suit
Canteen or refillable water bottle
Sunglasses
Sunscreen
Toiletries
Books for downtime
Binoculars
Bug spray
Camera
Laundry bag

List of Ranches (Alphabetical)

THE
RANCHES

——— ✳ ———

ARIZONA

Circle Z Ranch
Patagonia, Arizona

The Circle Z Ranch, founded in 1926, is nestled in a picturesque mountain valley at 4,000 feet, surrounded by colorful hills and dramatic mountain backdrops. The Circle Z is romantic, with its adobe buildings reflecting Spanish influences and early West simplicity. Circle Z is run by delightful resident managers and has been owned since 1974 by Lucia Nash, who fell in love with it when brought here by her family as a child. Ranch-bred horses and a variety of trails, coupled with delicious food and warm hospitality, bring guests back year after year. Circle Z is also recognized worldwide by birders who flock here to see some of the rarest species in the United States. You'll find all the easygoing pleasures of dude ranch life here; ride, relax, and unplug.

Address: P.O. Box 194, Patagonia, Arizona 85624

Telephone: 888/854-2525, 520/394-2525

Website: www.circlez.com

Airport: Tucson International or Phoenix Sky Harbor; private planes can fly to Nogales, 15 minutes away

Location: 60 miles south of Tucson, directly off Highway 82; 15 miles north of the Mexican border

Memberships: The Dude Ranchers' Association, Arizona Dude Ranch Association, American Quarter Horse Association

Guest Capacity: 40

Accommodations: Charming and comfortable. There are seven adobe country cottages with Southwest touches. Twenty-four rooms with private baths and showers. Laundry facilities and modem access available.

Rates: $$$- $$$$ American Plan.

Season: November to mid-May

Activities: Experienced wranglers lead twice-daily, all-day, scenic and picnic rides on a remarkable variety of trails across 5,500 acres of deeded ranch land and the contiguous Coronado National Forest. Rides are broken into small groups according to level of ability. Riding instruction, hiking, swimming in outdoor heated pool, and an-all weather tennis court.

Children's Programs: No planned Children's program. Children begin riding at age five with parental assistance. Table tennis, shuffleboard, horseshoes and basketball.

Dining: Ranch specialties include regional Southwestern dishes, home-baked breads, and desserts. Adult Cantina. BYOB.

Summary: One of Arizona's best! Easygoing spirit and charm prevail! Excellent riding and hiking. Unstructured other than riding and meals. Internationally known bird watcher's paradise at ranch and adjacent Nature Conservancy preserve.

Elkhorn Ranch
Tucson, Arizona

The Millers' Elkhorn Ranch is old-time dude ranching at its best! At 3,700 feet, the ranch sits in a secluded valley, surrounded by the picturesque Baboquivari Mountain Range, with canyons, rolling hills, mesquite, and open desert to the east. The ranch is small, informal, and well out of the city, with activities centering on the outdoors. It's a lovely part of the Southwest. The Miller family has been operating this riding ranch since 1945; today, it's run by the third generation — Charley and Mary Miller and Tom and Anne Miller. The Elkhorn offers excellent riding and a relaxed way of life for 32 guests. The ranch spirit encourages family group fun, but offers lots of time to be alone if you wish. The cabins and ranch buildings are designed in a Southwestern architectural style. With 10,000 acres and over 100 horses, unlimited riding and hiking are assured. The less adventurous can relax by the pool or outside each cabin. Bring your camera and binoculars — Arizona's birds are numerous.

Address: 27000 W Elkhorn Ranch Road, Tucson, Arizona 85736
Telephone: 520/822-1040
Website: www.elkhornranch.com
Airport: Tucson
Location: 50 miles southwest of Tucson, off Route 286, between mileposts 25 and 26
Memberships: The Dude Ranchers' Association, Arizona Dude Ranch Association, Altar Valley Conservation Alliance
Guest Capacity: 32
Accommodations: Guests enjoy Southwestern-style cabins that vary from one to two bedrooms, some with a sitting room and some with open fireplaces with mesquite firewood, all with private baths and electric heat. Cabins have tiled and cement floors with Mexican throw rugs, some original art, and all with bird feeders. Daily maid service and nightly bed turndown service.
Rates: $$$ - $$$$ American Plan.
Season: Mid-November through April
Activities: Some of the best riding in the country. Each morning at breakfast, Charley Miller meets with guests to discuss riding interests and options. As Charley says, "With six guides, we can keep our rides small. If someone really wants to ride, we sure try to accommodate them." And he does! With more than 100 horses, all levels of guided riding are provided on desert or mountain trails. All day and picnic rides. Tennis court and kidney-shaped, 50-foot heated swimming pool. Shuffleboard, table tennis, and horseshoe pitching are offered, as well as great country for bird-watching and hiking.
Children's Programs: Children of all ages are welcome, but are the responsibility of their parents.
Dining: Delicious home-cooked meals served buffet-style.
Summary: One of the old-time greats! Secluded among thousands of acres of unspoiled country, and run by one of the nicest families in the business. Many repeat families, couples, and singles. Newcomers always feel a part of the family, and family reunions are always welcome! Superb desert and mountain riding. Excellent ranch-raised horses and one of the best ranch riding programs in the country for all levels of horsemanship. Beginners can learn here, and advanced riders can be challenged. Great birding. Near Arizona-Sonora Desert Museum, Kitt Peak Observatory, Tubac, the Tohono O'odham Reservation, and the old Spanish missions of San Xavier and Tumacacori.

Flying E Ranch
Wickenburg, Arizona

The Flying E Dude ranch was established in 1946, and is hosted today by Andrea Taylor and fine staff. Experience a down-home, guest and working cattle ranch, hosting families, couples and singles that come to savor the ranch's wonderful spirit and friendly hospitality. Located in the Hassayampa Valley on the north edge of the Sonoran Desert, just four miles west of Wickenburg. Known as the "riding ranch" with an elevation of 2,400 ft and 20,000 acres of endless trails to ride and roam. Warm days, starlit nights, beautiful desert scenery, relaxed ambiance, family camaraderie, and privacy keep guests returning year after year. Only 17 rooms, the ranch offers wonderful food, served up family style, comfortable, clean accommodations, good horses for every rider, and fun activities in a friendly, informal ranch atmosphere.

Address: 2801 W Wickenburg Way, Wickenburg, AZ 85390
Telephone: 888/684-2650, 928/684-2690
Website: www.flyingeranch.com
Airports: Phoenix, Sky Harbor, Private plans and executive jets land at Wickenburg Municipal Airport (Wellik Field), across from the ranch
Location: On Highway 60, approximately 70 miles northwest of Phoenix Sky Harbor Airport: four miles west of Wickenburg's town center
Memberships: The Dude Ranchers' Association, The Arizona Dude Ranch association
Guest Capacity: 34
Accommodations: Guest rooms are immaculately clean, comfortable, electrically heated and air-conditioned, with delightful Western décor. All rooms have private baths, refrigerators, and wet bars.
Rates: $$$ American Plan.
Season: November to May
Activities: Two hour morning and afternoon horseback rides. The riding program includes beginner, intermediate, and advanced levels. Instruction available. Breakfast cookouts, lunch rides, Dutch oven cookouts and chuck wagon feeds with sunset rides. Beautiful heated pool with attached Jacuzzi, exercise room and sauna, shuffleboard, basketball, volleyball, horseshoe pitching, rock hounding, lighted tennis court, and miles and miles of hiking trails. Team penning offers the cowpoke a chance to work with the cattle and on special occasions you can experience a square dance in the barn loft.
Children's Programs: This is a family ranch where children and parents participate in activities together, no separate children's programs offered.
Dining: Offering delicious ranch food, including a made or order breakfast, buffet lunch, and a family style dinner in our lodge dinning room.
Summary: George and Vi Wellik established the Flying E Ranch. Today, host Andrea Taylor welcomes families to experience the ways of the west, and to find the magic the ranch extends to families and friends. The Flying E is a very special place.

Grand Canyon Bar 10 Ranch
In Arizona, near St. George, Utah

The lodge at the Bar 10 Ranch is located about nine miles from the north rim of the Grand Canyon. From this sandstone-brick lodge, you can see the distant grandeur of the canyon cliffs. For years, the Bar 10 Ranch has been a starting and ending point for guests on Colorado River rafting trips. The history and excitement of the Grand Canyon and the Colorado River are yours at the Bar 10, a working cattle ranch that boasts 60,000 acres and 400 head of cattle. The Heaton family hosts guests who come to experience Colorado River rafting trips and ranch tour packages. The Bar 10 offers a unique blend of remoteness and modern comforts. One guest wrote, "You have created an experience that enriches the lives of your guests! The Bar 10 Ranch is an unforgettable experience!" Hearty country meals, varied ranch activities, and genuine Western hospitality provide guests with a lasting Grand Canyon ranch experience! The Bar 10 office can be your one-stop shopping site for ranch tours and/or reservations with any of the numerous Grand Canyon river-rafting companies.

Address: P.O. Box 910088, St. George, Utah 84791
Telephone: 800/582-4139, 435/628-4010
Website: www.bar10.com
Airports: McCarren International, Las Vegas, Nevada; St. George Airport, Utah; direct charter flights from Las Vegas and St. George available; 4,280-foot by 40-foot runway at the ranch (radio frequency 122.9)
Location: 80 miles south of St. George, Utah (two-hour drive on dirt road, 30-minute flight); 200 miles east of Las Vegas (four-hour drive, 50-minute flight); most guests fly in
Guest Capacity: 50 overnight, more for day groups
Accommodations: For the adventurous, there are covered wagons for private sleeping on the hillside behind the main lodge — great for couples. Surrounded by lawns and desert landscape, the two-story Bar 10 lodge has comfortable dormitory-style rooms with bunk beds and common bathrooms. The main floor of the lodge is home to the Bar 10 Trading Post, which sells supplies, books, gifts, snacks, T-shirts, and other souvenirs.
Rates: $$ American Plan. Call for custom and package rates. Airfare, ATV tours, and helicopter rides extra.
Season: May through September; off-season dates available
Activities: The Bar 10 Ranch offers a variety of activities and tour packages, including Colorado River rafting trips, overnight packages consisting of one or more days at the ranch, wagon train, ATV tours, horseback pack trips, and scenic flights combined with part- or full-day ranch adventures. Ranch activities may include horseback riding, horseshoes, ranch demonstrations, trapshooting, hiking, billiards, volleyball, line dancing, and other group activities. Scenic helicopter rides available most days during the peak season (extra).
Children's Programs: No specific programs, but youth groups are welcome.
Dining: Cowboy, Dutch-oven dinners. BYOB.
Summary: Wonderful remote ranch located about nine miles from the north rim of the Grand Canyon, specializing in ranch tours and spectacular river-rafting packages. Many families, couples, business/incentive groups, and youth groups come for the day, some stay overnight, and others stay longer for various adventure programs. Most guests arrive by helicopter or airplane.

Hideout Ranch
Portal, Arizona

Hideout Ranch, a working cattle and guest ranch on the Arizona-New Mexico border, is founded on passion for ranching, horses, and cattle, combined with a deep appreciation for the role each played in settling the American West, underscored with an abiding love of history. Owners Craig and Tamara J Lawson offer an authentic and unique western experience, blending the great outdoors, fascinating local history, and breathtaking vistas on every trail. Centered between two majestic mountain-ranges - the Chiricahua of Arizona's and the Peloncillo of New Mexico - Hideout Ranch sits in the picturesque san Bernadiono Valley, with horseback riding at the center of ranch activities. The Lawsons guide guests along ancient mountain trails, across the desert floor, through washes carved by centuries of monsoon waters rushing off the mountains. Having already set their own inner cowboys on the trail to discovery, they ride side by side with guests, sharing the freedom of riding the range, gathering and moving cattle from pasture to pasture or into the corrals for branding and tagging. From horseback, the fabled wide open spaces stretch out from sunrise to sunset, and winter to spring, filling memories and campfire conversations for years to come.

Address: 11841 N. Hideout Ranch Road, Portal, AZ 856332
Telephone: 520/558-4433
Website: www.hideoutranch.com
Airports: Tucson, Arizona, and El Paso, Texas
Location: Fifty miles northeast of Douglas, Arizona, a historic border town, 150 miles from both Tucson, Arizona and El Pasoo, Texas
Guest Capacity: 12
Accommodations: Guests enjoy comfortable lodgings tucked inside the Coraonado National Forest. There are three cottages, two lodges with individual apartments, and a large ranch house, sleeping two to six depending upon the individual accommodation and the needs of our guests. Wildlife and scenic views are abundant, and the stay augments the Hideout Ranch experience perfectly.
Rates: $$$$ American Plan.
Season: Activities: Horseback riding is the main activity at Hideout Ranch. Riding and other aspects of horsemanship including trail rides, cattlework, lessons, and groundwork are part of the experience. The trails range from gentle slopes to soaring ridges, and wind through one of America's last pristine wilderness areas. Numerous other activities, all outdooors, are also available including hiking, birding, sight-seeing, and photography.
Children's Programs: No separate children's program.
Dining: Cowboy cooking, prepare authentically over an open fire in Dutch Ovens.
Summary: Guests at Hideout Ranch immediately realize the horses are the center of attention, and riding them is the reason for the ranch. Focusing on horses and riding gives Hideout guests every opportunity to hone their riding and horsemanship skills. The Lawsons have over forty years combined equine experience, and intentionally came to southeastern Arizona to ride, choosing their location specifically because of the easy access to hundreds of miles of mountain trails. Hideout Ranch is also a small working cattle ranch, and spending time with a small herd of purebred Black Angus beef cattle is an exciting extra guests will enjoy. Cowboying is a fading art, but not at the Hideout Ranch. As they say, "to set your inner cowboy on the trail to discovery, come hideout... on horseback."

Rancho de los Caballeros
Wickenburg, Arizona

Rancho de los Caballeros is one of the premier resort ranches in North America and recently celebrated its 67th season. Set amid 20,000 acres of beautiful desert scenery, the ranch has maintained a long tradition of excellence and continues to attract families, individuals, and groups who enjoy a host of recreational activities and first-rate personal service and comfort. Los Caballeros is well known for its 18-hole championship golf course, consistently ranked in the top five in Arizona and the spa at Los Caballeros. Many guests come just to play golf, others to play tennis, horseback ride in the open desert, sit by the pool, or just enjoy the relaxing atmosphere. The ranch offers superb conference facilities in the Palo Verde Conference Center, ideal for small and large groups of up to 175 people. Rancho de los Caballeros means "Ranch of the Gentlemen on Horseback," but it really stands for "excellence." Great people, great resort amenities, great golf, and great riding.

Address: 1551 S. Vulture Mine Road, Wickenburg, Arizona 85390
Telephone: 800/684-5030, 928/684-5484
Website: www.sunc.com
Airports: Phoenix Sky Harbor; private planes at Wickenburg Municipal Airport on a 5,000-foot paved runway, fuel available; call ranch for details
Location: Four miles southwest of Wickenburg; 56 miles northwest of Phoenix on Highway 60
Memberships: Arizona Dude Ranch Association
Guest Capacity: 175
Accommodations: A variety of casitas (79 of them) with sun patios and separate entrances are available. Each room is tastefully decorated in Southwestern style, including handcrafted furnishings from Mexico and Santa Fe. TVs, telephones with data ports, WiFi, and voicemail in all rooms. Business center with Internet access/computer station.
Rates: $$$$$$ American Plan.
Season: October through May
Activities: The ranch offers scenic beginner, intermediate, and loping rides. Riding instruction available. Breakfast, lunch, and dinner cookout rides, and occasional team penning. Full nature program with hikes, bird-watching, and more. Four tennis courts with resident tennis pro, heated swimming pool. Trap and skeet shooting extra; guns and instruction provided. Hot-air ballooning on-site, mountain biking, atv, and Jeep tours. Los Caballeros Golf Club's 18-hole course includes a head pro and several assistants, driving range, pro shop, locker rooms, golf carts, and rental equipment. Ask about the Turner Golf School. Food and beverages available at club grill. Full service spa.
Children's Programs: Excellent morning and evening programs for kids ages 5-12.
Dining: Menu features four-course meals.
Summary: One of the leading ranch resorts in America. Superb in every way. Excellent morning and evening children's programs. This historic guest ranch and golf club offers championship 18-hole golf—one of the top courses in Arizona. Golf and tennis pros on staff. Daily horseback riding. Excellent conference and spa facilities. Near Wickenburg.

Stagecoach Trails Guest Ranch
Yucca, Arizona

As Owner JP McCormick says, "We are literally in the middle of nature. Here we celebrate solitude, beauty and look off to the distant mountains; Buck, Hualappai and Mohave." The guests that come are those that truly appreciate nature and the environment. Some come after visiting the west rim of the spectacular Grand Canyon, and many others just to savor the magic of these incredible lands. Stagecoach Trails welcomes families, couples, singles, and is the only ranch that I know of that offers a full program including riding for the handicapped. It is truly one of a kind of in the world of guest ranches.

Address: 19985 South Doc Holliday Road, Yucca, Arizona 86438
Telephone: 866/444-4471
Website: www.stagecoachtrailsranch.com
Airport: Las Vegas, Nevada 2:15:00 north, Phoenix International 3 hours south
Location: 2 hours 15 minutes southeast of Las Vegas, 3 hours Northwest of Phoenix right off famous route 66
Memberships: Dude Ranchers Association, Arizona Dude Ranchers Association
Guest Capacity: 42
Accommodations: Buildings are Spanish Adobe style stucco all with a southwestern flair. All are decorated with a western theme with names like Rawhide, Stagecoach, Mustang and Outlaw. All rooms and suites are modern with private baths, air conditioning, heat and all handicapped accessible Rates: $$$ American plan.
Season: Year Round
Activities: Rides go out morning and afternoon. For guests staying 4-7 days, there are four-hour lunch rides and an all-day ride to the magnificent Mojave Mountains. Ask about the full moon wagon ride and the optional overnight sleep out under the stars. Hiking, ATV and wagon rides, swimming pool and hot tub. Fat-tire biking trails. Period Target shooting. Campfires and game nights.
Children's Programs: Children of all ages welcome. No formal kid's program.
Dining: Hearty ranch cuisine served buffet style. Lots to eat. Frontier Saloon - BYOB
Summary: The rugged beauty, amazing vistas, and tranquility of Arizona are only surpassed by the warmth of hospitality of the McCormick family. One of Arizona's newest guest ranches. Many come to relax and ride after a visit to the Grand Canyon. Wait till you see all those stars! An oasis into the magical Mojave Desert. Best for people who love nature and riding. Fully wheelchair accessible and special handicapped riding.

Tanque Verde Ranch
Tucson, Arizona

The Tanque Verde Ranch is a historic ranch dating to 1868, when the Carrillo family settled here and ran cattle up into the Rincon Mountains east of Tucson. Tanque Verde has evolved into one of the premier ranch/ resorts in the country, welcoming guests from around the world to a diverse program of riding, hiking, tennis, or just relaxing within a Sonoran-style architectural setting. Bob and Rita Cote, general manager Jim Bankson, and their dedicated staff provide guests with true Western hospitality every day of the year! The ranch continues to attract prestigious travel writers from around the world and is seen regularly in countless magazines and on television programs. Guests explore the fascinating Sonoran Desert through a comprehensive naturalist adventure program that is offered daily. A beautiful nature museum highlights the flora and fauna of the Sonoran Desert, complete with live-animal exhibits. The Cote family's philosophy is simple: Provide the very best in friendly, professional service in an exciting and stimulating environment for the entire family. Tanque Verde Ranch is truly an oasis in the desert, and without question one of the country's finest resort ranches.

Address: 14301 E. Speedway, Tucson, Arizona 85748
Telephone: 800/234-DUDE (800/234-3833), 520/296-6275
Website: www.tangueverderanch.com
Airport: Tucson, 35 minutes
Location: 15 miles east of Tucson at the end of East Speedway, in the foothills of the Rincon Mountains
Memberships: Arizona Dude Ranch Assoc., Dude Ranchers Association
Guest Capacity: 200
Accommodations: Seventy-six casita-style rooms, from historic Ramada rooms to spacious deluxe suites with whirlpool tubs and Southwestern decor. Most with adobe-style fireplaces, private patios, and large picture windows. All with telephones, WiFi and XM radio. Laundry facilities available.
Rates: $$$-$$$$$-plus American Plan.
Season: Year-round; including all holidays
Activities: Over 160 horses with daily guided rides. Adults may ride with children in the children's program. Daily beginner and intermediate horsemanship lessons. Slow scenic rides and some loping for the advanced rider. Breakfast all-day, and picnic rides. Fun gym - khanas in winter season. Cattle penning year round. All riding and instruction included. Five professional tennis courts (one Omni court), outdoor heated pool, indoor La Sonora Health Spa with massages, body treatments, and pedicures, Tai Chi also. Pool, saunas, whirlpool, and exercise room. Fishing, hiking, mountain biking, yoga and art classes, and bird walks. Over 175 species of birds seen at ranch. Golf at nearby courses.
Children's Programs: One of the most comprehensive, all-day. Kids 4-11.
Dining: Continental and American cuisine.
Summary: Internationally renowned year round ranch resort famous for its extensive instructional programs, including its superb children's program. One of the largest riding stables. Full Spa with a variety of treatments. Lots of Southwestern historical charm. Naturalists and nature museum.

Tombstone Monument Guest Ranch
Tombstone, Arizona

Tombstone Monument Guest Ranch is definitely one of a kind! The ranch was built to replicate Main Street of the turn of the century old west town. Opened in 2010, the ranch is located on one of Tombstone's original 1880s homesteads. The ranch is owned by the True family who have been in the dude ranch business for over 50 years operating their famous White Stallion Ranch outside Tucson. Under Russell True's direction, Tombstone has undergone extensive renovations, with extensive corrals and an arena. As Russell says "we want our guests to experience the old west and have created a really unique adventure back in time. Our Old West town sets the stage for western themed experiences, giving guests a glimpse of what the Wild West used to be." With its proximity to the old west town of Tombstone, the magic of the Arizona Desert and western hospitality the ranch will give you a lifetime of memories.

Address: 895 West Monument Road, Tombstone, Arizona 85638
Telephone: 520/457-8707
Website: www.tombstonemonumentranch.com
Airport: Tucson International
Location: 1 ½ hour southeast of Tucson
Memberships: Dude Ranchers Association, Arizona Dude Ranchers Association
Guest Capacity: 40
Accommodations: 17 different rooms, each with a special Western theme and individually decorated with a stylish interiors modeled from that historic time, with modern comforts. King or Queen Size beds, modern bathrooms and decorations make it easy to relax and enjoy the undisturbed sounds of nature. All rooms include air conditioning, free Internet WiFi and satellite TV. You can choose from four room categories: Standard, Deluxe, Junior Suite and Premium Suite.
Rates: $$-$$$ American plan.
Season: Year Round
Activities: Plenty of horses to choose from for slow and faster rides. Riding is varied in terms of terrain, speed and length. Ranch surrounded by ranching, mining, railroad, and Native American history. All-day rides go to the ghost town of Fairbank. Can ride to the town of Tombstone; old west style shooting, archery, tours of Tombstone, evening entertainment of music and poker.
Children's Programs: Children of all ages welcome. No formal kid's program.
Dining: Hearty ranch cooking. As they say, "No one leaves hungry." Meals are served or buffet style. Western saloon for adults.
Summary: One of Arizona's newest guest ranches just 3 miles from the famous town of Tombstone. The ranch serves up an Old West town themed adventure with a venue of horseback riding, cookouts, and plenty of Arizona sunshine. The ranch hosts families, couples, singles, weddings and corporate groups alike.

White Stallion Ranch
Tucson, Arizona

Just 17 miles from downtown Tucson, surrounded by rugged desert mountains, is White Stallion Ranch. In the 1960s, the True family bought this quiet, peaceful 3,000-acre ranch which looks out to Safford and Panther Peaks and the Tucson Mountain Range. "The only sounds you'll hear are those of the desert and the ranch," says Russell True, who, along with his brother Michael and their families, oversee this lovely desert ranch. Guests are impressed with the warmth and beauty of the land and the Trues' famous hospitality. The ranch features a herd of purebred Texas longhorn cattle and a rodeo each week with team roping, steer-wrestling, and barrel racing. Many movies and TV shows, including High Chaparral, were filmed here.

Address: 9251 W. Twin Peaks Road, Tucson, Arizona 85743
Telephone: 888/WSRANCH (888/977-2624), 520/297-0252
Website: www.whitestallion.com
Airport: Tucson International Airport.
Location: 17 miles northwest of Tucson.
Memberships: The Dude Ranchers' Association, Arizona Dude Ranch Association.
Guest Capacity: 90
Accommodations: The warmth of the Southwest is reflected in the architecture and immaculate and extensively landscaped grounds. The ranch has a warm, welcoming atmosphere that will make you feel immediately at home. Guest rooms are spacious and charming and situated throughout the ranch. There are 41 guest rooms and The Hacienda, a lovely and private four-bedroom, three-bathroom home perfect for larger families, girlfriend get-a-ways or small groups.Every guest room has a private patio with views of the cactus gardens, mountains, or corrals. Some suites include gas fireplaces or whirlpool bathtubs. Generous floor plans offer sunny, comfortable rooms with plenty of closet space. Adjoining suites create deluxe family suites. Friendly housekeeping staff cares for your needs daily and all guest rooms are supplied with eco-friendly soaps, shampoos and lotions. Hair dryers, mini-refrigerators and personal safes are found in all rooms.
Rates: $$$$ American Plan.
Season: Year-round.
Activities: Russell takes great pride in matching horses with riders. Children and adults may, if they wish, brush and saddle their own horses. Except on Sundays, there are four rides a day, usually two fast and two slow, and all-day rides into Saguaro National Park. If you think you're a fast rider, the ranch has a riding test for you. Breakfast and mountain rides. Team-cattle penning in arena is extremely popular with guests. Guided nature walks with trained naturalists along foothills of the Tucson Mountain Range, guided hiking program. Swimming pool, professional tennis court, indoor redwood hot tub, and rock climbing. AMGA, PCGI Certified Climbing Instructor will guide you climbing boulders and faces on the East end of the ranch. He has designed beginner climbs, intermediate and advanced climbs. Climbs are available from 2 hours and 4 hours to all day, based on your stamina and expertise. All the necessary climbing gear; helmets, shoes and hardware are provided. There is an additional charge for this new activity. Evening entertainment, massage, fitness room and sauna. Movie theatre, game room with a myriad of games. Sport court (volleyball, full court basketball, badminton).
Children's Programs: Children welcome and are parents' responsibility.
Dining: Breakfast menu-style, lunch and dinner buffet. Cookouts and special diets available.
Summary: The Trues' brand of hospitality and warmth is second to none! White Stallion blends the comforts of a resort with the hospitality of a traditional dude ranch. Excellent staff, immaculate grounds, delicious food, wonderful private desert setting, and one of the best values make White Stallion tops! Close to Tucson, but isolated and private.

ARKANSAS

— ★ —

Horseshoe Canyon Ranch
Jasper, Arkansas

Barry Johnson and his wife Amy met at a Wyoming dude ranch while at
Brigham Young University. Years later, they bought Horseshoe Canyon
Ranch to share their love of dude ranching with guests that come to recon-
nect with themselves and savor a rich tradition of Southern hospitality,
natural beauty, and the great outdoors. Together with their four children,
Cameron, Cody, Sierra and Creed, along with Barry's parents Martha and
Jerry, they run one of the best family dude ranches in the country. As Barry
says, "We offer a western family vacation filled with the natural beauty of
the Ozarks and fun for all; kids, parents, and grandparents." Welcome to
Horseshoe Canyon Ranch.

Address: HC 70 Box 261, Jasper, Arkansas 72641
Telephone: 870-446-2555
Website: www.horseshoecanyonduderanch.com
Airport: Little Rock, Arkansas 3 hours, Northwest Arkansas Regional,
Fayetteville, Arkansas, 2 hours
Location: 4 hours east of Tulsa, Oklahoma, 2 hours North and East of Fort
Smith, Arkansas
Memberships: The Dude Ranchers' Association,
Guest Capacity: 50
Accommodations: 13 handcrafted log cabins. Rustic with a western flair.
All have air conditioning, heat, and wood burning stoves for chilly nights. All
have full baths and views of the East Bluff, as well as covered porches to sit
back and relax.
Rates: $$-$$$$ American Plan.
Season: March to mid-November
Activities: Horses are matched to riders for the week. Typically, there are
morning and afternoon rides to places like Bear Bait, Bermuda Triangle,
and Crack House Alley, which are exciting, rugged and challenging. On
certain days there are trotting and loping rides for qualified riders. Sand-
stone rock-climbing is also a speciality at the Ranch, for both beginners and
experienced sport climbers. Swimming pool and canoe trips on the Buffalo
National river. Ask about the zip-line, fishing, canoe trips, elk viewing,
wagon rides, and target shooting.
Children's Programs: Kids of all ages welcome. Parents and children
interact together.
Dining: Home cooked ranch cuisine, weekly cookouts and campfires.
Summary: Spectacular Arkansas scenery, excellent horseback riding,
famous sporting rock climbing for all ages and experience levels. Southern
hospitality and great value make Horseshoe Canyon Ranch a jewel in the
Ozarks! Near the Buffalo National River for swimming, canoeing and fish-
ing is a special treat enjoyed by all. Great for family reunions and for small
corporate team building groups.

CALIFORNIA

—✴—

Alisal Guest Ranch
Solvang, California

The Alisal is one of the great resort ranches in North America. Opened in 1946, this 10,000-acre paradise really has it all: 50 miles of riding trails, two 18-hole championship golf courses, a private 100-acre lake, six tennis courts, and a lovely new fitness center and spa. In addition to first-class recreational amenities and lodging facilities, the ranch also has 2,000 head of cattle run separately from the guest operations. What also sets the Alisal apart is the level of personal service. General Manager David Lautensack continues to maintain a terrific spirit of hospitality, and personally gets out daily with his staff to meet and get to know his guests in the true spirit of great ranching hospitality. The Alisal — a tradition of excellence.

Address: 1054 Alisal Road, Solvang, California 93463
Telephone: 800/425-4725 , 805/688-6411
Website: www.alisal.com
Airports: Los Angeles, 2.5 hours; Santa Barbara with commercial jet service, 35 miles; Santa Ynez for private planes, five miles
Location: 40 miles northwest of Santa Barbara
Guest Capacity: 250
Accommodations: Seventy-three cottages and garden rooms scattered around the grounds which feature century-old sycamores range from one-room studios to executive suites with nightly turndown service. All are modern, with high ceilings, wood-burning fireplaces, and refrigerators. No TVs or telephones in the rooms, but they are available in public areas. Laundry facility available.
Rates: $$$-$$$$ Modified American Plan; includes breakfast and dinner. Numerous seasonal activity packages are available. Ask about the Roundup Vacation Package. Two-night minimum stay.
Season: Year-round; including all holidays
Activities: Two-hour trail rides go out twice each day, separated into walking, trotting, or loping over 50 miles of trails. Private rides and riding instruction available. Semiweekly breakfast rides, weekly guest rodeo (summer). Lake activities on Alisal Lake include fishing and boating. You can also fine-tune your archery skills under the skilled guidance of a certified archery instructor and you can learn the proper way to handle, sight and shoot an air rifle with our NRA instructor. The Ranch Golf Course is a par-72 California classic that winds past stately oak, sycamore, and eucalyptus trees. Six tennis courts. Pro shops for both tennis and golf, with professional instruction. Heated pool and whirlpool. Volleyball, shuffleboard, croquet and horseshoes. Game room with table tennis and billiards. The Alisal offers another way to renew body and spirit: Its state-of-the-art 6,000 square foot Fitness Center & Spa. Whether your goal is toning up in the well-equipped cardio room, an active workout in a private group fitness class, or pampering yourself with a signature spa treatment, the Fitness Center & Spa is guaranteed to enhance your Ranch experience.
Children's Programs: Extensive summertime and holiday programs, and a year-round petting zoo.
Dining: Dinner attire required. Contemporary regional cuisine created by acclaimed chefs.
Summary: One of the truly great year-round resort ranches in America with superb service and excellent cuisine. Summer children's program with fabulous petting zoo, horseback riding and 18-hole golf. Ideal for families and large corporate groups. Full resort amenities.

Circle Bar B Guest Ranch
Goleta, California

Tucked into the Refugio Canyon just 20 miles north of Santa Barbara sits the Brown Family's Circle Bar B Guest Ranch. Less than 2 hours from Los Angles and only 3.5 miles from the beach, this coastal mountain oasis is the ideal ranch getaway. The Circle Bar B has been welcoming visitors to its 1100–acre paradise since 1939. Guests appreciating a casual atmosphere come for the amazing horseback riding, tranquil surroundings, excellent food and warm hospitality. With a variety of trails and ride lengths, you will discover the Santa Ynez Mountains on horseback, meandering through fern-lined canyons over creek crossings, past a waterfall, and up to look-out points for magnificent views of the Santa Ynez Valley and Santa Barbara Channel Islands. In addition to fabulous accommodations, overnight guests have full access to the beautiful main lodge w/full bar, library, game room (ping pong, horseshoe pits, pool/Jacuzzi, mobile spa services, and seasonal dinner theatre. The escape, family reunion, corporate retreat or wedding, the Circle Bar B Guest Ranch is a perfect vacation destination.

Address: 1800 Refugio Rd., Goleta, Ca 93117
Telephone: 805-968-1113
Website: www.circlebarb.com
Airports: Santa Barbara Municipal Airport in Goleta
Location: 22 miles north of Santa Barbara at the Refugio State Beach exit off Hwy 101.110 miles north of Los Angles/LAX.
Guest Capacity: 68
Accommodations: Guests have 18 rooms and cabins to choose from in a variety of sizes and styles that sleep anywhere from 2 to 6 people. From Deluxe Ranch Rooms and Private Cabins to Creekside Cottages and Hillside Homesteads, we are sure to have something for everyone. Unwind and unplug; our rooms don't have telephones!
Rates: $$$ American Plan
Season: Year round, closed Christmas Eve and Christmas Day
Activities: On property horseback riding, horseshoes, game room (ping-pong, pool table, Foosball (main lodge with full bar and WIFI, library, a pool and Jacuzzi, and gorgeous hiking trails. Just a stones throw from the beach and some of the Central Coast's best shopping, wine tasting, and golf courses.
Children's Programs: Children of all ages love the Circle Bar B Guest Ranch! No formal program.
Dining: Hearty ranch cuisine.
Summary: Whether you're aiming to escape for a few nights or planning a group vacation, the Circle Bar B Guest Ranch is a coastal mountain gem. Guests can enjoy total relaxation or adventure out on horseback and beyond. The Circle Bar B Guest Ranch, where warm hospitality and coastal tranquility await you.

Coffee Creek Ranch
Trinity Center, California

Coffee Creek Ranch in the magnificent Trinity Alps has been creating life-long memories for families and children of all ages since 1976. Today, it carries on the tradition of welcoming families and lots of kids, who appreciate the camardarie and beauty here in one of California's most beautiful areas. Coffee Creek Ranch, named after the creek that flows through the property, covers 367 acres at the base of the majestic Trinity Alps Wilderness area. At 3,100 feet, Coffee Creek is in a river canyon surrounded by mountains. The ranch is not far from Trinity Lake and 13 miles from the Trinity Center Airport.

Address: HC2 box 4940, Coffee Creek Road, Trinity Center, California 96091
Telephone: 800/624-4480, 530/266-3343
Website: www.coffeecreekranch.com
Airports: Redding, Medford, OR (commercial) or Trinity center (3,000-foot runway), for small planes only. Transfers available.
Location: 278 miles north of San Francisco.
Memberships: The Dude Ranchers' Association, California Hotel Motel Association, Trinity County Chamber of Commerce.
Guest Capacity: 50
Accommodations: All 15 private cabins have porches. Most two bedroom cabins have one or two baths and wood-burning stoves and heaters. The one bedroom, one bath cabins have potbellied stoves to keep you warm and cozy. All cabins have bathtub/shower combinations. Handicapped accessible cabin or ranch house room with front porch is also available. Daily maid service and laundry facilities on premises.
Rates: $$$ American Plan.
Season: Easter to Thanksgiving.
Activities: Coffee Creek offers scheduled rides twice a day, including breakfast and twilight rides. Horsemanship clinics in the spring and fall. Line and square dancing, hayrides and bonfires, live music. Guided hiking, fishing in stocked pond, Coffee Creek, Trinity Lake, and Alpine Lakes. Fly-fishing is a favorite in Coffee Creek for native trout. Archery, badminton, volleyball, trapshooting, and rifle range (guns provided). Swimming in heated pool and paddle boats on the pond. Exercise room, Jacuzzi oversized outdoor spa (seats 14) enjoyed after a day in the saddle.
Children's Programs: Youth program for ages 3-17 Memorial Day to Labor Day.
Dining: All you can eat, family-style ranch meals.
Summary: Family-owned and operated since 1976, with a strong emphasis on families and children. A great place for a destination wedding, small meetings, or a reunion. Special theme weeks for adults only. Romantic weekends. Discounts offered throughout the season. June through September (with fall colors) have the best weather and lots of wildflowers. Conference room seats 40. Handicapped facilities. Nearby: Historical town of Weaverville and Chinese "Jess House" temple. Alpen Cellars Winery is a favorite.

Greenhorn Creek Ranch
Quincy, California

Greenhorn Creek Guest Ranch, with its magnificent pine forests, and crisp mountain air sits in the heart of Feather River country in the Sierra Nevada Mountains. The ranch is nestled on more than 600 acres and is surrounded by thousands of acres of the Plumas National Forest. Founded in 1962, the ranch has been a favorite destination for families and celebrities alike and continues to rise as a wonderful all-inclusive vacation destination. The ranch provides a western vacation experience for families, couples, singles, and businesses and corporations, and weddings seeking a unique, entertaining and educational experience.

Address: 2116 Greenhorn Ranch Road, Quincy, CA 95971
Telephone: 1-800-33-HOWDY, 800/334-6939
Website: www.greenhornranch.com
Airports: Just 70 miles from Reno/Tahoe Airport, close to private airstrips in both Quincy and Portola.
Location: 70 miles from Reno, and just 3 hours from Sacramento
Memberships: Proud Exclusive Members of The Dude Ranchers' Association
Guest Capacity: 100.
Accommodations: Rustic, cozy 1 and 2 bedroom cabins sleep up to 7 guests, while the main lodge room sleeps up to 4 people. Rooms offer a variety of bed arrangements including king, queen, double, twin and bunk bed accommodations. Each room/cabin has its own bathroom, and cabins offer a porch swing on the spacious covered porches. All cabins and lodge rooms offer various sleeping arrangements. Some have covered porches with swings.
Rates: Vary by season, duration of stay and availability. Call for promotional specials and discounts. Seniors and groups of 10 or more receive significant discounts.
Season: Off-peak season includes May through mid-June and mid-August through October, peak season includes mid-June through mid-August.
Activities: While horseback riding is the main activity at the ranch, there is also a huge variety of other activities and amenities that will keep everyone entertained from dawn till dusk. Each day provides several different activities including karaoke, line-dancing, frog races, poker night, guest rodeo events, volleyball, softball, horseshoe tournaments and more. If you don't want to ride, you can hike or mountain bike along mountain trails, relax by the heated pool, or enjoy catching the big one in the fully stocked trout ponds. Be sure to ask about the Equine Guided Education courses as part of your next stay.
Children's Programs: The ranch provides an onsite childcare service for small children in Kiddie Corral. For children 3-5 years old.
Dining: Guests enjoy 3 hearty family-style meals in chuck house and outdoor barbecue area.
Summary: When looking for a magical Northern California dude ranch experience, Greenhorn Creek Guest Ranch offers families a wholesome, all inclusive Western experience. This ranch has become very popular for reunions, weddings, business and corporate retreats, youth camps, special interest group events, and of course, family vacations.

Hunewill Ranch
Bridgeport, California

On the northeast side of Yosemite National Park sits one of California's greats, the Hunewill Ranch, an old-time family ranch that has attracted guests since 1930. The ranch is situated in the lovely, green, wide-open, cattle-ranching Bridgeport Valley, highlighted by the spectacular Sawtooth Ridge. It was founded by the great-great-grandparents of the present owners, the Hunewill family. The ranch runs about 2,000 head of cattle over 5,000 acres. While horseback riding is the main activity, hikers will find miles of trails, and anglers can enjoy nearby streams, lakes, and the awesome 4.5-acre, spring-fed pond filled with rainbow trout. The Hunewills say, "We love this ranch and enjoy sharing it with others." The ranch offers many wonderful things, including a beautiful setting, great hosts, and a relaxed Western atmosphere.

Address: P.O. Box 368 K, Bridgeport, California 93517 (summer); 205 Hunewill Lane, Wellington, Nevada 89444 (winter)
Telephone: 760/932-7710 (summer), 775/465-2201 (winter)
Website: www.hunewillranch.com
Airports: Reno-Tahoe International, Mammoth Lakes Airport, Bridgeport airport for private planes.
Location: 115 miles south of Reno, Nevada, on Highway 395; 50 miles north of Mammoth Lakes, California; five miles southwest of Bridgeport on Twin Lakes Road
Memberships: The Dude Ranchers' Association, Holistic Resource Management Institute, California Cattleman's Association.
Guest Capacity: 45
Accommodations: Bridgeport was one of the early gold-mining areas so the ranch buildings have a Victorian flavor. There are 12 cottages (24 rooms) each with private bath and porch, as well as the cozy Ranch House Suite. Guests dine in the ranch house, a lovely two-story Victorian built in 1880 and surrounded by tall poplars. Daily maid service. Laundry facilities available.
Rates: $$$$.
Season: May to mid- October, and 5 day November cattle drive.
Activities: Riding is the main attraction. Miles of open meadowland give riders of all skill levels the opportunity to ride to their maximum enjoyment. Three rides go out mornings and afternoons for beginning, intermediate, and advanced riders. Well-cared-for horses and great wranglers take guests on exhilarating lopes, splash rides, cattle moves, and visits to places like Eagle Peak, Buckeye Canyon, and Tamarack Lake. Beginners (both children & adults) appreciate special rides designed to build confidence and skills. Riding helmets provided upon request. Breakfast & lunch rides. Talent night, square dancing, bingo, roping practice, hay ride, campfire & sing-a-long, beautiful evening walks, volleyball, and horseshoes. For information about fly fishing on the 4.5 acre pond, go to kenssport.com.
Children's Programs: A kid's paradise! Though children are their parents' responsibility, they are included in all ranch activities.
Dining: Ranch-style—everyone eats together. Meals prepared by well-trained chefs.
Summary: One of California's great guest ranching families, ranching since 1861 and accommodating guests since 1931! Wide-open country surrounded by spectacular mountains. Riding is the main attraction. Ask about the colt-gentling, Big Fall Cattle Gather, Cattle Work Weeks, Bridgeport Rodeo in July, Special 4th of July week festivities, Fall color ride, Autumn getaways and 5 day November cattle drive. Massage therapist available.

Rankin Ranch
Caliente, California

The Rankin Ranch is one of California's legacies. Here in a secluded valley in southern California, Bill and Glenda Rankin, together with their children and grandchildren, share their love for people and the West. The Rankin family has been in the cattle business since 1863. On 30,000 acres in northern Kern County, things are pretty much as they always have been — the pace is slow and easy, the folks are warm and friendly. Over the years, lots of people have driven up the winding, slow-going road and down into this beautiful grassy valley to spend time at the ranch. Those who return yearly have a real appreciation for country living and are able to leave their businesses and professions behind. Here it's quality family time.

Address: P.O. Box 36, Caliente, California 93518
Telephone: 661/867-2511
Website: www.rankinranch.com
Airport: Bakersfield; free transportation available with one-week stay
Location: 42 miles northeast of Bakersfield, off Highway 58 via Caliente-Bodfish Road
Memberships: National Cattlemen's and Cattlewomen's Associations, California Historical Society
Guest Capacity: 50
Accommodations: Fourteen comfortable, wood-paneled duplex cabins are named after sites on the ranch, like Lightner Flat, Ruby Mine, and Rankin Hill. Each cottage room has a private bath, carpeting, and picture windows. Ask about the deluxe cabin. Daily maid service provided.
Rates: $$$ American Plan.
Season: Late March through early October
Activities: Daily one-hour morning and afternoon horseback trail rides are included. The rides vary from meadow flat-land to mountainous trails and from walking to the occasional gallop. Julia Lake and Walker's Basin Creek are stocked with rainbow trout. Bring your own fishing pole, and the cook will prepare your catch at any meal during your stay. Guests enjoy hiking trails throughout the ranch. If you let the cook know, he will pack a picnic for you. The ranch has lovely, shaded and heated swimming pool and hot tub. Here guests enjoy swimming, reading, or just plain relaxing. Recreation area with pool table, fooseball, shuffleboard, ping pong, horseshoes, archery and lawn sports. Petting farm for everyone to enjoy.
Children's Programs: Fully supervised seasonal children's programs. Ages 4-11.
Dining: Three hearty ranch-style meals. Rankin Ranch's famous guacamole dip and chips.
Summary: One of California's oldest and most famous cattle and guest-ranching families running an old-time, working cattle ranch for six generations. Hospitality reigns supreme! Enjoy wonderful, easygoing Western hospitality and kindness. Lots of space, peace, and quiet. Excellent for celebrating special birthdays, anniversaries, and family reunions. Featured in Better Homes and Gardens and Sunset magazines. Spanish spoken.

COLORADO

— ✶ —

Bar Lazy J Guest Ranch
Parshall, Colorado

The Bar Lazy J is the oldest continuously operating guest ranch in Colorado. It began entertaining guests in 1912, when it was known as the Buckhorn Lodge. It's situated right on the Colorado River at an elevation of 7,500 feet, about a half mile from the little town of Parshall. In 1995, Jerry and Cheri Helmicki bought the ranch to share their love of the great outdoors with people from around the world. A unique feature of the ranch is the beautiful Gold Medal trout river, offering anglers the opportunity to fish right outside their cabin doors. Horseback riding and fishing are the featured activities. Each day riders have a choice of walking, trotting, or loping rides. Because of Cheri's extensive teaching background, a strong emphasis is placed on children and families. Jerry and Cheri have put together a strong children's program with children's counselors and wranglers. At the Bar Lazy J, you can ride, fish, or relax listening to the Colorado River sing its song right outside your cabin.

Address: P.O. Box N, Parshall, CO 80468
Telephone: 800/396-6279, 970/725-3437
Website: www.barlazyj.com
Airport: Denver International, 100 miles
Location: 15 miles west of Grandby; 100 miles northwest of Denver
Memberships: The Dude Ranchers' Association, Colorado Dude and Guest Ranch Association
Guest Capacity: 42
Accommodations: Guests stay in 12 cozy log cabins named after wild flowers or fishing flies, which accommodate various family sizes. Most have wooden floors and enclosed covered porches overlooking the river, and all have rockers, bathrooms and thermostatically controlled heat. Ask about the family ranch house cabin that sleeps up to eight. Nightly turndown service and coffeemaker in each cabin.
Rates: $$$ American Plan.
Season: Late May through September
Activities: Most come here to fish, ride, and relax, not necessarily in that order! Gold Medal catch-and-realease fly-fishing with weekly fishing clinic. Stocked fishing pond for kids and those who don't wish to fish the river. Horseback riding for many levels of experience. Breakfast, half-day, and all-day rides take guests through aspen groves of the Arapahoe National Forest, along with sage and grazing cattle. Small groups (eight or fewer) go out on each ride. Scenic, moderate, and adventure rides. Other ranch activities include mountain biking, Jeep trips to the high country, guided hiking, swimming in the outdoor heated pool, relaxing in the large whirlpool tub, shuffleboard, horseshoes, and volleyball. River rafting on the nearby Colorado River.
Children's Programs: Extensive program operating from 8:30 a.m.-5 p.m. each day.
Dining: Meals are served family-style in the beautiful dining room, or on the porch overlooking the Colorado River.
Summary: One of Colorado's best children's programs for ages 3-12. The oldest continuously operating guest ranch in Colorado, located along the beautiful Colorado River. Lots of history. Buildings reflect wonderful old time atmosphere. Great for families, couples, and singles who enjoy the outdoors without a highly structured program. All cabins overlook the river. Two-thirds of a mile of the Gold Medal trout river, the Colorado River, runs through the ranch property.

Black Mountain Ranch
McCoy, Colorado

Black Mountain Ranch is located at 8200 feet in the heart of the Colorado Rockies, with 50-mile views, halfway between the famous ski towns of Vail and Steamboat Springs. A family run Ranch, Black Mountain offers an all-inclusive western adventure filled with rich ranching traditions and fun for all. Black Mountain truly offers a Colorodo Rocky Mountain high, and when you take a look at Trip Advisor, you will see what I mean. Guests rave about Black Mountain Ranch and come from as far away as Europe to savor the beauty, hospitality, and a host of outdoor activities that keep them busy from sunrise to sunset. As one family said so well, "Black Mountain Ranch is truly the best vacation ever!" Welcome to one of Colorado's best!

Address: 4000 Conger Mesa Road, McCoy, CO 80463
Telephone: 970/653-4226, 800/967-2401
Website: www.blackmtnranch.com
Airport: Vail/Eagle 1 hour, Denver 3 hours (150 miles) west.
Location: Half-way between Vail and Steamboat. Three hours west of Denver.
Memberships: The Dude Ranchers' Association, Colorado Dude and Guest Ranch Association
Guest Capacity: 40
Accommodations: Choose amoung 8 private cabins and 4 cozy suites, each featuring a private bath, fireplace and sitting area, and custom log furniture built on the ranch. Daily maid service and laundry facility for guests.
Rates: $$$$$ American Plan.
Season: June to mid-September.
Activities: Unlimited horseback riding and instruction. Weekly Longhorn cattle drive and optional overnight pack trip to Black Creek Camp. Whitewater rafting on the Colorado River one hour away. Skeet shooting and archery. Weekly trip to Rodeo, heated swimming pool with spectacular views, outdoor hot tub, roping cattle and weekly line-dancing.
Children's Programs: Children's counselors provide special activities for kids of all ages. Petting zoo.
Dining: Hearty western gourmet to wilderness cookouts. Several entrees nightly. Complimentary wine with dinner. Saloon with honor bar.
Summary: The May family's Black Mountain Ranch has created an outstanding dude ranch adventure for families, couples, singles and reunions. One of the best in Colorado. Relaxed atmosphere and beautiful mountain setting with spectacular 180 degree views over the Colorado River Valley and Flat Tops wilderness area over 50 miles away. All-inclusive, including fly fishing with limited instruction in three stocked ponds. Weekly long-horn cattle drive and optional overnight pack trip to Black Creek camp.

The Broadmoor's Ranch at Emerald Valley
Emerald Valley, Colorado

Just a short ride up the moutain from The Broadmoor, a distinctively Colorado experience awaits. The Ranch at Emerald Valley combines a unique retreat offering refined luxury with the rustic charm and inspiration of a wilderness enclave. This haven is the perfect destination for everything from an intimate getaway to a quintessential Colorado vacation for a group, family, and friends. During your stay at The Ranch, take the day to fly-fish in pristine mountain lakes, hike and bike scenic trails, or explore the mountains on horseback. Then unwind by soaking in an outdoor hot tub, sipping fine wine on a panoramic terrace while enjoying the beauty of a Rocky Mountain sunset. These experiences are all accompanied by The Broadmoor's luxury and impeccable service. A dedicated ranch staff and on-site Broadmoor chefs elevate this unique, all-inclusive hideaway beyond its 8,200 foot altitude. Fresh, locally sourced gourmet cuisine from The Broadmoor is presented at the grand lodge. Don't worry about the details, all meals, a selection of fine beverages, and ranch activities are included as part of your stay. What sets this experience apart from other mountain retreats is the option to be transported down the mountain to enjoy all the amenities The Broadmoor has to offer, including championship golf, a 5-Star spa, tennis, shopping, swimming pools, acclaimed dining and more.

Address: P.O. Box 1439, Colorado Springs, CO 80901-7711
Telephone: 866/443-8297
Website: www.broadmoor.com/experience-the-ranch.com
Airport: Denver International 75 minutes. Colorado Springs 15 minutes.
Location: 1 1/2 hours south of Denver. 8 miles from Broadmoor Hotel in Colorado Springs.
Memberships: Preferred Hotels and Resorts, Forbes and AAA 5-Star.
Guest Capacity: 32
Accommodations: Ten beautifully appointed cabins featuring luxury ammenties including rich furnishings and gas burning fireplaces.
Rates: $$$$$$ American Plan.
Season: May to mid-October
Activities: All activities are all taylored to guest wishes. Fly-fishing in pristine mountain lakes with guides. Daily horseback riding, mountain biking and guided hiking.
Children's Programs: Kid friendly for all ages, no formal program per se.
Dining: All meals freshly prepared and served by members of the Broadmoor's award winning culinary team. Three meals a day as well as appetizers at cocktail-hour nightly.
Summary: One of Kilgore's brightest new stars in the world of ultra-luxury guest ranches. Five star accommodations. World class service and cuisine. Superb mountain lake Fly-fishing and scenic mountain horseback trail riding. The ranch is owned and operated by the world renowned 5-Star Broadmoor Resort Hotel in Colorado Springs. Ranch guests may enjoy the best of both properties!

C Lazy U Ranch
Granby, Colorado

The C Lazy U is without a doubt one of the best year-round guest ranches in the world. C Lazy U mixes luxury with old-fashioned informality. The facilities and food are western, comfortable, and of superb quality. This 8,500 acre ranch has it all, from authentic western riding to an award-winning full service spa that will soothe your tired muscles and help you unwind. Family owned and very family-oriented. Families eat breakfast together, then the kids go off to camp and have the most fun they have ever had on vacation.

Address: 3640 Colorado Hwy 125 Granby, CO 80446
Telephone: 970/887-3344
Website: www.clazyu.com
Airport: Denver International
Location: Six miles northwest of Granby, off Highway 125; 95 miles west of Denver.
Memberships: The Dude Ranchers' Association, Colorado Dude and Guest Ranch Association
Guest Capacity: 105
Accommodations: The accommodations are comfortable with western elegance. The cabins have fireplaces, refrigerators, robes, snacks, humidifiers and vary from single rooms to family suites.
Rates: $$$$$ American Plan.
Season: Open year-round with four spectacular seasons to enjoy. Summer high season for families is Memorial Day weekend to Labor Day weekend. Fall is primarily for adults and groups. Winter Holidays and the winter season is family time. Spring is mainly for adults and groups.
Activities: Excellent progressive riding program: Fast, medium, and slow rides, depending on rider's ability; instructional rides for every level. Foundation horsemanship and ranch roping clinics available. Horses are assigned for the week and matched to each rider's ability. Adults and children ride separately, except on the weekly family ride. Two tennis courts, spring-fed heated pool; trap shooting; full fitness center; ropes course and zip line and a full service spa. Orvis endorsed fly-fishing and white-water rafting trips.
Children's Programs: Kids and adults do their own thing. Parents and kids love it! Extensive children's program for ages 3-12; teen program 13-17.
Dining: Superb cuisine. Guests enjoy happy-hour with appetizers before dinner in the cozy lodge bar, often accompanied by live grand-piano background music. Cookouts occur twice weekly.
Summary: Celebrating 97 years! In the world of guest ranching, C Lazy U is right up at the top. One of the most celebrated year-round destination guest ranches in the world. Renowned children's programs for kids and teens. Awarded the Condé Nast Traveler Readers' Choice Aware in 2015 for the #1 resort in Colorado, the #4 resort in USA and the 13th best resort in the world.

Cherokee Park Ranch
Livermore, Colorado

Cherokee Park is one of Colorado's oldest guest ranches. The lifeblood of dude ranching is the people, and so it is at Cherokee Park, with its western comfort and big helping of Southern hospitality. It's the Prince family's personal touches that make a stay at their ranch so memorable.

Address: 436 Cherokee Hills Drive, Livermore, CO 80536
Telephone: 800/628-0949, 970/493-6522
Website: www.cherokeeparkranch.com
Airport: Denver International, 100 miles.
Location: 100 miles northwest of Denver; 42 miles northwest of Fort Collins.
Guest Capacity: 40
Accommodations: As you greet the day in the Sunrise Room in the main lodge, the morning sun streams through a sky-blue Columbine flower etched in stained glass. Each sleeping room in the historic lodge, and every guest cabin along the north fork of the Cache La Poudre River, contains an original stained-glass art piece made by thhe ranch owner, Christine Prince. Each guest room and every cabin has a history, and all have been remodeled with Christine's special western touches: Quilts and refurbished antique dressers and furniture to create lots of authentic charm and a cozy feel. All accommodations offer porches, wonderful relaxing swings, hummingbird feeders, and lots of bright flowers.
Rates: $$$ American Plan.
Season: Mid-May through mid-September
Activities: Horseback riding is featured. There is also river rafting, swimming in the heated pool, mountain biking, relaxing in the hot tub, fishing in the ranch's stocked trout pond, fly-fishing on the Cashe La Poudre River, hiking, skeet shooting, and ranch-guided sightseeing trips to Rocky Mountain National Park and historic Laramie, Wyoming. Evening activities include hayrides, western dancing, campfires, cookouts, and sing-alongs. Once a week, there is an option for an overnight campout for parents and kids. You'll sleep under the stars and enjoy campfire cookout and camaraderie.
Children's Programs: One of the top children's programs in the country! Full-time counselors for ages 3-12. Older children can ride until the cows come home, while the younger set wrangles the rabbits, ducks, goats, and chickens.
Summary: One of the best children's programs for ages 3-12. Personal, caring attention with fabulous Southern spirit. Cherokee Park has something for everyone, whether you are coming with a young family, or bringing grandparents, everyone will feel at home and part of the Cherokee Park family.

Chico Basin Ranch
Colorado Springs, Colorado

Chico Basin Ranch is an 87,000 acre working cattle ranch southeast of Colorado Springs, Colorado. The ranch is managed by Duke Phillips, one of the finest gentleman and cattlemen I have met in all my travels. Together with his wife Janet, their children, and a fine crew, they run up to 1,800-head depending on the rainfall and grass. The Chico is dedicated to the enhancement and preservation of the natural world and western heritage. Their mission is to create a working ranch model that views the ranch as an ecological resource base, using cattle as an important tool to manipulate the surface of the ground to achieve conservation goals. This base supports a complementary mix of enterprises that emphasize sustainability, innovative management, and diversification as the keys to economic and ecological viability.

Address: 22500 South Peyton Highway, Colorado Springs, CO 80928
Telephone: 719-683-7960
Website: www.chicobasinranch.com
Airport: Daily flights from Denver to Colorado Springs—just 35 minutes from the ranch. There is a shuttle service offered to and from the ranch for a small fee.
Location: 35 minutes southeast of Colorado Springs, Colorado, 35 minutes northeast of Pueblo, Colorado, and about 2 hours from the Denver airport.
Memberships: Rocky Mountain Bird Observatory, The Quivira Coalition, Beefmaster Breeders United.
Guest Capacity: 12
Accommodations: Guests are hosted in a newly renovated adobe building out at May Camp, close to one of the ranch cowboys and his family. Two rooms are available for guests, and both rooms have one double bed and a set of bunks. There is one bathroom that is shared between the two rooms, as well as a full kitchen/sitting room. Washer and dryer available in the kitchen/sitting room. Fresh towels available throughout the week. Maid service provided if staying more than one week. It is very peaceful and quiet at May Camp, and on a clear night, tons of stars can be seen from the screened-in porch or from outside around the fire pit.
Rates: $$$$ American Plan.
Season: Year-round.
Activities: The Chico is a working cattle ranch where guests work alongside the crew each day. This is a life changing experience that is far removed from the hustle and bustle of the daily grind in the city. Most guests that come here want to contribute and take part in the daily ranching process, whether that be fencing, feeding, riding, sorting, branding, weaning, herding, or welding, to name a few. Guests are also welcome to relax and enjoy hiking on their own to one of the spring fed lakes for fishing, swimming, or viewing wildlife. Each and every day is different, and we encourage you to try and experience different things while you are here.
Children's Programs: No special children's programs.
Dining: Family style ranch cuisine, featuring Chico Basin Ranch grass-fed beef.
Summary: The Real McCoy. One of the finest working cattle ranches in America. The Chico is a very special place for those who want opportunities to learn about one of the oldest cowboy lifestyles in the USA. From the moment you step foot on the Chico, you will realize cowboy life is different. You will get to see first hand what it is like to live and work the land on a large modern day working ranch.

Colorado Cattle Company and Guest Ranch
New Raymer, Colorado

In the wide open spaces of Eastern Colorado, near the Nebraska border, is Tom and Darcy Carr's Colorado Cattle Company, a working cattle ranch that offers guests from around the world an exciting, hands-on experience of a lifetime. Here grasslands stretch as far as the eye can see. Guests, cowboys and cowgirls come together to savor old time goodness, a healthy dose of hospitality, and riding to your hearts' content. It's about wide-open spaces and working cattle operations from sunrise to sunset! As Tom and Darcy like to say, "We are a family and take great pride in the care of all our animals and stewardship of the land. We love sharing our special way of life with our guests, and fulfilling their dreams." Welcome to the Colorado Cattle Company!

Address: 70008 CR 132, New Raymer, Colorado 80742.
Telephone: 970/437-5345.
Website: www.coloradocattlecompany.com
Airport: Denver International.
Location: Two and a half hours east of Denver, 30 minutes from Kimball, Nebraska.
Memberships: Dude Ranchers' Association
Guest Capacity: 18
Accommodations: Guests sleep in either the original log bunkhouse or in one of the log cabin duplexes. All have private bathrooms, individual entrances, air conditioning and heaters, depending on the season. Living quarters look out to endless grass lands that stretch to the horizon. TV and Wi-fi access for those who need to connect.
Rates: $$$$$ American Plan.
Season: May through October.
Activities: Like all working cattle ranches, much depends upon time of year and weather. Activities include plenty of riding, no nose to tail, moving cattle, sorting, calving, gathering strays, vaccinating, branding, weaning calves, gathering bulls and fishing. Herd of 80 horses offers guests plenty of choices and plenty of riding. Ask about the overnight camp-out on horse-back.
Children's Programs: Adults only (18 years and older).
Summary: One of the best authentic working cattle ranch adventures in America. Here you will live the life of a working cowboy or cowgirl, enjoying seasonal working ranch activities. Those that come savor the wide open spaces, the hospitality, and 10,000 acres of riding ranch land. Adult only (18 and up). Great horses and staff.

Colorado Trails Ranch
Durango, Colorado

Over the years, Colorado Trails Ranch has earned one of the finest reputations in the guest-ranching business. It has always been famous for its outstanding riding and children's and teen programs. Today, Colorado Trails Ranch, along with its marvelous staff, continue to offer families a truly exceptional experience. Colorado Trails Ranch is geared to family fun and children. Located in the beautiful San Juan Mountains at 7,500 feet, just outside the famous town of Durango, the ranch offers a comprehensive western riding program. In addition, an extensive guided fly-fishing program has been developed, with over two miles of private water. At Colorado Trails, you'll also enjoy the western town atmosphere, complete with a trading post that offers old-fashioned ice-cream treats. Colorado Trails Ranch is one of Colorado's best all-round family ranches.

Address: 12161 County Road 240, Durango, Colorado 81301
Telephone: 800/323-3833, 970/247-5055
Website: www.coloradotrails.com
Airport: La Plata, 18 miles from ranch.
Location: 12 miles northeast of Durango on County Road 240; 200 miles north of Albuquerque, New Mexico; 350 miles southwest of Denver
Memberships: The Dude Ranchers' Association, Colorado Dude and Guest Ranch Association, American Quarter Horse Association, American Paint-Horse Association.
Guest Capacity: 55
Accommodations: All guest cabins have been replaced with new, larger cabins over the past four years. All cabins have a private bath for each bedroom, a living room, carpeting and great covered porches. Complimentary guest laundry is available.
Rates: $$$$-$$$$$ American Plan.
Season: Early June to October
Activities: Western riding instruction for beginners through advanced riders. Guided fly-fishing program. Ask about Mesa Verde trip. Heated swimming pool and whirlpool spa. Archery, rifle shooting, trapshooting (guns provided), hiking, river rafting plus power-tubing on Vallecito Lake. Golf, guided Mesa Verde trips, team penning, old fashioned Melodrama.
Children's Programs: One of the best and most extensive programs for children ages 5-17.
Dining: Home cooked, hearty ranch food.
Summary: Outstanding ranch for families, with exceptional program for children ages 5-17. Caring and personable staff. Full Western riding and fly-fishing programs. Ask about adults-only weeks, family reunions, horsemen's week, fall art program, and the exciting trip to Mesa Verde Indian National Park (ancient Puebloan cliff dwellings). Nearby: The famous Durango Silverton narrow-gauge train.

Coulter Lake Guest Ranch
Rifle, Colorado

Coulter Lake Guest Ranch is one of the few western guest ranches that overlooks its own charming lake. The Ranch is nestled in a small moutain valley on the western slope of the Rockies, deep in the White River National Forest at 8,100 feet. In operation since 1938, Coulter Lake retains that Old West flavor. The ranch is surrounded by some of Colorado's most scenic mountain country, stretching for miles in all directions, virtually unchanged since Native American times. Forests of quaking aspen and spruce overlook meadows of wildflowers. Coulter Lake guest Ranch has been kept small, intimate, and rustic. Family members of all ages will love and savor this extra-special mountain hideaway.

Address: 80 County Road 273, Rifle, Colorado 81650
Telephone: 800-858-3046, 970/625-1473
Website: www.coulterlake.com
Airports: Grand Junction; Eagle County Airport, Gypsum
Location: 21 miles northeast of Rifle
Memberships: Colorado Outfitters Association
Guest Capacity: 30
Accommodations: Eight rustic cabins stand on the mountainside among the quaking aspen trees. They vary in size and can sleep 3-10 people. Lakeside and Forest Haven are by the lake. Each has a private bath, some have fireplaces, most have porches. Ranch generates its own power.
Rates: $$$$ American Plan.
Season: Year-round.
Activities: Riding includes short excursions to Little Box Canyon, Long Park, and Pot Holes. All-day rides to Irish Point and Little Hill. Breakfast, lunch, and dinner rides during the week. Fishing for trophy rainbow trout in stocked lake or in Alpine streams and lakes (some equipment available). Hiking to beautiful Rifle Falls, horseshoes, volleyball, occasional cattle drives, swimming, archery, skeet and target shooting. Rafting and hot springs in nearby Glenwood Springs. Guided photographer safari on horseback. Hunting package with licensed outfitter available. Winter: Meals and lodging for snowmobiles and cross country skiers. Guided snowmobile rentals and tours available at additional charge.
Children's Programs: Fun-filled days for children ages 4-16.
Dining: Country cookin' with a flair. Breakfast ride, lake side, and mountain top dinner rides weekly. Special diets are accommodated with advance notice. BYOB.
Summary: Coulter Lake is one of the few guest ranches in the world that has a beautiful lake-side setting. Here you can commune with nature, enjoy looking out each day over the pristine lake, ride to your heart's content over a myriad of trails. Fishing, swimming, boating, white water rafting on the Colorado River, and hearty ranch cuisine. An old fashioned family ranch that shares the best of the outdoors, wonderful family traditions, and great hospitality. Weddings, family reunions, and intimate business groups welcome. Featured in National Geographic Traveler Magazine.

Drowsy Water Ranch
Granby, Colorado

Drowsy Water Ranch is exactly what you imagine a classic mountian dude ranch would be. This 600-acre ranch is in the beautiful Rocky Mountains, bordered by thousands of acres of backcountry and the Arapahoe National forest. Situated in a private valley at 8,200 feet and surrounded by shimmering aspen and scented pine, Drowsy Water is authentic and offers its guests genuine Colorado hospitality. The log cabins are situated along Drowsy Water Creek, which meanders through the ranch. The Foshas are hosts and owners. Ken, Randy Sue, and their sons Justin and Ryan, offer a quality horse program for beginners to experienced riders and a full program for children of all ages. There's old fashioned goodness to this ranch. It brings to mind another century, when people were less hurried and really cared about treating each other right.

Address: P.O. Box 147, Granby, CO 80446
Telephone: 800/845-2292, 970/725-3456
Website: www.drowsywater.com
Airport: Denver
Location: 90 miles west of Denver; six miles west of Granby, off U.S. 40
Memberships: The Dude Ranchers' Association, Colorado Dude and Guest Ranch Association   .
Guest Capacity: 55
Accommodations: Guests enjoy comfortable, log cabins that are sheltered in stands of aspen and pine overlooking Drowsy Water Creek and the ranch ponds. Cabins have covered porches. The largest sleeps nine and looks out over the children's fishing pond. The cabins accommodate two to nine people. The sleeping lodge has another eight rooms, all with private baths.
Rates: $$$-$$$$ American Plan.
Season: June to mid-September
Activities: One hundred fine horses provide all the riding you could possibly want. Ken and Randy Sue have raised many of their own horses and have a personal commitment to helping each guest become a better rider. Faster loping and slow ambling trail rides go out mornings and afternoons, and all-day mountain rides travel to beautiful vistas at 10,500 feet. Ranch cattle penning. Riding here will get you to some spectacular high country and views of the Continental Divide. River rafting, guided hiking, hayrides, fishing (equipment for beginners provided). Heated pool and whirlpool. Mountain bikes available.
Children's Programs: This is one of the top children's ranch programs in the country. Parents may participate in kid's activities.
Dining: Home cooked, hearty meals.
Summary: The Fosha's are one of the great dude ranch families in the West! An excellent children's program. Drowsy Water is one of the country's top family owned and operated ranches for parents and infants on up; also great for couples and singles.

Elk Mountain Ranch
Buena Vista, Colorado

High in the Colorado Rocky Mountains is a gem of a ranch called Elk Mountain, located in the heart of the largest collection of 14,000-foot peaks in the lower 48 states, and the white-water capital of Colorado. What makes Elk Mountain shine so brightly are the incredible spirit of owners Tom and Sue Murphy, the beauty of the countryside, off-the-beaten-path charm, and spectacular views out to the incredible mountains. Nestled away among aspen and pine trees, this charming ranch is ten and a half miles off the main road and surrounded on all four sides by the San Isabel National Forest. Here you will rest and recharge, you will watch hummingbirds dance, and you and your family will savor hospitality second to none — warm, friendly, and sincere. Elk Mountain has hosted guests since 1981, and today offers families, couples, and singles a western experience that you will remember for a lifetime!

Address: P.O. Box 910, Buena Vista, Colorado 81211
Telephone: 800/432-8812, 719/539-4430
Website: www.elkmtn.com
Airports: Colorado Springs or Denver
Location: 120 miles southwest of Denver; 90 miles west of Colorado Springs; 20 miles southeast of Buena Vista. Ranch will send you a detailed map.
Memberships: The Dude Ranchers' Association, Colorado Dude and Guest Ranch Association
Guest Capacity: 30
Accommodations: The main lodge houses the dining room with fireplace, cowboy and mining artifacts, sitting room, library, sundeck, and the upstairs Elk guest suite. There are six one and two-bedroom log cottages with private baths and queen or king-size beds, and the Pioneer Lodge has three private rooms and baths, all tastefully furnished. Eight-person hot tub and large deck. A gift basket awaits your arrival. Sue loves flowers and has colorful arrays everywhere. The ranch generates its own electricity. Lights are out at 11p.m.
Rates: $$$ American Plan.
Season: Late through mid September
Activities: Horseback riding in small groups. Spectacular 360-degree views on rides, where you will see the largest collection of 14,000+ ft. peaks in the lower 48 states. Excellent horse orientation program. Weekly brunch trail ride overlooking Brown's Canyon. Weekly white-water rafting on the Arkansas River. Auto trips to Aspen for the views and shopping. Rifle marksmanship and trapshooting (guns provided). Trout fishing in two stocked ponds (fishing gear is available). Archery, mountain biking, horseshoes, and volleyball. Massage a la carte.
Children's Programs: Full children's program offered for ages 3-7. Petting zoo.
Dining: Great, hearty ranch food.
Summary: One of Colorado's real gems! Wonderful, remote, charming small family-oriented ranch. Terrific hosts and excellent staff who love what they do—and it shows. Great for families, couples, and singles who enjoy an outdoor wilderness setting. Great trading post ranch store. Massage available. Near: Buena Vista (the white-water capital of Colorado) and the largest collection of mountains higher than 14,000 feet.

Elk River Guest Ranch
Steamboat Springs, Colorado

Elk River Guest Ranch was built back in the 1950s and has hosted guests who savor its location in the heart of some of Colorado's most beautiful and picturesque beauty. The ranch was dormant for a number of years and was purchased in 2014 by a wonderful young woman named Bex, and her husband Scott. Bex began dude ranching as a child and always dreamed of one day having her own guest ranch. Finally her dream came true, and at the age of 28, she shares her love of life, dude ranching, and the great outdoors with guests that come to enjoy both on-ranch and off-ranch activities. Unlike many guest ranches, Elk River encourages its guests to explore the surrounding areas and use the ranch as a base camp for a host of outdoor adventures including trail rides, off-ranch biking, white-water rafting, and hiking. The ranch is very small and accomodations are simple. What makes it shine is its location and the heart and hospitality that Bex shares with all that pass through her ranch gates. Bex comes from Tennessee, and her Southern roots combine with her contagious smile and cowboy hat, offering second-to-none gooness and heart!

Address: P.O. Box 1080, Clark, Colorado 80428
Telephone: 970/879-1946
Website: www.elkrivergr.com
Airports: Hayden/Steamboat Springs Airport.
Location: 20 miles north of Steamboat Springs.
Memberships: Dude Ranchers' Association, Colorado Dude Ranch Association.
Guest Capacity: 15
Accommodations: Four simple cabins, all with the views of the horses getting wrangled in the morning, and at the height of the summer season, close enough to hear the Elk River across the road wind its way through the valley. Aspen, Evergreen, Bear's Den and Riverside cabins have a fireplace, gas or wood stove. All sleep anywhere from 2-6 guests, have one or two bedrooms and a bathroom, kitchen, and small living room area. Daily housekeeping available.
Rates: $$$, American plan
Season: Summer: June through middle of September; Winter: lodging available
Activities: Horseback riding up (arena instruction, barrels, poles, other arena activities, half day trail rides, all day trail rides, optional overnight camp trip); mountain biking, hiking, Whitewater rafting, fishing, archery, western dancing, cookouts, campfires, Steamboat Pro Rodeo Series.
Children's Programs: No minimum age to come to the ranch; 6+ ride on their own. Families enjoy vacation together.
Dining: Healthy ranch cuisine; special-diet friendly, saloon and cookouts.
Summary: A very small, simple guest ranch with amazing Southern heart and soul. Bex and husband Scott offer a flexible on and off-ranch experience in the heart of the Colorodo Rockies. Modest accommodations, good western food, proximity to the famous ski town of Steamboat Springs, and in the heart of Colorodo's magical scenery. Affordable and flexible program.

4 UR Ranch
Creede, Colorado

The present owners bought the 4UR in the early 1970s. The same time-less qualities of nature, history, fly-fishing, and hospitality continue to make the 4UR Ranch a delightful experience. The ranch is high (8,500 feet) in the San Juan Mountains of southwestern Colorado, and the old CF and I Flurspar Mine from the early 1900s keeps a watchful eye over it. For discriminating fly-fishing guests, there is private fishing on the Rio Grande and Goose Creek; the two Lost Lakes are at 11,000 feet. July and August are the ranch's busiest family months. September is a favorite for fisherman.

Address: P.O. Box 340, Creede, Colorado 81130
Telephone: 719/658-2202
Website: www.4urranch.com
Airports: Alamosa via Denver; 6,800 foot paved airstrip in nearby Creede with hangar facilities for guests.
Location: 222 miles southwest of Denver, 60 miles west of Alamosa, eight miles southeast of Creede off Highway 149.
Guest Capacity: 50
Accommodations: Guest facilities consist of three delightfully remodeled 1950s cedar-shake mini-lodges. Rooms share a common breezeway porch, but each has its own entrance with numerous rockers. All rooms have private baths, thermostatic heating, daily maid service, and nightly bed turn-down. A family cottage is available at certain times of the year. The main lodge, with its dining and living rooms, splendid valley views, bar and game room, is the center stage for evening socializing. Laundry service is available (extra).
Rates: $$$$$ American Plan. Children's rates available.
Season: Early June through September
Activities: Fly-fishing, riding, and hiking are main activities. Fly-fishing on river and in alpine lakes with instruction available by request. Each evening fisherman roll the dice to select their own half-mile stretch of water for the following morning's fishing. Flies and equipment available. Breakfast, morning, afternoon, and all-day horseback rides through very scenic country; beginning to advanced riding with emphasis on natural horsemanship. Heated swimming pool, log bathhouse with sauna, hot sulfur baths, whirlpool. Massage room, hiking, and rafting available. 13-station sporting-clays course.
Children's Programs: Counselor for kids over age 5. Full day activities program from 9 a.m. to 5 p.m.
Dining: Fine Dining, cookouts, and kids menu.
Summary: Superb guest ranch on scenic Goose Creek, famous for its excellent fly-fishing; 7.5 miles of private waters. Family oriented during July and August; mostly adults during September. Hot sulfur pool. Special 4UR fly-fishing school, natural horsemanship and weekly kid's gymkana. Excellent for families with kids. Wonderful for those who love to fish and ride.

The High Lonesome Ranch
De Beque, Colorado

The High Lonesome Ranch is one of Colorado's Best multi-sport adventure ranches. Located on the Western slope of the Colorado Rockies, the ranch encompasses 400 square miles of deeded and permitted lands, stretching far and away from big-city life. From mountain forests, grasslands, spring creeks and alpine mesa's, the ranch is a mecca for wildlife and multiple ranch adventures. What makes the High Lonesome Ranch unique among ranches today is its size and the opportunity to create-your-own guest ranch experience. It's your vacation, and you are the boss to select from an abundance of sporting options, including guest ranch packages, Orvis-endorsed fly-fishing and wing-shooting, corporate and group retreats, weddings and family reunions. As they say at HLR, "There are places and experiences that touch your soul, and where the rest of the world simply falls away." Here you may discover majestic wildlife, abundant trout, spring creeks, wild horse herds, magnificent rock formations, western hospitality second to none, and skilled guides that cater to your every wish. Without question, the staff at HLR will create for you memories that last a lifetime. One guest said it best, "The passion and purpose of the HLR staff is as grand and beautiful as the landscape." Welcome to the fabulous High Lonesome Ranch.

Address: 0275 County Road 222, De Beque, CO 81630
Telephone: 970/283-9420
Website: www.thehighlonesomeranch.com
Airport: Denver International, Grand Junction Regional Airport
Memberships: Colorado Dude and Guest Ranch Association, Orvis endorsed Fly-fishing and Wing-Shooting, Dude Ranchers' Association.
Guest Capacity: 38
Accommodations: At the epicenter of the ranch are the headquarters and cookhouse. Guests select from a variety of homes and cabins perfect for families, corporate groups, and wedding venues. Ask about the Guest House, Pond House, Forshay Cabin, Homestead House, Castle Rock Camp and McCay Fork Camp. Conference facilities centered at headquarters.
Activities: Do as much or as little as you please. Guests can select from a myriad of outdoor adventures including hourly or day-long trail rides with instruction, extensive fly-fishing or wing-shooting, equestrian geocaching, weekly wild horse viewing with picnic, ranch sorting and sporting clays. Heated pool and campfires.
Children's Programs: Parents interact with kids. No set program per se. All ages welcome.
Dining: Executive chef prepares inspired, world-class cuisine. Farm to table family-style meals with culinary flare! Excellent in every way. Wine included.
Summary: One of Gene Kilgore's rising stars in the world of guest ranching! A sporting ranch adventure second to none. Orvis-endorsed fly-fishing and wing-shooting. Excellent for family reunions, corporate events, and intimate wedding venues. 400 Square miles of raw, majestic, and uncivilized landscapes. Ask about their sister property, The K-T Fly-fishing Lodge.

The Home Ranch
Clark, Colorado

Welcome to The Home Ranch, one of North America's finest summer and winter guest ranches. Since 1980, this magnificent property has been hosting families, couples, and singles who come to savor the postcard-perfect setting along with rustic elegance, a host of outdoor summer and winter activities, and superb cuisine. Host and general manager Clyde Nelson, along with a superb staff serves up one of the finest guest ranching experiences. As you walk to the main lodge, you'll pass under an arch with a sign that says, "Welcome Home." And for everyone who comes for a stay, that's exactly how it feels. The Home Ranch—a real Rocky Mountain high.

Address: Box 822, Clark, Colorado 80428
Telephone: 970/879-1780
Website: www.homeranch.com
Airport: Hayden airport
Location: 18 miles north of Steamboat Springs, off Highway 129
Memberships: The Dude Ranchers' Association, Colorado Dude and Guest Ranch Association, Relais & Chateaux, Orvis endorsed.
Conference Capacity: 30
Guest Capacity: 45-50
Accommodations: Each beautiful log cabin is wonderfully furnished and set in a grove of aspen trees, ensuring privacy. Each has its own hot tub on a covered deck, great for total relaxation at the end of a day's ride. There are also rooms on both levels in the handsome main lodge. A wonderful 2,500-square-foot, two-floor, hand-hewn log cabin for large families is available as well. All rooms with nightly turndown service, flowers, and robes. Laundry facilities available.
Rates: $$$$$$ American Plan.
Season: June through mid-October; mid-December through March
Activities: Guests young and old can do as much or as little as they wish. The only emphasis at The Home Ranch is on everyone having fun! You're assigned your own horse for the duration of your stay. It's up to you how much you ride inside the adjoining one-million-acre Routt National Forest. Interested guests are taught how to saddle and bridle their horses, and learn about natural horsemanship. Rides go out in small groups each day accompanied by a wrangler. The ranch raises many of its own quarter horses. Heated swimming pool, fishing and fly-casting in the stocked pond or Elk River, and fly-fishing instruction. Extensive hiking program with nature guides. A full winter program offers skiing, snowshoeing, and much more.
Children's Programs: Complete children's program for ages six and up.
Dining: Excellent, mouth-watering gourmet meals.
Summary: The Home Ranch is a charming, world-class year-round luxury guest ranch, now celebrating 36 years. In a magnificent setting, the ranch is open all seasons. The ranch is an exclusive Relais & Chateaux property with superb cuisine thanks to long-time Chef and Manager, Clyde Nelson. Yoga and natural horsemanship programs. Kids and teens programs are among the best. The ranch's riding program is varied, with many different options for riding. Winter skiing and snowshoeing, group retreats in the fall or spring.

Lane Guest Ranch
Estes Park, Colorado

Lane Guest Ranch is celebrating its 62nd year of continuous operation
in 2015. Host and owner Lloyd Lane has developed one of the most suc-
cessful summer ranch experiences in North America. His secret is best
described by guests who write, "The staff was wonderful, the food excellent,
and there were plenty of activities! Staff, food, scenery were all top-notch—
we've never been to a more loving resort." Lloyd's success has come about
because he offers a wide choice of activities besides horseback riding, and
a superb children's program, all in one of the prettiest areas of Colorado
— right next to Rocky Mountain National Park. Welcome to Lloyd Lane's
famous "Colorado Vacation."

Address: P.O. Box 1766, Estes Park, Colorado 80517
Telephone: 303/747-2493
Website: www.laneguestranch.com
Airport: Denver International; shuttle available (extra)
Location: 67 miles northwest of Denver; 12 miles south of Estes Park, off
Highway 7
Memberships: American Hotel and Motel Association, Estes Park Chamber
of Commerce
Guest Capacity: 60
Accommodations: Log-sided units accommodate 2-6 people. Twenty-five
units are comfortably furnished with queen-size beds, private baths, patios,
hammocks, TV, DVD, VCR, and 1000 movies, complimentary stocked
refrigerators. Most units have their own private hot tubs. Early morning
wake-up coffee brought to your room when you wish. Ask about the Doctor's House or the Governor's House for family reunions. One-day laundry
service offered. Free house wines & beers.
Rates: $$$ American Plan.
Season: June to August
Activities: Daily ranch activity sign-up sheet with lots of programs.
Horseback riding (except Sunday) in Rocky Mountain National Park and
Roosevelt National Forest. Wine and cheese rides for adults; two overnight
pack trips weekly. Guided hikes, scenic photography hikes, and expert
trout fishing guides. Landscape drawing and silversmith classes. Heated
outdoor pool, sauna, and hot tub. White-water rafting about two hours
away. Massage available (masseuse on staff). Fitness center and mountain
bikes. Wildlife viewing trips (one of the largest elk hers in the US). Golf and
tennis nearby. Gift shop. Evening entertainment includes a magic/comedy
show, Karaoke, and a pianist at the Sunday shrimp, champagne, and hors
d'oeuvres welcome party.
Children's Programs: Extensive program with counselors; full child care
available for infants and older children during the day.
Dining: Guests have a choice of a dozen dinner entrées; breakfast, lunch
at pool.
Summary: Lloyd Lane has celebrated more than 62 years of operation.
2010 Gene Kilgore Rancher of the Year. The ranch is only 67 miles from
Denver and near Rocky Mountain National Park. Lloyd will loan a video
of the park so you can see one of the the the most beautiful areas of Colo-
rado where guests hike, ride, & fish. Come here to enjoy a wide variety of
activities, food, and entertainment. High staff-to-guest ratio (30 staff to 60
guests). One of the best children's programs for infants on up. Lots of fami-
lies and couples. European-type concierge and satellite Internet access.
Pets welcome. Advertised in The Wall Street Journal for over 50 years.

Laramie River Ranch
Glendevey, Colorado

The spirit of Bill and Krista Burleigh's Laramie River Ranch is captured by this guest quote: "Our family loves riding and fishing, and we got to do plenty of both. Laramie River Ranch is blessed with exceptional scenery offering incredible horseback rides. With a mile and a half of the Laramie River running through the property, there is plenty of opportunity for great fishing. The area is stunningly beautiful." The ranch is located in the Laramie River Valley of northern Colorado, not far from the Wyoming border. In 1995, Bill and Krista bought this historic ranch, which was homesteaded in the late 1800s and had entertained guests for over 50 years. Today, along with sons Christopher and Alex, they share their way of life in this remote river valley. Here you will experience side-by-side horseback riding, private fishing, and a host of naturalist-led activities.

Address: 25777 N. County Road 103, Jelm, Wyoming 82063
Telephone: 800/551-5731, 970/435-5716
Website: www.lrranch.com
Airports: Laramie, Wyoming, and Denver, Colorado; free pickup from Laramie
Location: 42 miles southwest of Laramie; 150 miles northwest of Denver
Memberships: The Dude Ranchers' Association, Colorado Dude and Guest Ranch Association
Guest Capacity: 25
Accommodations: The lodge, built in the 1880s and renovated in 1996, has a living room with an old stone fireplace, two open porches with rocking chairs, and a large enclosed porch overlooking the Laramie River. Choose one of seven rooms in the historic lodge, or one of five cozy log cabins that sit along LaGarde Creek and the Laramie River. One guest wrote, "We loved being on the river, listening to the sound of rushing water, windows wide open!" Homemade cookies and fresh flowers in your cabin are just a couple of the nice, friendly touches here. Daily maid service. Smoke-free policy.
Rates: $$$$ American Plan.
Season: Early June through mid September
Activities: Morning, afternoon, cookout and all-day rides in small groups are available for riders of all abilities. There is an abundance of open terrain suitable for loping. Guests are welcome to help groom and saddle their own horses. Riding instruction and horse education programs throughout the week. After a good day in the saddle, you can enjoy a swim in the river and a soothing soak in the riverside hot tub. Overnight pack trips. Fishing for wild brown and rainbow trout. Fly-fishing instruction provided, with guide and gear available. Other activities include cattle penning, tubing down the river, birding, hunting for wildflowers, roping a steer dummy, exploring beaver dams, volleyball, horseshoeing and dancing.
Children's Programs: Activities are family-oriented, so parents and children can explore the ranch together. Full child care for infants
Dining: Hearty meals, served family-style. Special diets catered to.
Summary: Bill and Krista Burleigh have created one of the best family guest-ranch experiences in Colorado. Excellent horseback riding and fly-fishing. One family summed it up: "The amount of activities was perfect for us, not too much, not too little, and we really appreciated the optional aspect. We had time for hiking, riding, reading, visiting, and napping."

Latigo Ranch
Kremmling, Colorado

What a view! At 9,000 feet, looking out to the spectacular Continental Divide, the air is crisp and the hospitality sincere. Nature lovers will enjoy the breathtaking scenery and the abundance of wildflowers and wildlife on thousands of acres. Latigo Ranch runs summer and winter programs, from hayrides in summer to cross-country skiing in winter. Here you can ride, hike, swim, and fish. When you and your family are at the ranch for whatever season you pick, you can be sure of one thing... many special memories. If you want to have some stimulation conversations, just ask your host about their interesting educational backgrounds. The George and Yost families who own and operate the Latigo Ranch often engage in provocative discussions with their guest. Mostly, though, everyone takes in nature's beauty and serenity. As one of the guests wrote, "Between the depth of instruction in nature and riding, combined with the spirit of kindness that permeates the ranch, our experience was grand!"

Address: P.O. Box, 237, Kremmling, Colorado 80459
Telephone: 800/227-9655, 970/724-9008
Website: www.latigotrails.com
Airports: Denver
Location: 130 miles northwest of Denver; 55 miles southeast of Steamboat Springs; 16 miles northwest of Kremmling.
Memberships: The Dude Ranchers' Association, Colorado Dude and Guest Ranch Association.
Guest Capacity: 38
Accommodations: Guests stay in contemporary log duplexes and one fourplex nestled in the pine forest. Each is carpeted with sitting room and fireplace or wood-burning stove. All have refrigerators and Latigo's famous homemade caramel corn. Daily maid service.
Rates: $$$$ American Plan; all-inclusive, gratuities included, no extras.
Season: Sumer: June to October; Winter: Mid-December to April
Activities: The main emphasis is on the horseback riding and the quality of instruction for all levels on the trials, as well as in the arena. The Ranch prides itself on a high wrangler-to-guest ratio, so ride groups are small and be better tailored to fit guests' ability levels and interests. Rides include morning, afternoon, all-day, breakfast, sunset, and overnight pack trips to Dakota Cliff or High Rock Creek. Riding at 9,000 feet with 360-degree views and serenity offers a genuine Rocky Mountain high. Heated swimming pool, fishing in streams and ranch pond. Jim Yost offers fly-fishing instruction. Lots of hiking and rafting incuded nearby. Be sure to ask about weekly team cattle penning and fall cattle roundup!
Children's Programs: Optional fully supervised program for children ages 3-13 while adults are riding.
Dining: Ranch fare with variety and gourmet touches.
Summary: One of the best summer and winter guest ranches in Colorado. Spectacular panoramic views. On a clear day, you can see for 100 miles from the ranch's 9,000 foot perch. Latigo Ranch is known for four things: its hospitality, scenery, horse program, and winter cross-country skiing.

Lost Valley Ranch
Deckers, Colorado

In the world of guest ranching, Lost Valley Ranch is right at the top. The qualities that make the Lost Valley Ranch so unique are the superb staff and fabulous children's/teen program. Everyone at the ranch exudes a caring and enthusiastic spirit, and guests quickly become friends. Lost Valley has been in the ranching business for more than 100 years. This year-round guest ranch is a private island in the middle of 40,000 acres of the Pike National Forest. At Lost Valley, adventure is combined with fun. If the number of returning guests is any indication, they are doing everything right. Walt Disney stayed here years ago, and said, "If I had this place, I would do all that I could not to change its character." This is one of the best family ranches in the business.

Address: 29555 Goose Creek Road, Sedalia, Colorado 80135-9000
Telephone: 303/647-2311
Website: www.lostvalleyranch.com
Airports: Denver or Colorado Springs.
Train: Amtrak to Denver.
Location: Two hours southwest of Denver; 1.5 hours northwest of Colorado Springs; 12 miles southwest of Deckers.
Memberships: The Dude Ranchers' Association, Colorado Dude and Guest Ranch Association.
Guest Capacity: 90
Accommodations: The 24 cabin suites (one, two, and three bedrooms) all have living rooms, fireplaces, refrigerators, covered porches with swings, full private tub/shower baths, and amenities such as daily maid service, oversized towels, coffeemakers, and delightful cowboy hat amenities baskets. To ensure peace and quiet, the cabins are nicely spaced among the pine. No TVs or telephones. Laundry facilities are available. Smoke-free policy in dining room and cabins.
Rates: $$$$$ American Plan.
Season: March through November
Activities: All levels of western riding. With 150 horses and 200 head of cattle, the ranch encourages guests to participate in a host of fun activities, including some ranch and cattle work. Try the quality fishing in Goose Creek, which runs through the property, or drive 20 minutes and wet your fly in the world-famous Cheasman Canyon on the South Platte River. Orvis endorsed fishing guides are available. Heated outdoor swimming pool, three whirlpool spas, two plexi-paved tennis courts, trapshooting, and guided hiking. Ranch store. Seasonal cattle and horsemanship weeks.
Children's Programs: This is one of Lost Valley's strongest attractions. A superb collegiate staff supervises children and teens. Babysitting available.
Dining: Down-home ranch cooking served.
Summary: Lost Valley Ranch is celebrating 55 years in Dude Ranching! One of the top family guest ranches in North America. Excellent staff and superb children's and teens' programs, nightly entertainment, family square and barn dancing, melodramas. Riding, seasonal cattle roundups and special horsemanship weeks. Great for family reunions and off-season conference groups. A true destination vacation.

Rainbow Trout Ranch
Antonito, Colorado

Rainbow Trout was built back in the 1920s when its 18,000 square-foot log lodge and cabins were used as an exclusive sportsman's retreat by anglers and their families–thus its name. Today Doug, Linda, David and Jan Van Berkum carry on this great tradition. As in years gone by, Rainbow Trout is a haven for families who come to rejoice in natural beauty, horseback riding, fly-fishing, and being together. Rainbow Trout serves up plenty of warm and friendly hospitality. Guests can enjoy varied riding, fish the Conejos River, join in evening activities, and savor all the family fun. There is white-water rafting out of Taos, sightseeing in Sante Fe, or riding along the Cumbres & Toltec Scenic Railroad. At Rainbow Trout Ranch, guests have the best of the Colorado Rockies with convenient proximity to New Mexico.

Address: 1484 FDR 250, Box 458, Antonito, Colorado 81120
Telephone: 800/633-3397, 719/376-5659
Website: www.rainbowtroutranch.com
Airport: Alamosa (available pickup extra); guests also fly into Albuquerque, New Mexico or Colorado Springs.
Location: 2.5 hours north of Sante Fe, New Mexico
Memberships: The Dude Ranchers' Association, Colorado Dude and Guest Ranch Association.
Guest Capacity: 60
Accommodations: Fifteen old-time cabins with names like Deer, Birch, Cottonwood, and Cougar are situated above the main lodge and interspersed among the aspen and pine. They range in size from two bedrooms and one bath to three bedrooms and two baths. Most cabins have living rooms and fireplaces. All have covered porches. Daily housekeeping. Laundry room
Rates: $$$$ American Plan.
Season: Late May through September
Activities: Horsback riding and fishing are the most popular ranch activities. You'll have your own horse for the week. Five to eight riders per ride, divided accoring to guest's wishes and abilities, as well as family rides. Weekly overnight packtrip for teenagers and adults. The ranch's Conejos River and its tributaries are known for great fishing. Personal instruction and some gear available. Serious anglers should ask about the local professional guide service. Heated swimming pool, hot-tub, volleyball, basketball, hiking and trapshooting. Exhilerating white-water rafting on the Rio Grande near Taos, New Mexico
Children's Programs: Excellent supervised children's program for ages 3-5, 6-11, and teens.
Dining: Hearty, home-cooked family style meals.
Summary: Excellent children's program! You'll find the best of Colorado and the enchantment of northern New Mexico. Great for families who want to be together but enjoy activities for varied interest and ages. Historic lodge with views of the valley. Varied horseback riding and supberb fishing in the Conejos River. Kids especially enjoy riding in Doug's century-old wagon. Near Santa Fe and Taos, New Mexico.

Smith Fork Ranch
Crawford, Colorado

Smith Fork Ranch is located in the western Colorado Rockies, midway between Aspen and Telluride. Nestled in the West Elk Mountains, the ranch straddles three miles of the Smith Fork River Valley and is surrounded by over a million acres of national forest and wilderness, with endless trails for spectacular vistas on horseback rides or hiking. Towering mountains filled with aspen and pine, high mountain meadows and streams filled with wildflowers, wildlife, and wild trout make for a breathtaking environment. The ranch itself first hosted guests in the late 1930s. The Hodgson family discovered it a decade ago, and after meticulous renovation — adding luxurious touches, slate-tiled bathrooms, and a covered dining pavilion — have elevated this ranch to a world-class mountain hideaway. History, beauty, adventure, and luxury all in one." The London Daily Telegraph reported, "It is, without a doubt, one of the most peaceful, welcoming and thoughtfully run places I've ever stayed."

Address: P.O. Box 401, Crawford, Colorado 81415
Telephone: 970/921-3454
Website: www.smithforkranch.com
Airports: Montrose, Aspen, Eagle/Vail, Grand Junction, and Gunnison.
Location: Eight miles east of Crawford, Colorado; five hours west of Denver; about 30 minutes from the north rim of the Black Canyon of the Gunnison National Park.
Memberships: The Dude Ranchers' Association, Colorado Dude and Guest Ranch Association.
Guest Capacity: 26-28
Accommodations: Three log cabins, each with decks facing the mountains and gas log stoves for crisp Colorado nights accommodate two to four guests. A large log guesthouse has five guest bedrooms with private baths, a living room with river-rock fireplace, sun porch, and wraparound porch. The River Cabin has three spacious bedrooms, rock fireplace, screened porch and deck with hot tub, and accommodates three couples or two large families. Workout and massage rooms also available.
Rates: $$$$$ American Plan.
Season: June through October.
Activities: Spectacular trail riding, outstanding fly-fishing, and hiking. Guided trail rides range from two hours to all-day picnic rides. Afternoon cocktail ride to watch the sunset, and an evening ride to a riverside cookout. Campfire, cowboy sing-alongs and hayride are also part of this western Colorado experience. Fly-fishing on three private miles of the Smith Fork River, seven ponds, and backcountry mountain drainages for Colorado rainbow trout, brookies, brown, and cutthroats. Complimentary, top-quality equipment and knowledgeable guides are provided. Guided and self-guided walking/hiking trails with picnic spots along the river. Long-bow archery, roping, and Natural Horsemanship. Stargazing through the ranch telescope.
Children's Programs: A paradise for young people. Families interact together.
Dining: Food and wine are a specialty. Trained chef prepares dishes that celebrate fresh, organically grown and raised produce, game, lamb, and beef.
Summary: A charming luxury ranch in the heart of the Colorado Rockies with Superb accommodations, excellent cuisine and stellar wines. Wonderful fly-fishing program and horseback riding. Featured in the coveted Hideaway Report by Andrew Harper.

Sylvan Dale Guest Ranch
Loveland, Colorado

An easy commute, just a little over one hour from Denver International Airport is where you will find Sylvan Dale's 3200 acre Dude Ranch, nestled in the Colorado Foothills along the banks of the Big Thompson River. Family owned and operated since 1946, the Jessup's invite you to "saddle up" for an experience you won't soon forget. The ranch raises and trains registered Quarter Horses so you can count on a responsive mount to partner with in the arena and on the trail. With the elevation of only 5,200 feet, you will have no high altitude adjustment for you and your family, which makes the ranch ideal for multi-generational family reunions! In addition to offering family Dude Ranch vacations, Sylvan Dale is also known for their famous Cowgirl Round Up's and Adults Only Week for those preferring a kid-free vacation! They also host corporate events, B&B stays, wedding/receptions and have wonderful "off-season specials". The ranch has been featured in a number of publications. Outbound Holidays ranks Sylvan Dale Guest Ranch second only to Disney World and better than Hawaii, New York, and Las Vegas, for a kid friendly vacation. They carry the gold certification from Green Life, and were awarded "2008 Environmental Business Award for Small Members" by the Fort Collins Area Chamber of Commerce making Sylvan Dale a leader in the growing "Green Movement."

Address: 2939 N. County Road 31 D, Loveland CO 80538
Telephone: 877-667-3999
Website: www.sylvandale.com
Airports: Denver.
Location: 55 miles northwest of Denver and 18 miles east of Estes Park off Highway 34.
Memberships: CGRA,DRA, Green Hotel Association.
Guest Capacity: 30
Accommodations: Comfortable Country! You'll enjoy the warmth of home in a peaceful, riverside setting. Individual and family units are available. Antiques are throughout the 26 lodging units, dining hall and gathering areas. Several units have fireplaces, porches or decks, and their guest houses have full kitchens. All accommodations are TV and telephone free, but free internet and cellular access is available.
Rates: $$$$ - American Plan.
Season: Year-round. Full Dude Ranch Program mid-June – August.
Activities: Enjoy horseback riding, hayrides, guided hikes, world class fly-fishing, rock climbing, trap shooting, white water rafting and more! Tennis courts, game room, swimming pool and a hot tub are available to all guests. A variety of evening activities are designed for all ages, & include Western dancing, a rollicking ranch party, cowboy entertainment, campfires, family softball, and an ice cream social….just good ol'fashioned family fun! Close to Rocky Mountain National Park, Loveland and Estes Park, there is plenty of off ranch sight-seeing and shopping opportunities, but guests rarely leave the ranch!
Children's Programs: Supervised youth programs for ages 3-12.
Dining: A wide variety of wholesome family style meals.
Summary: One of Colorado's best! Celebrating 70 years. As they say at Sylvan Dale, come "Discover Your Inner Cowboy!" Sylvan Dale Guest Ranch is a great place for people of all ages. Terrific for off-season corporate events, reunions and weddings as well! Great Fun! Great Food! Great Folks!

Tumbling River Ranch
Grant, Colorado

The Gordons' Tumbling River is one of the most famous family and children's ranches in America. Second-generation hosts Scott and Megan Dugan along with their three children serve up Western hospitality high in the Colorado Rockies. At 9,200 feet, the ranch is in Indian country, on the banks of Geneva Creek and in the middle of Pike National Forest. The property consists of an upper ranch, which was built as a mountain retreat in the 1920s, and the Pueblo house, featuring carved beams and adobe walls, which was built by Taos Indians for the daughter of Adolph Coors. One of the best features at Tumbling River is the extensive children's program, with caring college-age counselors. Tumbling River Ranch, in one word, is terrific, and it brings out the very best in families and children.

Address: P.O. Box 30, Grant, Colorado 80448
Telephone: 800/654-8770, 303/838-5981
Website: www.tumblingriver.com
Airports: Denver.
Location: Four miles north of Grant; 62 miles southwest of Denver
Memberships: The Dude Ranchers' Association, Colorado Dude and Guest Ranch Association.
Guest Capacity: 55
Accommodations: Accommodations are in the main lodge and the Coors family Pueblo house. There are also eight cabins around the ranch with names like Indian Hogan, the Frenchman's Cabin, Big Horn, and Tomahawk. All have fireplaces, arched ceilings, and king or queen-size beds, or bunk beds for kids. Some are real logs, some log-sided; all porches have swings and colorful planters, and many bird feeders are scattered about.
Rates: $$$$ American Plan.
Season: Mid-May through mid-October
Activities: A wide variety of activities: scenic high country riding with weekly riding clinic and instruction for all levels; half-day and all-day rides; family rides, kids' rides, and an overnight ride for adults and kids ages 12 and older. Hiking to breathtaking 14,000-foot vistas. Fly-fishing with instruction in stocked ponds, streams, and mountain lakes. The heated swimming pool has a full-length cabana with tables and two hot tubs. Massage therapist available. Weekly river rafting on the Arkansas River (extra).
Children's Programs: Tops! Excellent morning and afternoon supervised western programs for children ages three through teens.
Dining: Healthy well balanced family style meals. Serving elegant adult dinners.
Summary: One of the great family dude ranches in the West. Excellent family ranch with outstanding children's program for infants to teens! Wonderful entertainment. Hosts and staff are tops! Wait until you see the marvelous old ranch trading post and the Pioneer Club, a marvelous 4,000 square foot recreation facility that hosts weekly square dancing, live music, kids club activities, indoor games, and arts and crafts. Also wonderful for destination weddings in the Spring and Fall. Near Towns of Georgetown, Fairplay, and Breckenridge.

Vista Verde Ranch
Steamboat Springs, Colorado

Tucked away in a secluded valley with hay meadows, aspen groves, and mountain vistas, Vista Verde is more than just a riding ranch. It offers tremendous diversity for those who want to experience other guided adventures like mountain biking, rock-climbing, river rafting, and even hot-air ballooning. Small with attention to detail; active, very relaxing and unpretentious. With a beautiful lodge and cabins, a trained chef, wide-ranging activities, and a superb staff, Vista Verde is one of the best! Vista Verde's winter program adds a unique element to the typical guest ranch experience with cross-country skiing, sledding, snowshoeing and sleigh rides.

Address: P.O. Box 770465, Steamboat Springs, Colorado 80477
Telephone: 800/526-7433, 970/879-3858
Website: www.vistaverde.com
Airport: Hayden Airport just 40 miles away
Location: 25 miles north of Steamboat Springs
Memberships: The Dude Ranchers' Association, Colorado Dude and Guest Ranch Association
Guest Capacity: 50
Accommodations: Named after surrounding mountains, log cabins are nestled up against an aspen covered hillside, overlooking the valley floor. Handsomely furnished, they include woodstoves, full baths, and comfortable porches that overlook the meadows and forest. All have private outdoor hot tubs and master suites for Mom and Dad. Three spacious rooms with splendid views are upstairs in the lodge. Fresh flowers, baskets of snacks, and a fridge full of beverages welcome guests. Daily service and evening turndown provided. Wireless internet available in the Main Lodge.
Rates: $$$$$$ American Plan.
Season: Summer: June through October; Winter: Christmas through March.
Activities: The riding program offers in-depth instruction and helpful clinics in the indoor arena for all levels of experience. Half-day and all day rides as well as cattle work and team penning are also options. Guided hiking trips head into the Mt. Zirkel wilderness area as guests choose the level and length of experience they desire. An extensive mountain biking program provides thrills for novice as well as expert riders beginning in the Terrain park and moving out on to single track trails. Fly-fishing guides offer a personalized opportunity for beginning anglers on stocked ponds and for more experienced anglers on private waters. Rock-climbing, rafting, a photography workshop, and hot air ballooning add to the variety of possible adventures. Evening entertainment ranges from campfires to a barn dance and Cowboy Music Show.
Children's Programs: A complete supervised children's program is offered for youngsters 6-17 years.
Dining: Award-winning chefs prepare meals that walk the line between fancy and ranchy.
Summary: One of America's top year-round luxury sporting ranches in North America. Featured in National Geographic Traveler. Lots of wilderness, superb food, and lots of good company. Excellent fly-fishing and incredible mountain biking program. With so many on and off-ranch adventures, this is more than just a riding ranch. Ask about winter, when it's Vista "Blanca." Near Famous ski town of Steamboat Springs.

Waunita Hot Springs Ranch
Gunnison, Colorado

For over 50 years three generations of the Pringle family have hosted guests looking for that authentic western vacation in a wholesome, safe, family atmosphere. Near the Continental Divide at 8946 feet, the ranch borders the Gunnison National Forest. A noted health spa during the early 1900's, the abundant natural hot springs water now feed the giant private pool and spa which is perfect for soaking after a long day of horseback riding. Forest permits allow for miles of scenic trails from flowery meadows to spectacular mountain peaks. Kids love the open space to safely roam, catching frogs from the creek, playing catch in the yard and befriending all the small ranch animals that call Waunita home. A full week of western activities await with something to please everyone in the family. Whether it's the ride to canyon creek camp, razr trip to Little Baldy, or singing at the evening hayride, enjoy a week at Waunita as "The Best Week of Your Year!"

Address: 8007 county road 887, Gunnison, Colorado 81230
Telephone: 970-641-1266
Website: www.waunita.com
Airport: Gunnison.
Location: 27 miles east of Gunnison; 150 miles west of Colorado Springs, off Highway 50.
Memberships: The Dude Ranchers' Association, Colorado Dude and Guest Ranch Association.
Guest Capacity: 35
Accommodations: Two lodges designed for family occupancy all units with private baths, and robes for the short walk to the hot springs pool. Large common areas include fireplaces, billiard/Library room and the dining hall. Laundry facility is available. The square dance hall on the 2nd floor of the barn is also used for a weekly western music show.
Rates: $$$ American Plan.
Season: Summer June-September. Off-season B&B and groups October-April
Activities: Your own horse for the week will take you on a variety of trails and terrain, from flowered meadows to snowcapped peaks. Guided rides are scheduled in small groups, rides vary from beginner walking rides to more advanced rides with loping. Arena games for the kids and cattle penning for the adults. The high ride to Stella Mountain's 12,500 summit is breathtaking. Three cookout rides and an overnight at the forest camp on Canyon Creek are weekly highlights. Scenic Razr 4x4 trips. Evening activities include hayride, square dance, skeet shooting, and Western music. Stream and lake fishing available off site.
Children's Programs: Most activities are designed for family participation. There is a full time children counselor with special activities "just for the kids". Kid's fishing pond.
Dining: Emphasis in the kitchen is on homemade, fresh, plentiful and tasty. Where else can you get such food as "made from Scratch" muffins, biscuits, rolls, cakes, pies, pancakes and cookies. There are also lots of salads, veggies and meats. At any time of the day you can help yourself to the fruit bowl, hot chocolate, tea and coffee, with a guest refrigerator to "raid" for that late night snack. We are glad to accommodate special diets or food allergies with prior notice. In keeping with the family atmosphere, BYOB wine or beer in moderation is allowed at meals or in your room only.
Summary: One of the great family –owned and operated guest ranches. Magnificent giant hot springs pool, terrific mountain scenery in a wholesome family atmosphere.

Wind River Christian Ranch
Estes Park, Colorado

Wind River Ranch is a Christian Family Dude Ranch located 7 miles south of the quaint mountain town of Estes Park. Nestled between Twin Sisters Mountain and the 14,259 Longs Peak, Wind River blends the rustic history of this historic ranch. The barn was built in 1889, the ranch house and several cabins were built in the 1920's and have been elegantly remodeled. Executive chefs prepare meals, wranglers will guide you through scenic Rocky Mountain National Park, and exceptional staff will provide entertaining programs that children will enjoy. The program is packed with fun days and entertaining nights, but everything is optional, so you can be as active or relaxed as you like – it is your vacation.

Address: P.O. Box 3410, Estes Park, CO 80517
Telephone: 970-586-4212; 800-523-4212
Website: windriverranch.com
Airports: Denver (DIA).
Location: 7 miles south of Estes Park off Highway 7, the ranch is 75 miles from the Denver Airport (DIA).
Memberships: Colorado Dude and Guest Ranch Association, Christian Camping and Conference Association.
Guest Capacity: 55
Accommodations: Quaint mountain cabins are perfectly tucked away in the aspen and pine forests of the property. Each cabin has a wonderful porch with willow rocking chairs for you to enjoy the amazing views. Cabins have newly remodeled master bedroom suites with new mattresses, renovated master bathrooms with granite counter tops, slate walk-in showers, and a great rustic elegance feel.
Rates: $$$ American Plan.
Season: Late May – Early October
Activities: Guests can ride every day and arrange for personalized riding lessons at no extra charge. Adults can attend the optional morning bible study with featured guest speaker. Other activities include climbing wall and zip-line, hiking in Rocky Mountain National Park, rafting on the Cache Le' Poudre River, golfing and shopping in Estes Park, frisbee golf, soaking in new resort swimming pool and hot tub, lake kayaking, and many more. Each day will have events like square dancing, a kid's rodeo, a family Olympics, and lots of laughter at the ranch "Hootenanny". Three nights a week offer a fireside gathering in the upper meadow where praise and worship songs are sung by the fire and visitors hear a short message from the guest speaker of the week. Roasting marshmallows as often as possible.
Childrens Program: All ages welcome, excellent kids' and teen programs. The ranch also has a brand new nursery for the little buckaroos.
Dining: Hearty ranch cuisine.
Summary: Wind River Ranch and Ministry celebrates Christian family values, wholesome fun and plenty of western charm. It is a place where life slows down and time together with family is maximized; here you and your family will re-charge your spiritual batteries and grow closer to one another. You will make memories that not only last a lifetime, but nourish a lifetime!

Zapata Ranch
Mosca, Colorado

Zapata Ranch is a 103,000-acre ranch owned by The Nature Conservancy of Colorado, where guests can ride through and learn about the conservation of 2,500 herd of bison, integrate themselves into daily life on the ranch, and participate in extensive nature programs. Managed by Tess Phillips Leach, Zapata Ranch is nestled at the base of Southern Colorado's Sangre de Cristo Mountains and shares a border with the United States' newest National Park: The Sand Dunes National Park & Preserve.

Address: 5305 State Hwy. 150/Mosca, CO/ 81146
Telephone: 800-5-ZAPATA or 719-378-2356
Website: www.zranch.org
Airport: Denver
Location: 4 hours southwest of Denver, 2.5 hours northwest of Santa Fe, 30 minutes northeast of Alamosa and bordering the Great Sand Dunes National Park.
Memberships: Dude Ranchers' Association, Colorado Dude & Guest Ranch Association, Center for Holistic Resource Management.
Guest Capacity: 30
Accommodations: Each guest room is equipped with either two double beds or a single king and its own private bathroom. The lodge is built on the original Zapata homestead with buildings that date back to the late 1800's and is surrounded by extensive grounds. The buildings, which include The Lodge, Bunk House and Stewart house, are all restored for comfort and rustic charm. Daily maid service and laundry facilities are included.
Rates: $$$$: American Plan
Season: January – November
Activities: Two programs, Ranching With Nature and The Great Outdoors Experience will give you the opportunity for a one-of-a-kind, fully customizable vacation. Whether you want to help move cattle from one pasture to the next, monitor water levels and grass growth, participate in a traditional branding, ride through the Sand Dunes National Park Summit with 14,000-ft peaks, go on an interpretive walk through grasslands and learn about bison as a conservation species, or white-water raft down the Arkansas River, the staff is here to make this the vacation of your lifetime.
Children's Programs: No specific Children's Program. Best for older children.
Dining: Zapata Ranch serves its own grass-fed beef and bison, along with local produce. The style is down-home gourmet, and meals are served family-style in dining room.
Summary: Spectacular setting. A rider's dream: great horses, excellent wranglers, stunning scenery and fabulous food. One of the most unique ranches in North America, bordered by the Sand Dunes National Park and Sangre de Cristo Mountain range. 103,000 acres with bison and cattle. Wide range of activities and programs offered both on the ranch and at nearby locations. Working ranch opportunities and educational, conservation and nature experiences. Be sure to ask about Branding Week, Buffalo Roundups, Sandhill Crane Photo Trip, Painting and Photography Workshops, Horsemanship & Roping Clinics and Corporate/Family Retreat Capacities.

GEORGIA

—✳—

Southern Cross Guest Ranch
Madison, Georgia

Southern Cross Guest Ranch is a year-round guest ranch & horse farm, conveniently nestled in Central Georgia's Historic Heartland and within an hour drive from Atlanta. Home to well over 150 quality Paint and Quarter Horses, the ranch is best known for its exceptional hands-on horseback riding program, unguided riding opportunities, and peaceful, comfortable setting. Southern Cross Ranch is, at its core, a family-owned and operated horse farm that values and respects its animals. SCR has been raising quality Paint and Quarter Horses for over 25 years. For over a decade, SCR has been welcoming guests to visit and share the indescribable joy of being around these magnificent creatures. Over two dozen foals are born on the ranch from March-June each year. Everyone has virtually unlimited opportunities to touch, photograph, and interact with many of the foals and other horses. If you are a horse lover or are simply curious about horses, you've found the right place. You'll be able to watch horses grazing from every porch, deck, dining room, and even from the pool. The philosophy is simple: It can't be a horse lover's paradise if it's not a horse's paradise first.

Address: 1670 Bethany Church Rd., Madison, GA 30650
Telephone: 706/342-8027
Website: www.southcross.com
Airport: Atlanta, GA.
Location: Just a 1 hour drive from the Atlanta Airport.
Memberships: Professional Assoc. of Innkeepers, AQHA, APHA.
Guest Capacity: 35
Accommodations: Nicely appointed guestrooms with private bath, HDTV, DVD, A/C, free wifi, and King sized beds. Rooms are available in five categories. Premium rooms feature balconies, whirlpool baths, and fireplaces. Some rooms feature both a king and queen bed to accommodate families.
Rates: $-$$$.
Season: Year-round.
Activities: Guided and unguided horseback riding is the featured activity at Southern Cross. The climate in Georgia is great for horseback riding year-round. The relaxed program even allows guests the unique opportunity to ride on their own if they desire, but small guided groups are always available. Guests are encouraged to groom and help tack the horses for a true hands-on and bonding experience. If you're not into horseback riding and don't wish to start, there are non-riding plans with reduced rates to meet your needs. While you'll find many ways to relax and unwind at Southern Cross, there is no shortage of other activities. On site you can enjoy the pool, hot tub, mountain bikes, basketball, fishing pond, game room, hiking, visiting horses in the pasture, throwing horseshoes, etc. Attractions nearby include golfing, tennis, boating, skeet shooting, kayaking, museums, historical tours, and shopping.
Children's Programs: Children are parent's responsibility.
Dining: Three full meals are served daily, buffet style. Each meal is prepared fresh and made from scratch.
Summary: Family owned bona-fide horse ranch with emphasis on horseback riding year round. Both guided and unguided rides. Convenient to major airport (Atlanta) and many regional attractions as well (theme parks, museums, etc.) Hearty food, great horse selection, and comfortable, modern accommodations.

IDAHO

— ✶ —

Diamond D Ranch
Stanley, Idaho

The Diamond D is located in one of Idaho's hidden valleys. Most guests come by car and savor the long and winding gravel road up and over Loon Creek Summit, which eventually switches back down into the beautiful Salmon River Mountain Valley. This slow but scenic drive is breathtaking and gives everyone a chance to slow down and unwind to the pace that they will enjoy for their week, or two or more, at the ranch. The Diamond D is remote. On all sides, it's bounded by millions of acres of wilderness and plenty of wildlife. Arriving at the ranch, you feel the same exhilaration the early gold miners must have felt when they exclaimed, "Eureka! We have found it!" The Demorest family has been running this wonderful ranch since 1951. No telephones—nothing but pure Idaho wilderness and wonderful family hospitality. The Diamond D is one of Kilgore's diamonds in the rough!

Address: P.O. Box 1555, Boise, Idaho 83701 (winter).
Telephone: 800/222-1269; Summer: 208/336-9772;
Cell: 208/861-9206; Winter: 208/336-9772
Website: www.diamonddranch-idaho.com
Airport: Boise, 45 minutes by charter plane, four hours by car; air charter service available from Boise to the 2,600-foot dirt airstrip four miles from the ranch.
Location: 75 miles north of Sun Valley, off Highway 75; the ranch will send you a map.
Memberships: Dude Rancher's Association.
Guest Capacity: 40
Accommodations: Three comfortable two-bedroom cabins a short walk from the main lodge and near Loon Creek, one large four-bedroom cabin that sleeps 10, one-bedroom suites including the honeymoon/anniversary suite. Several upstairs lodge rooms. All rooms and cabins have electricity and modern bathrooms. A hydroelectric generator powers ranch. Email/Internet available. Guest laundry.
Rates: $$$ American Plan.
Season: June through October
Activities: Lots of activities are available each day. Evening and morning sign-up sheets for horseback riding with lessons available, hiking to back country hot spring, and gold panning. Ask about guided hikes to Mystery Lake, a 3,000-foot climb, and the ride to Rob's Hot Springs and Pinyon Peak rides (tremendous lookout point at 10,000 feet). The Diamond D offers 3 - 7 day pack-trips to hot springs, mountain lakes, and historic ranches, as well as backpacking trips. Modern swimming pool with adjacent hot tub, skeet and target shooting, and archery. Fly-fishing in the private lake and many streams. Guides and equipment available. Volleyball, kickball, and horseshoes on the lawn in front of the lodge. Each summer, the ranch hosts numerous weddings and renewals of vows in the beautiful, hand-built rock chapel overlooking Loon Creek, which also offers a Sunday service.
Children's Programs: Fully supervised programs for children under age six.
Dining: A variety of tempting meals are served ranch-style.
Summary: One of Kilgore's real diamonds in the rough! Incredible setting! One of the great family-run ranches for families on the headwaters of Loon Creek, which is a tributary of the Middle Fork of the Salmon River. Lovely, remote ranch in the heart of some of Idaho's most pristine wilderness, with all the comforts of home and its own private lake. The area is full of Western lore, gold mines, and Native American stories. You'll want to see the old mining town of Custer and the Yankee Fork gold dredge.

Idaho Rocky Mountain Ranch
Stanley, Idaho

Spectacular! Nestled between the breathtaking White Cloud and Sawtooth Mountains, the historic 900 acre Idaho Rocky Mountain Ranch is unique among western adventure ranches. The Ranch offers beautifully renovated luxury appointed accommodations, gracious hospitality, excellent food, casual atmosphere and some of the world's best outdoor recreation, without the crowds. Surrounded by more wilderness than anywhere in the continental United States, the distant majestic craggy peaks, alpine lakes, winding Salmon River and extensive trail system beckon you for adventures including hiking, biking, horseback riding, fishing, rafting, ghost town and museum visits. The Ranch's natural hot springs swimming pool and breathtaking views from the famous front porch with its old hickory rocking chairs, invite soothing relaxation. The knowledgeable and caring staff will help you arrange your ideal vacation from the host of available activities on the ranch and offsite. Built in 1930 and listed on the National Register of Historic Places, the Ranch is the ideal home-base for exploration of one of the most spectacular and least traveled regions of the United States.

Address: HC 64 Box 9934, Stanley, Idaho 83278
Telephone: 208-774-3544
Website: www.idahorocky.com
Airport: Boise, 130 miles, Sun Valley (Hailey), 64 miles; Stanley airstrip, 10 miles.
Location: 50 miles north of Sun Valley/Ketchum, on the Salmon River-Sawtooth Scenic Byway, one of the Top 10 Scenic Drives of the Pacific Northwest.
Memberships: National Trust for Historic Preservation, Nature Conservancy, Associate Member Dude Ranch Association, Idaho Dude Ranch Association.
Guest Capacity: 50
Accommodations: Beautifully preserved 7,400 square foot hand-hewn log main lodge houses the great room, dining room, and four guest rooms with queen beds and private baths. Seven beautifully renovated duplex log cabins, the 3-room Family Cabin and Honeymoon Cabin have Oakley stone fireplaces, private baths and twin or king beds.
Rates: $$$$ - Including meals, à la carte activities program.
Season: June through September
Activities: Natural hot springs swimming pool, fly-fishing the Salmon River and ranch stocked catch-and-release fishing pond with paddleboat, mountain bikes and trails, hiking, and horseback rides. Weekly BBQ's, Dutch-oven and wood-fired brick oven dinners, star gazing, sunset and wildlife viewing, children's program. Offsite activities: rafting the Salmon and Payette Rivers, rock-climbing, unlimited hiking, biking and fishing opportunities, numerous pristine alpine lakes, ghost town and museum visits, Sawtooth Fish Hatchery, Sawtooth National Recreation Area.
Children's Programs: Children are the responsibility of parents. Three nights a week there is children's dinner and activities.
Dining: Multi-course dinners are innovative and elegant.
Summary: Spectacular! One of the most incredible views I've ever seen. On national register of historic places. Authentic western luxury cabins and à la carte activities program. Outstanding outdoor recreation opportunities without the crowds, relaxed atmosphere and activity schedules, freedom to choose activities for a personalized vacation. Historic architecture, natural hot springs pool, fine food and amenities, knowledgeable and gracious staff.

McGarry Ranches
Rexburg, Idaho

Theron and Jean McGarry were both born and raised in the upper Snake River Valley to ranching families. They raise Hereford, Black Angus cattle and registered Quarter Horses on the ranch. The main ranch is located on approximately 250 acres with large shade trees, gardens, and various types of flowers. With the exception of branding and tagging, the ranch work is done from Quarter Horses. The tack is checked daily, and most of the saddles are custom / handmade.

Address: 6140 W. 5000 S., Rexburg, Idaho 83440
Telephone: 866/593-4455
Website: www.mcgarryranches.com
Airport: Daily flights from Salt Lake City, Utah and Denver, Colorado to Idaho Falls, Idaho. The airport is just 30 minutes away from the ranch. A pick-up service is offered to and from the ranch for a small fee.
Membership: Dude Ranchers' Association.
Guest Capacity: 4 rooms, up to 8 guests.
Accommodations: Guests are hosted in 2 log cabins with 2 rooms each. Three single beds available in three of the rooms. One room has a double bed and one single bed. Housekeeping is provided if staying more than one week. Meals are served family style in the main ranch house. Breakfast is served at 7:00 a.m., lunch is prepared and packed into coolers to be taken to the mountains. Evening meals are served around 6:00 p.m. depending on when guests get back from working the cattle and/or after ranch chores are completed. The main ranch house is located on a peninsula surrounded by water from the Snake River and large shade trees.
Rates: $$-$$$$ American Plan.
Season: May 15 through the end of October.
Activities: McGarry's is a working cattle ranch, where guests work alongside the cowboys. Moving cattle, branding, sorting, weaning and fencing are all in a day's work.
Children's Programs: Minimum age for children is 8 years old.
Dining: Family style ranch meals.
Summary: McGarry Ranches is a 7th generation ranch that has been in this area since the early 1900s. The ranch started with 640 acres and grew to over 55,000 acres. This has always been and is currently, a working cattle operation. The McGarry's own and run, depending on the time of year, two thousand head of cattle. Guests come from all over the world to experience ranch life as it has been done for generations. Come ride with the ranch cowboys and become part of the McGarry Family.

Red Horse Mountain Ranch
Harrison, Idaho

Idaho's Red Horse Mountain Ranch is a vacation getaway and retreat for those who savor the spirit of adventure, relaxation, and friendly western hospitality. Rich in history, the ranch dates back to the 1940's when it began hosting dudes. Today those traditions live on, and now, as host Cory Inouye says, "We offer a wonderful program for families who want to get away from it all and enjoy the myriad of activities we offer together with our special brand of western hospitality." Red Horse Mountain Ranch is recogrnized as one of the great guest ranches in Idaho and the West with activities for all. If there are three words that sum up Red Horse, they are adventure, food and friends. Here you'll truly discover the luxuries of silence, the wind on your face and the stars shining brightly. As Cory says "The essence of a ranch vacation nourishes the heart and soul. It is all about watching children blossom and finding time for yourself to find peace away from the daily grind. Here we pride ourselves in the care we give our guests and the memories that are made." Red Horse Mountain takes you back and shares old fashioned goodness that bring out the best in all of us.

Address: 11077 East Blue Lake Road, Harrison, Idaho 83833.
Telephone: 888/689-9680, 208/689-9680
Website: www.redhorsemountain.com
Airports: Spokane, Washington (GEG), private planes use St. Maries or Coeur d'Alene, Idaho.
Location: Five miles east of Harrison, off Highway 97; 78 miles southeast of Spokane; 28 miles southeast of Coeur d'Alene.
Membership: Dude Ranchers' Association, Idaho Outfitter and Guides Association.
Guest Capacity: 48
Accommodations: Comfortable two-story log cabins and suites with private baths. Numerous hot tubs and a heated swimming pool. Daily laundry service. 7000 square foot main lodge with spacious dining; multiple meeting facilities; outdoor amphitheater.
Rates: $$$$ American Plan.
Season: Year-round.
Activities: Daily horseback riding, scenic, advanced, all-day, and lunch rides. Additionally, kid's program (ages 3-11). Incredible challenge course and climbing wall. Downhill mountain biking, pond fishing, bike tours, sporting clays, hiking, 3D archery, morning fitness hiking, massage and yoga, kayaking tours, boat tours, bass fishing, geo-cacheing. Walk & wade or drift boat fly-fishing and whtiewater trips (extra). Winter offerings include cross-country skiing, sledding, snowshoeing, ice fishing, and snowmobile trips.
Children's Programs: Extensive program from Memorial weekend through Labor Day weekend for ages 3-11.
Dining: Classically trained chefs offer a blend of western ranch cuisine and Pacific Northwest favorites, made with fresh, regional ingredients.
Summary: One of Idaho's best! Excellent for families and corporate team buliding. Red Horse Mountain Ranch is located one hour south of Coeur d'Alene, Idaho and offers a full service, all-inclusive dude ranch vacation from May through October. The ranch includes a famous kid's program packed with outdoor activities and horseback riding (ages 3 and up) every day from Memorial Weekend through Labor Day. All inclusive rates. Incredible challenge course and climbing wall. Additional activities include massage, and fly-fishing on the beautiful St. Joe river. Red Horse Mountain Ranch is well known for its surprising amount of activities, wonderful horses, extensive kid's program, delighful staff, and old west flair. Special weeks include Wine Tasting and Girl's Getaways. Airport shuttles are available.

Western Pleasure Guest Ranch
Sandpoint, Idaho

On a winter day in 1939, Janice's grandpa packed up his family and left Colorado. Their destination was his beautiful dream ranch in northern Idaho. This ranch is now known as the Western Pleasure Guest Ranch. Since 1990, Roley and Janice Schoonover, and her parents, ranchers Jim and Virginia Wood, have transformed this fourth generation family owned and operated cattle ranch into one of Idaho's quality guest ranches. Guests enjoy riding through the 1100 acre cattle ranch or into the national forest. The ranch is located in northern Idaho's scenic Panhandle region famous for Lake Pend Oreille, one of the largest freshwater lakes in the United States, and Schweitzer Mountain, a premier skiing destination for the Northwest. Hosts Roley and Janice share their love for their family ranch along with the rich history, beauty, and traditions of the area. Western Pleasure is for folks who appreciate sincere, real country hospitality, while enjoying beautiful handcrafted log accommodations.

Address: 1413 Upper Gold Creek Road, Sandpoint, Idaho 83864
Telephone: 208/263-9066; 888-863-9066
Website: www.westernpleasureranch.com
Airports: Spokane, Washington, 90 miles.
Location: 90 miles northeast of Spokane, Washington; 60 miles north of Coeur d'Alene Idaho; 16 miles northeast of Sandpoint, Idaho.
Memberships: Idaho Outfitters and Guides Association; Dude Ranch Association, Idaho Bed and Breakfast Association.
Guest Capacity: 20
Accommodations: Three log cabins and six lodge rooms. The handcrafted log cabins are secluded among tall pines to assure privacy. Each cabin can accommodate up to six yet is cozy enough for two with one bedroom. Loft, bathroom, and woodstoves for cool evenings. The lodge provides six comfortable guest rooms with private baths. A large great room where guests gather features a big river-rock fireplace. In the downstairs rec room, relax while playing a game of pool or while watching a favorite John Wayne movie.
Rates: $$$ American Plan. Three-day minimum stay.
Season: Year-round.
Activities: Horseback riding is the main activity, with varied terrain including ridges, forests, valleys, logging roads, and meadows. Slow, medium, and fast rides. Arena instruction. Ride mornings and afternoons for 2 - 2.5 hours, plus weekly all day rides. Ask about the Big Hill panorama, Grouse Creek Falls, and Gold Ridge scenic rides. Group wagon and private buggy rides, too. There is an 18-hole golf course less than 10 miles from ranch. Evening entertainment includes camp fire music, horsedrawn wagon rides, and a dinner cruise on Lake Pend Orielle. Winter: Guests enjoy horsedrawn sleigh rides and cross-country skiing. Year-round hot tub.
Children's Programs: Hands on experiences with their horse is the centerpiece of program.
Dining: Family-style meals. Ranch raised all natural beef. BYOB.
Summary: One of Idaho's best. Great for those who appreciate genuine country folks who love their family ranch and care about the land, their heritage, and Western traditions. Lots of heart here. Wonderful country spirit. Beautiful northern Idaho scenery. Evening horse and teamdrawn buggy/wagon rides. Ask about the summer youth camps and family reunion packages. Near one of the country's largest freshwater lakes and Schweitzer Mountain.

MONTANA

—✦—

Averills' Flathead Lake Lodge
Bigfork, Montana

Flathead Lake Lodge is on the shores of the largest freshwater lake in the West, encompassing 2,000 private acres that border national forest. Featured on Good Morning America and Live with Regis and Kathie Lee, and written up in Better Homes & Gardens, Sunset, and Bon Appétit magazines, and a Mobil 4-Star property, this full-service dude ranch features the best of two worlds. For those who like water, there are all kinds of lake activities. If you'd rather be on horseback than on water skis or in a sailboat, there is an abundance of horse and rodeo activities available. In northwestern Montana, the lodge is 35 miles from one of nature's greatest wonders—Glacier National Park. The lodge was started in 1945 by the Averills and is operated by second generation Doug and Maureen Averill, along with their children and general manager Kevin Barrows. One word sums this up—tops!

Address: Box 248, Bigfork, Montana 59911
Telephone: 406/837-4391
Website: www.flatheadlakelodge.com
Airport: Kalispell.
Train: Whitefish, 30 miles.
Location: One mile south of Bigfork; 17 miles south of Kalispell.
Memberships: The Dude Ranchers' Association, Montana Dude Ranch Association.
Guest Capacity: 120
Accommodations: The historic main lodge is a beauty, with a rock fireplace, dining facility, saloon, and three upper sleeping rooms. The south lodge has 15 rooms, and there are 13 two and three-bedroom log cottages/cabins and two larger deluxe log cabins. Everything radiates warmth and charm.
Rates: $$$$$$ American Plan.
Season: May through October
Activities: Daily children and adult horseback riding, arena horse games, cattle penning instruction, and ranch rodeo. Breakfast, lunch, and dinner rides. Wilderness hiking—ask about Jewel Basin. Heated pool right next to Flathead Lake. Four tennis courts. Extensive lake activities and private beach. Sailing on two historic 50-foot Q-class sloops, canoeing, lake cruising, and water-skiing. Fly-fishing instruction available. White-water rafting and float-fishing available. Kayaking, river tubing, and mountain biking.
Children's Programs: Tremendous college staff. Ages 3-12 participate in organized children's program. Baby-sitting for younger kids available.
Dining: Social hour each evening in the private Saddle Sore Saloon. Enjoy steak barbecues, fresh seafood.
Summary: One of the leading resort ranches in North America. Extensive children's program where kids are catered to, not just accommodated. Fabulous lakeside setting on 28-mile long Flathead Lake, with extensive lake activities. Horseback riding through private Elk Preserve, which is available for viewing and photography. Be sure to have a huckleberry milkshake in Bigfork. Run by an old-time ranching family with a 70 percent family return rate. Near Glacier National Park. Golf nearby.

Bar W Guest Ranch
Whitefish, Montana

A great western vacation for all ages is what the Bar W Guest Ranch in Whitefish is all about. The Bar W is open year-round and ready to treat you with true Western Montana hospitality from the moment you arrive. Beautiful vistas and rolling ridges adorn the Montana countryside of this cozy dude ranch. Located on Spencer Lake, there are 3,000 acres available for horseback riding and all kinds of outdoor activities. Almost all guests, amilies, adults, singles and groups alike – have a tendency to think they are miles away from civilization here. But just 3.5 miles down the road from this serene wilderness is the vibrant resort town of Whitefish, offering shopping, dining, theater, and nightlife. The Bar W is nestled at the base of Spencer Mountain, between two pine-covered ridges. The ranch consists of a 6,200 square foot lodge, cabin suites, indoor and outdoor horseback riding arenas, stables, a barn, play meadow, an entertainment area, and a gazebo on the lake all helping to make the Bar W an idyllic piece of paradise for guests to soak in all year long.

Address: 2875 Highway 93 West Whitefish, MT 59937
Telephone: 856-828-2900, 406-863-9099
Website: www.barwguestranch.com
Airport: Kalispell, 15 miles (Glacier International Airport) Airport code (FCA)
Location: 4 miles west of Whitefish, Montana 23 miles west of Glacier. National Park, 30 mile north of Flathead Lake.
Memberships: Dude Ranchers Association.
Guest Capacity: 42
Accommodations: The main lodge is 6,200 square feet of classic and traditional western informality. The lodge has 6 guest suites, three common areas, and a game room. There is no shortage of great views from the decks that overlook the back horse pasture, the arena, and even the wildlife rich wetlands surrounding Spencer Lake. In addition to the lodge, there is also the meadow cabin overlooking south pasture. There are two suites, each with private bath, living area, and decks.
Rates: $$$ American Plan.
Season: Year-round.
Activities: The Bar W offers scenic horseback riding in the mountainous Montana terrain surrounding the ranch, the foothill country of the Rocky Mountain Front range, and the wide open praire of the Blackfeet Indian Reservation, in addition to indoor and outdoor arenas. The Bar W is a horseman's dream. The ranch has horses and a tailored riding program to fit all experience levels. By the middle of the week, you may be out in the pasture rounding up the cattle, and team penning. When the riding is done, the day is not over. There are wagon-ride dinners, skeet shooting, archery, guided hikes, fishing and swimming in Spencer Lake.
Children's Programs: Kids programs tailored to the families.
Dining: Meals served family style, everything is homemade western fare.
Summary: One of Montana's best. Fabulous location, great staff, terrific home cooked meals and comfortable accommodations. Above all, the Bar W Ranch is about providing true western hospitality to guests. It is near Glacier National Park, one of the most spectacular parks in the world.

Covered Wagon Ranch
Gallatin Gateway, Montana

The Covered Wagon Ranch, built as a Dude Ranch in 1925, remains one of the oldest operating Guest Ranches in the Gallatin Canyon. Retaining its historic western character, you will experience old-time charm and true family hospitality. Located three miles from the northwest corner of Yellowstone National Park and surrounded by the Gallatin National Forest, the Covered Wagon Ranch is noted for their excellent horse string and superb horseback riding opportunities. Taking daily rides in a multitude of directions from the ranch, guests travel some the most beautiful backcountry in the world teeming with mountain wildlife, and meadows full of wildflowers. Treasured by families for generations, the small, personal character of the ranch of decades ago remains a tradition today.

Address: 34035 Gallatin Road, Gallatin Gateway, Montana 59730
Telephone: 406/995-4237
Website: www.coveredwagonranch.com
Airport: Bozeman and West Yellowstone.
Location: 54 miles south of Bozeman and 34 miles north of West Yellowstone on Hwy 191.
Memberships: The Dude Rancher's Association, Montana Dude Rancher's Association.
Guest Capacity: 24
Accommodations: Ten original historic log cabins varying in size from one to two-bedrooms with private bathrooms. Log beds and furnishings, along with character bedding and décor add to the comfort and historic nature of the cabins. Most have wood stoves, and all have a covered porch with log rocking chairs for your afternoon siesta, reading comfort, relaxation, or visiting. A log lodge serves as the dining hall, and guest living room. An old historic log recreation hall includes a pool table, foosball table, and comfortable furniture in front of the stone fireplace.
Rates: $$$$ American Plan.
Season: June 1 through late September.
Activities: The primary activity of the ranch is horseback riding, and the program is very informal, allowing our guests to determine their own daily schedule. Welcoming novice through experienced riders, wranglers personally "fit" a horse to each guest for their full stay. Full day lunch rides, short full day rides, or half day rides are offered each day, and are scheduled during breakfast, allowing guests to best schedule their day. Rides are typically limited to a maximum of 6 riders, and are most likely to be two to four, with one to two wranglers per group. Guests will seldom, if ever, experience the same trail twice, as the riding opportunities are extremely varied. Along with the excellent riding, the ranch is adjacent to the Gallatin River and Taylor Fork of the Gallatin which offer blue-ribbon fishing opportunities. The Madison and Yellowstone Rivers are easily reached from the ranch as well. White-water rafting, mountain biking, golf, and tennis are available nearby. Tours of Yellowstone can be arranged, or you can visit the park on your own from the ranch as the entry is only 34 miles down the road.
Children's Program: No structured children's program. Children 6 and above are welcome to ride.
Dining: Hearty ranch cuisine served family style in the lodge. BYOB.
Summary: Just off the Gallatin Gateway Road, this is a wonderful little historic ranch with the old-time dude ranch spirit rich in Western hospitality. Very small and unassuming, a great base camp for a host of outdoor adventures during your summer visit to Montana, and just down the road from Yellowstone National Park.

Elkhorn Ranch
Gallatin Gateway, Montana

Welcome to one of Kilgore's authentic old-time dude ranches. The Elkhorn Ranch was started in the early 1920s by Grace and Ernest Miller, and is still run by the Miller's. Located one mile from the northwest corner of Yellowstone Park, Elkhorn is at 7,000 feet in a beautiful valley surrounded by the Gallatin National Forest and the Lee Metcalf Wilderness. It is a gateway to incredible natural beauty, mountain scenery, and loads of wildlife. From ranch headquarters, rides and hikes go out in all directions. Since the early days, Elkhorn has been famous for its superb riding program, for its dedication to preserving our Western heritage, and for uniting families. Today, as in years gone by, the ranch combines old-fashioned Montana-style hospitality, rustic warmth, and natural beauty. At Elkhorn, they still serve up the West the way it used to be.

Address: 33133 Gallatin Road, Gallatin Gateway, Montana 59730
Telephone: 406/995-4291
Website: www.elkhornranchmontana.com
Airports: Bozeman and West Yellowstone.
Location: 60 miles south of Bozeman, off Highway 191; 30 miles north of the west entrance to Yellowstone Park.
Memberships: The Dude Ranchers' Association, Montana Dude Ranch Association.
Guest Capacity: 40
Accommodations: Fifteen original log cabins radiate old-time Western charm and the early spirit of dude ranching. Most were built in the 1930s. Each is set apart from the others and varies in size, sleeping one to eight persons. All have colorful Hudson Bay foot blankets and comforters; and squeaky wooden floors. All have electric heat in the bathrooms, and most have woodstoves in the sitting areas. All have porches, most covered, and guests spend a good deal of time on them relaxing, reading, reflecting, and visiting. Nightly turndown. Laundry facilities available.
Rates: $$$$ American Plan.
Season: Mid-June through September.
Activities: This is a western riding ranch. Beginners will feel just as much at home as experienced riders. Everyone gets their own horse for the week. Great emphasis is placed on safety. Each morning at breakfast, guests are signed up individually for the day's riding, which starts at 10 a.m. Groups usually go out with six to eight people and two wranglers. All-day rides three times a week. Fishing rides twice a week. No riding on Sundays. Because there's such diverse riding, guests will seldom take the same ride twice. Fly-fishing enthusiasts will enjoy the Madison, Gallatin, and Yellowstone Rivers, all Blue Ribbon trout streams. Swimming in the ranch's spring-fed pond for the brave, and unlimited hiking. Keep your eyes open—there is lots of wildlife to see, including bear, wolves, elk, and moose.
Children's Program: Excellent all-day children's program, ages 6-12.
Dining: Home-cooked meals served buffet-style.
Summary: One of the classic, old-time dude ranches, with lots of authentic Old Western charm! Founded in 1922. Emphasis on horseback riding for all ages. One of the country's top children's programs. Excellent fly-fishing on Blue Ribbon waters. Close access to Yellowstone National Park (a must), and white-water rafting nearby. One week minimum stay preferred.

G Bar M Ranch
Clyde Park, Montana

Welcome to one of Montana's great full time ranching families, and when they say the welcome mat is out and the coffee pot is on, they mean it! Brackett Creek Valley, in the sage covered, rolling foothills of the Bridger Mountains, is home to the G bar M guest ranch. The Leffingwell family has operated this 3,200 acre cattle ranch since 1900 and has welcomed guests since the early 1930s. This part of the country was made famous by one of North America's early explorers and mountain men, Jim Bridger. The Leffingwell family offers a very speical, hands-on experience. At the G bar M, you can join in the daily activities that are part of this cattle/guest ranch, or you can enjoy everything at your own pace. The entire ranch has been designated as a game reserve, where wildlife can enjoy a safe and natural habitat. As Pat says, "We believe it is important to live in harmony with the land and to encourage eagles, elk, deer, and even hummingbirds to be a part of the ranch." While most guests come from the United States, some come from as far away as Europe and Australia to experience great Montana hospitality and ranching.

Address: Box 29, Clyde Park, Montana 59018
Telephone: 406/686-4423
Website: www.gbarm.com
Airport: Bozeman.
Location: 26 miles northeast of Bozeman, off State Highway 86.
Memberships: The Dude Ranchers' Association.
Guests Capacity: 17
Accommodations: Main lodge with dining room, fireplace, and four bedrooms, and a ranch house with two bedrooms and fireplace. Also two rustic log cabins, each with full bath and one with fireplace.
Rates: $$$ Full American plan.
Season: Year-round.
Activities: The ranch raises and trains most of their own horses. The riding emphasis is on Natural Horsemanship. Horses are matched to guests riding abilities. Guests may participate in various kinds of cattle work, mostly herding, changing pastures, checking fences, or placing salt licks for the cattle. Things are always busy, as the Leffingwells look after not only their own ranch, but several neighboring ranches' riding chores as well. Because this is an operating cattle ranch, you're expected to fit into the varied daily program unless you wish to entertain yourself by reading, hiking, or fishing for part or all of the day. Ranch fishing for rainbow trout in Brackett creek.
Children's Programs: Children are parent's responsibility. Best for older children.
Dining: Guests, ranch hands, and wranglers all eat together. Hearty ranch cooking.
Summary: Small, working, family-run cattle and horse ranch, with wonderful old-time Montana hospitality. "The coffee pot is always on here," and your're welcomed into the family! Great for families as well as singles and couples. Natural Horsemanship program. More open-riding than trail riding. In fact, the ranch discourages head-to-tail riding.

JJJ Wilderness Ranch
Augusta, Montana

The Triple J Ranch is run by Ernie and Kim Barker. Here in the pure mountain air, the emphasis is on enjoying the great outdoors, unwinding, relaxing, and having fun. The ranch lies in a valley at 5,500 feet in the Rocky Mountain Front Range of the Lewis and Clark National Forest, above the beautiful Sun River Canyon and Gibson Lake (7 miles long). The Barkers specialize in family vacations and emphasize horseback riding, hiking, and trout fishing. For the more adventurous and pioneers of heart, Ernie takes fabulous pack-trips to remote mountain lakes and through pine forests of the famous Bob Marshall Wilderness. The Barkers have hosted people from around the world over the years. They have a saying, "Let us show you some new horizons." Indeed, they will!

Address: Box 310, Augusta, Montana 59410
Telephone: 406/562-3653
Website: www.triplejranch.com
Airport: Great Falls.
Location: 80 miles west of Great Falls, 25 miles northwest of Augusta at the end of Sun River Canyon Road.
Memberships: The Dude Ranchers' Association, Professional Wilderness Outfitters Association.
Guest Capacity: 20
Accommodations: Twenty-four well-maintained, fully insulated, one to four-bedroom log cabins (each one sleeps two to nine) and luxury six-bedroom Ridgetop Lodge. Each features comfortable beds, electric heat, bathrooms with tub/shower, and a rock fireplace or woodstove. The cozy cabins are close to the clear mountain stream that winds through the property. All have front porches for relaxing.
Rates: $$$ American plan.
Season: June through mid-October.
Activities: The emphasis is on horseback riding consisting of horsemanship instruction followed by half day and a full day rides. Also, there are hiking opportunities, guided non-technical mountain climbing, and nature hikes to learn to identify wildflowers, trees, and birds. Trout fishing in the ranch trout ponds or nearby Gibson Lake and Sun River. Cookouts on Mortimer Vista, 4 miles north of the ranch. Optional overnight pack-trips. Also available are 5 - 8 day pack-trips that take in the incredible beauty and mystique of the Bob Marshall Wilderness.
Children's Programs: Parents interact with kids.
Dining: Healthful meals served family style in the main lodge.
Summary: One of the top ranches in Montana, and one of the top pack-trips in the Country! The Triple J is a small and personal ranch. You will discover new dimensions to life after spending a week with the Barkers. The ranch was included in a feature article on the Bob Marshall Wilderness in National Geographic magazine.

Lone Mountain Ranch
Big Sky, Montana

Lone Mountain Ranch is one of the country's premier multi-season guest ranches. What makes this ranch so special is its location in the heart of so much beauty and so many outdoor recreational activities. Here you'll discover nature and enjoy first-rate family guest-ranching in the summer, a world-class Nordic skiing program in the winter, and an Orvis endorsed fly-fishing program year-round. The ranch is in Montana's famous Gallatin Canyon, just down the road from Big Sky Ski and Summer Resort and thirty minutes from Yellowstone National Park. Throughout each week, naturalists lead hikes to teach visitors about the Yellowstone area's spectacular natural wonders. Activities vary, including spotting soaring eagles, identifying wildflowers, learning about geology or old Indian trails, taking early morning trips to hear bugling elk, and visiting Yellowstone. Whether you're horseback riding, hiking, mountain biking, fishing, skiing, or just daydreaming, the Lone Mountain crew will show you Montana's best.

Address: P.O. Box 160069, Big Sky, Montana 59716
Telephone: 800/514-4644, 406/995-4644
Website: www.lmranch.com
Airport: Bozeman.
Location: 40 miles south of Bozeman, off Highway 191.
Memberships: The Dude Ranchers' Association, Montana Dude Ranch Association, Cross-Country Ski Area Association.
Guest Capacity: 75
Accommodations: Twenty-four well maintained, fully insulated, one to four-bedroom log cabins (each one sleeps two to nine) and luxury six-bedroom Ridgetop Lodge. Each features comfortable beds, electric heat, bathrooms with tub/shower, and a rock fireplace or woodstove. The cozy cabins are close to the clear mountain stream that winds through the property. All have front porches for relaxing.
Rates: $$$$$ American Plan.
Season: Summer: Late May to mid-October; Winter: Early December to late March.
Activities: Superb summer and winter programs. Summer includes fly-fishing, naturalist-led hikes, horseback riding, mountain biking, canoeing, and relaxing. Riding instruction with no more than eight on a ride. Award-winning, Orvis endorsed fly-fishing on some of the best Blue Ribbon trout streams in the country. White-water rafting, golf, and scenic tram-ride nearby. In winter, the ranch offers wonderful downhill and cross-country skiing packages and snowshoeing.
Children's Programs: Full-day programs (optional) for ages 4-18.
Dining: Exceptional food created by trained chef. Winter sleigh-ride dinner.
Summary: One of North America's leading summer and winter guest ranches. Excellent for those who want a flexible on and off ranch program with close proximity to Yellowstone National Park! Children's and naturalist programs. Year-round Orvis endorsed fly-fishing with guides and instruction. Winter includes cross-country and downhill skiing packages at Big Sky Mountain. Great for spring and fall conferences. Superb cuisine! September and October best for adults with kids back in school. Year-round Yellowstone National Park tours.

McGinnis Meadows Cattle Guest Ranch
Libby, Montana

Welcome to one of the country's leading Buck Brannaman-style horseman-ship guest ranches. Here guests, both seasoned and novice riders, will learn excellence in horsemanship, and the art and spirit that embodies this wonderful way of life. McGinnis Meadows Cattle & Guest Ranch is oper-ated by owners Shayne and JoAnne Jackson and general Managers Dori and Randy Bock. Located in northwest Montana, the ranch was home-steaded in the 1890's by the Davis family. Cattle moved onto the scene in the 1920's, and in 1998 it opened its doors as a cattle and guest ranch us-ing the Buck Brannaman style of horsemanship, which is based on the 300 year old Vaquero tradition. As Shayne says, "This method is both gentle and effective and creates a unique bond between horse and rider."

Address: 6220 McGinnis Meadows Road, Libby, Montana 59923
Telephone: 406/293-5000
Website: www.mmgranch.net
Airport: Glacier International Airport, Kallspell; Spokane, Washington.
Location: 1.5 hours west of Kalispell, 40 minutes east of Libby; 200 miles east of Spokane.
Guest Capacity: 15
Accommodations: Three rooms in the lodge are single and double oc-cupancy, and six handcrafted, Amish built log cabins sleep up to four. Each has a queen size bed with denim down comforters and Pendleton wool blankets, as well as fluffy robes, complimentary slippers, plush towels for bath and hot tub use, and water bottles for rides. Rooms in the lodge have individual private baths and are close to the coffee pot and private deck.
Rates: $$$-$$$$ American Plan; six-night minimum Sunday to Saturday. Off-peak rates available.
Season: April- November 1
Activities: Here the spirit is all about the Buck Branaman style of horse-manship. The wranglers are trained in this style of riding and experienced in this way of life. With three guests per wrangler, quality individual at-tention is provided. Each day during the main season guests can choose to ride, move cattle out on 15,000 acres of summer range, practice team penning and cutting steers, further their horsemanship skills in the heated indoor arena, outdoor arenas, or out in the meadows, or ride through the open and timbered countryside. Side-by-side riding is featured. Call ahead for the year's horsemanship and cattle working schedules. Riding and nonriding guests also enjoy hiking and mountain biking along abandoned logging trails, swimming and fishing in nearby lakes, and guided fly-fishing and white water raft trips on the Kootenai and Flathead Rivers.
Children's Programs: No structured children's progam. Best for kids 10 and older.
Dining: Fine Western cuisine. Wine served at dinner.
Summary: The experience of a lifetime! One of the country's top Buck Brananman-style horsemanship cattle and guest ranches, with custom tack and extensive programs about horses, working with cattle, and roping demonstrations. Roping for experienced ropers. Lots of hands on work with cattle and horsemanship. For those who want to experience and learn about natural horsemanship McGinnis Meadows is one of the best!

Mountain Sky Guest Ranch
Emigrant, Montana

Mountain Sky goes way back to the early days of dude ranching. Originally it was the famed Ox Yoke Ranch, run by an old Montana family. Today, managed by Yancey and his fine staff, the ranch has guests hailing from around the globe. Together they have succeeded in blending the excellence customarily expected in a fine hotel with the casualness and sincerity of a Western ranch. It's in the magnificent Paradise Valley, home of the famous Yellowstone River. Just as in the early days, great emphasis is placed on the family. The staff go out of their way to ensure that both the young and the young-at-heart are happy and having one of the greatest experiences of their lives. Mountain Sky offers clean, fresh air, outstanding scenery, tranquility, luxuriously renovated Western accommodations, and fine dining. At this ranch, "the sky's the limit."

Address: Box 1219, Emigrant, Montana 59027
Telephone: 800/548-3392, 406/333-4911
Website: www.mtnsky.com
Airport: Bozeman.
Location: 60 miles southeast of Bozeman; 30 miles south of Livingston, 30 miles north Yellowstone National Park.
Memberships: The Dude Ranchers' Association, Montana Dude Ranch Association.
Guest Capacity: 80
Accommodations: Thirty luxury units, some that sleep up to ten; modern baths with fine amenities, large picture windows, and sitting rooms. The older, more rustic cabins have been preserved, keeping the Old West charm, with stone fireplaces or wood-burning stoves, pine furniture, and small front decks. All of the cabins have inviting front porches with hanging flower baskets. A bowl of fresh fruit is brought to each cabin daily. Yellowstone City, the newly refurbished main lodge, radiates warmth and comfort, with three stone fireplaces, a hand-hewn trussed ceiling, and braided rugs. It has a lounge, cozy bar, dining room, and for the musically inclined, a Yamaha grand piano.
Rates: $$$$$-$$$$$$ American Plan.
Season: May to late October
Activities: Extensive riding program for all levels. Rides go out daily except Sunday. Swimming in heated pool. Hot tub and sauna. Daily guided nature hikes. Tennis court. Fly-fishing on the Yellowstone River; guides can be arranged. Fishing on the ranch in a stocked trout pond. Big Creek is minutes from your cabin door. Ask about the ranch's own golf course! Off-ranch river rafting and Yellowstone National Park tours extra. Daily massage available.
Children's Programs: Exceptional children's program for infants to teens. One of the best in the country!
Dining: The food... wow! Gourmet, five-course dinners to authentic ranch cookouts.
Summary: One of America's premier ranches, and one of the oldest operating dude ranches in the U.S. Excellent historic, old-time ranch with superb children's program for infants on up, fine dining, and service second to none. Excellent fly-fishing and horseback riding. Ideal for high-level corporate meetings. River rafting on the Yellowstone River, private golf course. Specialty weeks: Visions of Yellowstone, Flavors of the West, Fall roundup & painting workshop. Near Yellowstone National Park (30 miles).

Nine Quarter Circle Ranch
Gallatin Gateway, Montana

One of Montana's legends! Since 1946, from early June to mid-September, the Nine Quarter Circle Ranch has been doing what it does best—welcoming families. High in the Montana Rockies in its own secluded mountain valley, the ranch is seven miles from the northwest corner of Yellowstone National Park. There's a five-mile drive up a winding, scenic dirt road until the ranch is visible. Taylor Fork, a fly-fishing river, runs through the ranch, and the log cabins overlook the green, grassy meadows with the striking mountain peaks in the distance. One of Montana's most famous, the ranch is run by Kim and Kelly Kelsey and their two young sons, Konnor and Kameron, and daughter Kyleen. Kim and Kelly are the son and daughter-in-law of the founders, Howard and Martha Kelsey. As the Kelseys say, "Two things can never change or end, the goodness of nature and man's love for a friend." You'll find both here.

Address: 5000 Taylor Fork Road, Gallatin Gateway, Montana 59730
Telephone: 406/995-4276
Website: www.ninequartercircle.com
Airport: Bozeman or the ranch airstrip; contact ranch for airstrip fact sheet.
Location: 60 miles south of Bozeman.
Memberships: The Dude Ranchers' Association, Montana Dude Ranch Association.
Guest Capacity: 65
Accommodations: Twenty one four bedroom log cabins with log furniture and hand-sewn quilts. Most have woodstoves and porches. The cabins are named after guests, such as Hubbards' Cupboard and Wihtol's Wickiup. All cabins have private or family baths. The main lodge has a huge rock fireplace. The Kelseys have a clever "Medallion" award board for guests who have returned year after year; it's hanging in the dining room. Some guests have medals representing over 30 years. Guest laundry facilities.
Rates: $$$ American Plan.
Season: Mid-June through mid-September.
Activities: Riding, fly-fishing, hiking, and wildlife viewing. Plenty of horses. The ranch raises and trains over 120 Appaloosas. Four or five rides, ranging from kiddie rides to advanced rides, daily go to vistas like Inspiration Point, Sunken Forest, and Alp Basin. Two all-day rides and an overnight pack-trip go out weekly, including the Kelsey Killer, "for those who want a real thrill." Great fly-fishing on the Gallatin River and the ranch's own Taylor Fork (which runs through the ranch), fly-fishing guide on staff and included with activities. Individualized instruction and local fishing trips included in ranch stay. Stocked trout pond for casting and kids' catch-and-release fishing. Limited loaner fly-fishing rods and retail fishing shop on ranch. A spring-fed "swimming pool" for hardy swimmers.
Children's Programs: Full program for kids ages infant to nine years.
Dining: Children and teens eat early while parents enjoy happy hour. Meals are home-cooked and family-style.
Summary: One of Montana's most famous ranches, and one of the oldest continuously operating dude ranches in the West since 1912. Wonderful family-run ranch for families with children throughout the summer. Adults only in the fall. Great riding and fly-fishing. Ideal for young families with kids of all ages and for grandparents, too. Appaloosas bred and trained on the ranch. Ask about the fall Bugle Rides! Private airstrip. Ranch store. Near Yellowstone National Park, Museum of the Rockies in the Western college town of Bozeman.

Parade Rest Guest Ranch
West Yellowstone, Montana

Parade Rest Guest Ranch is near one of the world's most famous parks—Yellowstone National Park—and in the heart of some of North America's best fly-fishing country. With Grayling Creek literally at the back door, and Blue Ribbon trout streams surrounding it, Parade Rest offers a parade of outdoor activities, natural beauty, and for those so inclined, lots of rest. There's no timetable or regimented activity list. Your time is your own, and you may do as much or as little as you please. Life at Parade Rest is informal. Mornings and evenings are cool, with midday temperatures in the mid- to high 80s. Parade Rest Ranch is a small dude/fly-fishing ranch—your home away from home while fishing or touring Yellowstone National Park and the surrounding area.

Address: 1279 Grayling Creek Road, West Yellowstone, Montana 59758
Telephone: 800/753-5934, 406/646-7217
Website: www.paraderestranch.com
Airports: West Yellowstone or Bozeman, Montana; Idaho Falls, Idaho.
Location: Nine miles north of West Yellowstone, on Highway 287; 90 miles south of Bozeman, off Highway 191.
Guest Capacity: 50
Accommodations: Fifteen turn-of-the-20th-century log cabins with one to four bedrooms. All are named after famous fishing rivers nearby. All have porches, wood-burning stoves, bathrooms, and comfortable beds; the newest is the Aspen Cabin. Several of these cabins are along Grayling Creek. The Gallatin Lodge recreation room is a happy gathering spot for reading, visiting, playing games, and listening to music.
Season: Mid-May through September.
Activities: Very few areas in the country offer such diverse fishing. Through the ranch flows 1.5 miles of Grayling Creek, an excellent fly-fishing stream. Nearby are Madison, Gallatin, Firehole, and Gibbon. Full guide service is available, just let the ranch know what you'd like to do, and they will arrange it for you. Parade Rest is well known by all the local fly-fishing guides. Horseback riding is geared to beginner and intermediate riders. Rides are accompanied by a wrangler and vary from one hour to four hours. Whitewater raft trips 40 miles from ranch. Bicycling and hiking on many ranch trails. Six-person hot tub outside Gallatin Lodge next to Grayling Creek. Yellowstone Country Van Tours (extra charge) are a great way to see the area's sights—great for fly-fishing widows and kids. Guests are picked up at the ranch for full-day or half-day tours. Evening wildlife tours in Yellowstone, Jackson/Teton tours, and others.
Children's Programs: Children are welcome and are the parents' responsibility.
Dining: Even if you're late from your fishing excursion, dinner will be waiting for you. The warm, friendly atmosphere is matched by great, hearty ranch cooking.
Summary: Since the 1920s, Parade Rest Guest Ranch has been hosting guests who appreciate the old-time dude ranch spirit, easygoing pace, and world class fly-fishing in surrounding area. It is a great place to call home while touring Yellowstone National Park (a must-see) and fly-fishing in Blue Ribbon waters.

The Ranch at Rock Creek
Philipsburg, Montana

The Ranch at Rock Creek is a bright star in the world of ranch vacations. Owner Jim Manley spent 20 years vacationing at many of the West's top ranches, while also searching for a property that 'had it all.' He found it set among 10 square miles of rugged Montana ranchland between Bozeman and Missoula, in the secluded Rock Creek Valley. Here, guests experience limitless outdoor recreational opportunities including horseback riding among the ranch's sprawling wildflower meadows, and guided fly-fishing on the four private miles of Rock Creek that wind through the property. Outstanding accommodations, superb cuisine enhanced by an inspired wine list, two rustic saloons, and a full-service spa await guests at the end of each day. Together they create a place that offers the feel of the 'true West' without sacrificing true comfort. Welcome to The Ranch at Rock Creek.

Address: 79 Carriage House Lane, Philipsburg, Montana 59858
Telephone: 877-786-1545
Website: www.theranchatrockcreek.com
Airports: Missoula, Butte, and Bozeman. Personal shuttle services are available and included.
Location: 1.5 hours southwest of Missoula, 2.5 hours west of Bozeman, 1.5 hours northwest of Butte.
Memberships: Relais and Chateaux.
Guest Capacity: 60
Accommodations: The Ranch at Rock Creek features the 9-room Granite Lodge, 5-bedroom Bear House, three-bedroom River House, Bluebird Cabin, The Loft, Wrangler, eight luxury riverside canvas cabins, and Trapper, a unique part-canvas, part-stone and wood luxury canvas cabin. Interior spaces and rooms are individually decorated and appointed with a unique combination of Western antiques and custom furniture to reflect an authentic Montana ranch with a sophisticated sensibility. Nightly turndown.
Rates: $$$$$$, American plan
Season: Year-round.
Activities: For families, couples, friends, weddings, and corporate groups, everything at The Ranch at Rock Creek is designed with individual tastes, preferences, and needs in mind. Horseback riding with instruction on trails that meander among 6000+ acres, guided fly-fishing on over four private miles of Blue Ribbon Rock Creek, hiking, swimming in heated pool, wildlife watching, mountain biking, archery, paintball, ropes course, and sporting clays are all popular pursuits. Excursions off-site include trips to ghost towns and historic mines, fishing trips to other nearby waters, and golf. In winter, a full activity program makes The Ranch a superb home base for the holidays. Movie theater and bowling alley too!
Children's Programs: While there is not a dedicated children's program, children are always very welcome. For very young children, The Ranch recommends a nanny accompany the family.
Dining: The Ranch's culinary-trained chef produces magnificent organic cuisine.
Summary: In the Gene Kilgore world of ultra-luxury guest ranches, The Ranch at Rock Creek is right up at the top. Exclusive Relais & Chateaux member and Forbes 5-Star. Featured in Andrew Harper's coveted Hideaway Report. It is outstanding in every way, offering the finest in cuisine, invigorating outdoor activities, stunning accommodations and amenities. Luxury glamping. It's truly one of the world's great ranch experiences.

63 Ranch
Livingston, Montana

One of the first dude ranches in Montana to be chosen as a National Historic Site, the 63 Ranch is one of the oldest ranches in the business. It's still run by the same family that started it in 1930. At an altitude of 5,600 feet, you listen to the soothing sounds of Mission Creek as it tumbles down its rocky course through the ranch on its way to the Yellowstone River. The 63 offers guests an eye-opening view of what the early West was all about. Here you'll enjoy weekly cattle rides and fulfill your childhood dreams of being a cowboy or cowgirl. In July and August, the 63 offers an overnight pack-trip each week (limited to four guests) into the high country of the Absaroka-Beartooth Wilderness. There's also plenty of riding, fishing, hiking, and Indian lore. The 63 knows the spirit of old-time dude ranching and welcome guests from all over the United States and many foreign countries.

Address: Box 979, Livingston, Montana 59047
Telephone: 888/395-5151
Website: www.63ranch.com
Airport: Bozeman, 50 miles; or a small airstrip for private planes, six miles
Location: 12 miles southeast of Livingston.
Memberships: The Dude Ranchers' Association, Montana Dude Ranch Association.
Guest Capacity: 30
Accommodations: Eight comfortable one to four-bedroom cabins with wonderful log furniture, all different and unusual. All have baths and showers; some are heated with gas, others with electricity. Double and twin beds. All arriving guests find a cotton bandana on their pillow, fresh seasonal wildflowers, and the 63 Ranch newspaper. Daily maid service and coin-operated laundry facilities. Guest telephone and soda machine.
Rates: $$$$ American Plan. Rates vary depending on the season. Children's and pack-trip rates. One week minimum stay, Sunday to Sunday.
Season: Mid-June to mid-September.
Activities: The 63 is known for its horses and excellent high-country scenic and open-meadow riding. Western lessons available. Lessons in arena each Monday for all guests. Picnic and barbecue rides. Blue Ribbon fly-fishing (ask about "Montana's First Best Place for Fishing" pamphlet). Ranch pond also stocked with cutthroat trout for children and fly-casting practice. Swimming in a pond (for the courageous), hiking, history lessons, homestead ride, and evening nature walk.
Children's Programs: Best for children six and older who can participate in ranch and family activities.
Dining: Beautiful dining room furnished with Molesworth furniture dating from the 1930s. Hearty ranch cooking.
Summary: One of Kilgore's great historic ranches in America. Wonderful classic, old-time historic dude ranch with emphasis on riding and families. Weekly cattle rides. First Montana dude ranch to be listed on the National Register of Historic Places. Near historic town of Livingston, Yellowstone National Park, and world class fly-fishing on the Yellowstone River and numerous spring creeks.

Sweet Grass Ranch
Big Timber, Montana

"A genuine old-time working-cattle guest ranch, with unlimited riding as the main emphasis. Guests are welcome to take part in all pleasures of ranch life," say Sweet Grass hosts and owners Bill and Shelly Carroccia along with family members Page and Pat and Rocco and Annie, who radiate warmth and sincere Western hospitality. The Sweet Grass Ranch is secluded in the Crazy Mountains 40 miles outside the small town of Big Timber. Cattle and dude ranching have been in the family since 1880. The Carroccias limit the number of guests so that everyone will actually feel like family. Families from all over have come to enjoy the beautiful open, rolling country; the foothills, and the magnificent high alpine country. Share in the ranch activities if you like, or do your own thing. Life is unstructured. Sweet Grass Ranch is a place where the whole family can enjoy the great outdoors. Ride, fish and savor the Old West.

Address: 460 Rein Lane, Big Timber, Montana 59011
Telephone: 406-537-4477
Website: www.sweetgrassranch.com
Airport: Billings or Bozeman; pickup service available (extra).
Location: 120 miles northwest of Billings, 40 miles northwest of Big Timber. Driving directions will be sent to you.
Memberships: The Dude Ranchers' Association, Montana Ranch Vacation Association, National Register of Historic Places, National Cattlemen's Association.
Guest Capacity: 20
Accommodations: Guests are housed in eight rustic log cabins (built between 1928 and 1935), or in four rooms on the second floor of the main house, some with living rooms and fireplaces. Lots of authentic old-time charm here. Private baths in all cabins; shower house available. Coin operated laundry facilities. In the main house there's a marvelous burl second-floor railing and banister.
Rates: $$. American Plan. Children's rates available. One-week minimum stay. Many guests stay 10 days to two weeks. Most arrive and stay Sunday to Sunday.
Season: Early June through mid-September.
Activities: Every day is different. Those who wish to participate in ranch work like checking and salting livestock, trail-clearing, and doctoring cattle may do so. In addition, excellent half-day and all-day rides go out every day except Sunday. These may be working or scenic walking, trotting, and loping rides. Bareback and dinner rides along with pack trips and cattle work are things you may enjoy, too. Riding instruction is available on request at no charge. Fishing in alpine lakes and on the Sweet Grass River, which runs through the ranch. Swimming in the creek for the hardy and brave; bird-watching.
Children's Programs: No special programs. Very flexible (old-time, ranch style) riding for kids. Children are welcome and are included in all ranch activities. Baby-sitting can be arranged.
Dining: Home-cooked and served family-style in the circa-1925 main lodge. Ranch-raised Montana beef, and homemade ice cream. Sandwich packed lunches are served on all-day rides and trips.
Summary: The real McCoy! A wonderful, old-time Western Montana guest and cattle ranch. This rustic ranch serves up plenty of authentic Western spirit and genuine hospitality. Sweet Grass is a riding ranch. No set schedule; do as much or as little as you please. Cattle work. It's completely private, at the end of the road.

320 Guest Ranch
Big Sky, Montana

Located in the Gallatin Canyon, not far from the famous year-round resort of Big Sky, is the 320 Guest Ranch. It is situated on the Gallatin River, adjacent to the U.S. 191 corridor from Bozeman to Yellowstone National Park and at the mouth of the Buffalo Horn Creek access—gateway to the million-acre Gallatin National Forest, which joins Yellowstone. The ranch first hosted guests back in 1905. Today the ranch is owned by David Brask, who notes, "The folks who truly enjoy the 320 Guest Ranch experience appreciate our proximity to some of Montana's finest natural wonders and our flexible ranch spirit. We go out of our way to make it easy for our guests to come and go as they please, fly-fishing, hiking, riding, or traveling to Yellowstone, Bozeman, or Big Sky. The diversity of accommodations—from one-room cabins to three-bedroom log homes—no minimum-stay requirement, and its size allow the ranch to cater to a wide variety of needs, from corporate groups to weddings to families and couples, who come to enjoy all the freedom we offer."

Address: 205 Buffalo Horn Creek, Gallatin Gateway, Montana 59730
Telephone: 800/243-0320, 406/995-4283
Website: www.320ranch.com
Airport: Bozeman, 50 miles.
Location: 12 miles south of Big Sky; 36 miles north of West Yellowstone, off Highway 191.
Guest Capacity: 200
Accommodations: Accommodations have all the creature comforts that you would expect in an upscale facility. Seven three-bedroom log homes, 12 riverfront two-bedroom cabins complete with kitchenettes and fireplaces, and 38 single cabins—some with fireplaces, some with kitchens. All have telephones and cable TV. Daily maid service.
Rates: $$$ American Plan.
Season: Summer: June to early October; Winter: Mid-December to mid-March.
Activities: Summer: Guests come to do a host of activities on and off the ranch, including horseback riding and fly-fishing. Six different rides go out Monday - Saturday. One-hour to all-day rides best suited for beginner to intermediate riders. Fully equipped fly shop on ranch with rental gear available. Casting instruction on private stocked ponds. Superb fly-fishing in area and local guides available. Ask about the Gallatin, Madison, and Yellowstone Rivers for fishing. Hiking, river rafting with local outfitter, and day trips to Yellowstone Park. Winter: Backcountry and downhill skiing at Big Sky; snowmobiling and sleigh rides.
Children's Programs: Children are welcome, but no formal program.
Dining: Seasonal full breakfast and full Western-style dinner a la carte.
Summary: 320 Guest Ranch offers one of the most flexible, independent summer and winter programs in the world of guest ranching. Guests savor the riverside setting and the freedom to choose from a host of outdoor activities, both on and off the ranch. A variety of upscale accommodations and summer and winter programs. Nearby: Yellowstone National Park and Big Sky Resort.

Triple Creek Ranch
Darby, Montana

One of Andrew Harper's favorite hideaways in the world! Triple Creek Ranch is an exclusive ultra-luxury mountain hideaway almost at the foot of beautiful Trapper Peak, just outside the tiny town of Darby. This "diamond in the rough," adults-only property was built in 1986 to create a wilderness retreat for those who yearned for nature's wildness, but wanted to experience it with luxurious amenities. Kyle Whyhard and Molly Smith manage Triple Creek, and together with a wonderful staff has created a haven of rest, relaxation, and mountain splendor. Triple Creek is without a doubt one of the best in the world!

Address: 5551 West Fork Road, Darby, Montana 59829
Telephone: 406/821-4600
Website: www.triplecreekranch.com
Airports: Missoula; private planes to Hamilton with 4,200-foot airstrip; helicopter pad at ranch; airport pickup available.
Location: 12 miles south of Darby; 74 miles south of Missoula.
Memberships: Relais & Chateaux, Orvis, Andrew Harper Q Club.
Guest Capacity: 60
Accommodations: Choose from cozy cedar to luxury log cabins. Each is tastefully furnished. Refrigerators are fully stocked with an array of beverages, and there's a full complimentary supply of liquor. For those who wish, there are satellite TV/DVDs. The larger luxury cabins have massive, handcrafted, log king-size beds, double steam showers, and a private hot tub on the deck looking out into the forest. Telephones with wireless internet in each cabin. Daily housekeeping and turn down service provided.
Rates: $$$$$$ American Plan.
Season: Year-round; all holidays; closed March.
Activities: An informal program that caters to each couple or individual. Horseback riding, hiking, white-water river rafting, swimming in the outdoor heated pool. For those who especially want to fly-fish, Triple Creek offers a customized Orvis guided program. Tennis court and swimming pool. Bird and wildlife watching and photography. Serious golfers can drive to the Hamilton 18-hole golf course. While snowmobiling in the winter is a specialty, there's also a variety of cross-country skiing and downhill opportunities for both beginning and advanced skiers
Children's Programs: Children under 16 are allowed only when a family or group reserves the entire ranch.
Dining: Fantastic executive chef prepares meals that vary and are designed to tempt even the most finicky diners.
Summary: In Gene Kilgore's world of ultra-luxury ranches, Triple Creek is up at the top. #1 Hotel in the World Travel + Leisure 2014, and awarded Andrew Harper Hideaway Report Best of the best! One of the world's leading luxury adults-only ranch/hideaways. Superb and friendly staff with personalized service second to none. Quiet, restful, intimate, romantic atmosphere (great for honeymoons), with gourmet cuisine and full room service. Individual telephone line and number and wireless internet in each cabin. Triple Creek may be booked for family reunions and corporate retreats. Triple Creek Ranch and its sister ranch the CB offer guests over 27,000 acres of largely undeveloped Montana countryside.

NEBRASKA

Rowse's 1 + 1 Ranch, LLC
Burwell, Nebraska

The 1 + 1 Ranch is an authentic working cattle ranch owned and operated by Jerry and Tammy Rowse. Situated on over 7,000 acres, they run
800 cow/calf pairs and 50 horses. Come as a guest and leave as a family
friend. Here you will have a day-to-day experience second to none living
the life of real working cowboys and cowgirls.

Address: 46849 833rd Road, Burwell, Nebraska 68823
Telephone: 308/346-58530
Website: www.1plus1ranch.com
Airport: Omaha, Nebraska
Location: 190 miles west of Omaha, 100 miles north of Grand Island, NE,
6.5 hours NE of Denver.
Memberships: The Dude Ranchers' Association
Guest Capacity: 10
Accommodations: Six beautiful and spotless rustic log single and double
cabin rooms, accented in authentic cowboy style with private baths. Rock-
ing chairs on the porches to watch the wonderful Sand Hills sunsets.
Rates: $$$ American Plan.
Season: Mid-May to November.
Activities: You can expect at least 6 hours of riding a day. A wide variety
of riding opportunities include working cattle, roping, long rides in wide-open
pastures, checking cattle and fixing fences. Once Jerry has assessed your
riding ability, he will then assign ranch work accordingly. Typically you will
have your own horse for the entire week. Each guest saddles and cares
for their own horse. Riding lessons along with team penning, feeding and
grooming colts, campfires, fabulous star gazing, and good old fashioned
family fun.
Children's Programs: Adults only.
Dining: Delicious home cooked meals are renowned. As Tammy says,
"Down home cooking, and plenty of it!" Three meals plus snacks are served
family style. From thick juicy steaks with mashed potatoes and gravy to
decadent homemade desserts, you won't be disappointed! Tammy grows a
large garden so fresh produce is always available in season. Special needs
such as vegetarian diets can be accommodated with advance notice.
Summary: The Rowse Family serves up one of the best authentic working
Ranch experiences in the country. Adults-only (18 and up), wonderful hos-
pitality, ranch cooking and as much working ranch experiences you could
ever ask for. It is really an adventure of a lifetime, and the real McCoy!
Wide-open Nebraska landscapes and real ranch life and hospitality. Ask
Tammy about the history, and Nebraska's famous Sand Hills.

NEVADA

—★—

Cottonwood Ranch
Wells, Nevada

At 6,200 feet, the Cottonwood Ranch is in Nevada's high desert country on Cottonwood Creek in the O'Neil Basin of Elko County, one of the largest cattle-producing counties in the United States. This working ranch runs 500-head of cows, calves, and bulls, and 80-head of horses over 2,000 acres. The fourth-generation Smith family leases more than 30,000 acres from the forest services and Bureau of Land Management. Renie and adult children Kim, Agee, and his wife, Vicki, go out of their way to ensure that each guest is well looked after. Cottonwood offers city folks a chance to really get away from it all and experience life the way it used to be. The Smiths have been in the ranching business in this part of Nevada since the 1920s. Today, their guests travel a good distance to experience their hospitality at this way-off-the-road paradise. The high mountain cow camp is right in the middle of Nevada's summer home to hundreds of elk and mule deer. Wildnerss pack-trips lasting almost a week take guests into the isolated and beautiful Jar-bidge Wilderness, where one can see dramatic views of mountain peaks, quaking aspen, willows, and meadows filled with sunflowers and lupine.

Address: HC 62 Box 1300, O'Neil Route, Wells, Nevada, 89835
Telephone: 775-275-0593
Website: www.cottonwoodguestranch.com
Airport: Elko, Nevada or Twin Falls, Idaho.
Location: 70 miles north and west of Wells, Nevada. Call ranch for details.
Memberships: Nevada Outfitters and Guides Association, Nevada Cattle-man's Association.
Guest Capacity: 10
Accommodations: A modern seven-bedroom, open-beam lodge with a deck offering panoramic views has three rooms with double beds, four rooms with twin beds and bunk beds. Bathrooms are both private and shared.
Rates: $$$ American Plan. Pack-trip rates available.
Season: May to September.
Activities: Unlimited riding and western ranch life! For years, the Smiths have been known for their horse drives and high-country pack-trips. Today, as in years gone by, they welcome guests to participate in their weekly cat-tle ranch activities. The Smiths will show you some of Nevada's magnificent country. Seasonal cattle roundup and horse drive for experienced riders.
Children's Programs: Best for older children who love to ride.
Dining: Hearty, home-cooked, real ranch meals.
Summary: One of Nevada's old-time ranching families. Authentic working ranch serving up wonderful western hospitality. Magnificent wide-open, pristine landscapes. The long drive in is worth every minute! Thirty miles off the paved highway and 70 miles from the nearest town. Tremendous high desert beauty, with the Jarbridge Mountains forming the backdrop. Horse drives, wilderness pack-trips, and high mountain cow camp. As they say, "If you've been hankerin' for a touch of the old West, you'll find it here." And so you will!

NEW MEXICO

—⋆—

Concho Hills Guest Ranch
Magdalena, New Mexico

Concho Hills Guest Ranch is all about nature, huge skys, horses, distant mesas and Sante Fe style charm. For two years, Tim and Marilyn Norris searched the West for a setting that combined the good ol' Western way of life with a magnificent setting and seclusion. A place where city folks could come to truly get away from it all and join in camaraderie, savoring rich, western heritage, history, and pure natural beauty. In 2014 they opened Concho Hills, and today they offer guests a slice of heaven and a piece of paradise. The ranch is located 35 miles from the closest town on the historic Magdalena Stock Highway, where for over a hundred years ranchers drove their cattle to the trail head. Completely surrounded by public lands and National forest, the ranch has access to 2 million acres of varied country-side; from Ponderosa forrested mountains and rocky canyons to pinon and juniper dotted foothills and grass covered plains. The ranch offers diverse riding, scenery and ranching activities. As one guest wrote, "This is one of the few places left where one can relax and let time unwind." And so it is. Welcome to Concho Hills.

Address: 1522 Remuda Trails, Magdalena, New Mexico, 87825
Telephone: 575-772-5757
Website: www.conchohillsranch.com
Airport: Albuquerque, NM.
Location: 2.5 Hours south of Albuquerque, New Mexico.
Guest Capacity: 14
Accommodations: Six beautiful tiled rooms built in 2014 in a large one-story casita, each with period antiques and lots of Southwestern charm. Twin and queen size beds, fluffly bath towels, and all are climate-controlled and smoke-free. A gorgeous main house for meals and guest gatherings. All look out to spectacular views of the New Mexico landscape and distant mountains. Daily maid service and central laundry facility.
Rates: $$$ American Plan.
Season: Year-round.
Activities: All activities are tailored, for the most part, to individual guest wishes. In the heart of New Mexico cattle country, the ranch is primarily a riding ranch, with a small herd of yearling cattle. Guests participate in horse care, riding lessons, wildlife viewing, and an assortment of Western ranch activities. Because the ranch is so small, guests get a lot of individual attention, and can do as much or as little as they please. Riding the wide-open spaces, photographing the magestic scenery, and maybe even a little roping.
Children's Programs: 12 years and older. Parents and kids interact together.
Dining: Hearty Western cuisine and special mexican favorites. BYOB.
Summary: Quiet, beautiful, and the food and fellowship are fantastic! A charming New Mexico styled guest ranch with rich Western heritage in the heart of cattle country. Wide-open countryside on the border of the San Mateo mountains and the St. Augustine plains. Small, secluded, and run by a wonderful couple, Tim and Marilyn Norris. Excellent for singles, couples, and older family gatherings. Fantastic night skies! 34 miles from the closest town. Make sure you have a full tank of gas!

Geronimo Trail Guest Ranch
Winston, New Mexico

Geronimo Trail Guest Ranch, situated in the 3.3 million acre Gila National Forest in some of the most breathtaking, untouched country in America, is a real western adventure. This is the birthplace of Geronimo and the homeland of the Chiricahua Apache. Long before the Apache, the Mimbres people lived here (750 -1150 AD). Famous for their exquisite "black on white" pottery, considered the finest prehistoric pottery in the Americas, guests ride or hike to their ancient dwellings, pit houses and cliff dwellings, see their petroglyphs and discover shards of their pottery. Outlaw and cowboy hangouts are here to explore, and the wildlife is abundant: elk, mule deer, wild turkey, javelin, eagles and dozens of kinds of birds. Geronimo Trail Guest Ranch is a small family owned ranch. Meris and Seth Stout offer warm hospitality, a relaxed atmosphere – no fixed schedules, delicious food, outstanding horses, comfortable, attractive accommodations and a commitment to making a vacation at Geronimo Trail the best guests have ever had. The focus is on horseback riding in breathtaking country. Horseback or hiking takes guests through beautiful forests of Ponderosa pine, across open meadows, down into astounding deep canyons with sheer towering walls and crystal clear streams, and to the heights such as "The Top of the World," where the views go on forever.

Address: 1 Wall Lake Road, Winston, NM 87943
Telephone: 575-772-5157
Website: www.geronimoranch.com
Airport: Albuquerque, NM or El Paso, TX
Location: 4-hour drive from either Albuquerque or El Paso. 2 hours from Truth or Consequences, NM
Memberships: The Dude Ranchers' Association, AQHA, APHA
Guest Capacity: 15
Accommodations: Cabins nestled among tall Ponderosa pines. "Apache" sleeps up to 6. Full bath. Sitting area with table, chairs. Porch. Native American décor. "Cowboy," half of duplexed cabin. Sleeps up to 5. Full bath, sitting area with table, chairs. Small porch. Cowboy and horses décor. "Outlaw," half of duplexed cabin. Sleeps up to four in two bedrooms, one with queen, the other with bunk bed. Full bath. Sitting area. Small porch. Cowboy and horses décor. All cabins have propane fireplaces.
Rates: $$$ American Plan.
Season: March 1 – January 31
Activities: Horseback riding in the glorious Gila National Forest guided by the capable hand of Meris Esterly. Short rides, half day rides, all day picnic rides, overnight adventures. Informal riding lessons, arena riding and horseback games. Hiking to cliff dwellings, petroglyphs, and in search of Mimbres artifacts. Small swimming pool. Fishing in Taylor Creek. Library. Rec Hall where guests dance (line and country western) enjoy musical entertainment, watch western movies. Campfires with s'mores, western entertainment, singing and guitar, sing-a-longs, star gazing.
Children's Programs: Children's are parent's responsibility.
Dining: Southwestern Ranch cooking served family style.
Summary: Small family owned ranch with emphasis on horseback riding in the magnificent Gila National Forest. Land of the early Mimbres, homeland of the Apache. Pit houses, caves, cliff dwellings, petroglyphs. Unforgettable western adventure. Good food, comfortable accommodations, warm hospitality, great horses, and moderate climate. Be sure to get detailed directions - it is an incredible drive to the Ranch!

The Lodge at Chama
Chama, New Mexico

Welcome to The Lodge at Chama, owned by the Jicarilla Apache Nation! Here men and women come to enjoy privacy amid 36,000 acres of unspoiled mountain and forest scenery. The Lodge at Chama provides first-class amenities and excellent service. Over the years, the lodge has hosted many business and industry leaders. Because it hosts only 42 people at any one time, guests quickly feel at home. For high-level board meetings or high-level rest and relaxation, The Lodge at Chama has what it takes for guests who appreciate one of the finest sporting lodges in the world. The lodge's fine staff tailors everything to each guests' preferences, so whether you come to fly-fish, hike, hunt, or view wildlife, The Lodge at Chama is without a question one of the world's best!

Address: 16253 S. Hwy 84, Chama, New Mexico 87520

Telephone: 575/756-2133

Website: www.lodgeatchama.com

Airport: Albuquerque; private jets to Pagosa springs. Call regarding ranch airstrip.

Location: 100 miles north of Sante Fe; 90 miles west of Taos; 45 miles southeast of Pagosa Springs.

Guest Capacity: 42

Accommodations: Twenty-one guest rooms, each with private bath and upscale amenities and four suites with fireplaces.

Rates: $$$$$$ American Plan. Special rates for full lodge rental.

Season: Year-round; all holidays.

Activities: The lodge is known for its legendary fly-fishing, wildlife viewing, and big-game hunting. The lodge will send you a detailed brochure and video outlining the activities. As well as fly-fishing during the summer and fall, guests may hike, tour the ranch to view vistas and wild game (including one of the world's largest private elk herds) or take part in sporting clays and wildlife photography.

Children's Programs: Children welcome. No formal program. Best for older kids who love to fly-fish.

Dining: Superb cuisine, gourmet ranch fare.

Summary: One of Kilgore's top ultra sporting lodges, where luxury, exclusivity, scenery and wildlife reign supreme! One of North America's finest wildlife ranches, specializing in high quality outdoor recreation for business executives, corporate groups, and exclusive family gatherings. Delicious cuisine, and tremendous wildlife viewing. Superb lake and stream fly-fishing and world-class big-game hunting. One of the world's largest private elk herds.

NEW YORK

—★—

Ridin-Hy Ranch Resort
Warrensburg, New York

This is a year-round family resort ranch in the timberlands of Adirondack State Park and along the shores of beautiful spring-fed Sherman Lake. The ranch is owned and operated by Andy and Susan Beadnell and their three sons. Since 1940, when the ranch was started by Susan's father, the property and guest accommodations have grown. Today, the ranch hosts 175 guests who enjoy the privacy of the resort's 800 acres. Most guests come from New York, Connecticut, New Jersey, and Massachusetts. As one happy guest said, "There are not many resorts where you can catch good-sized bass in the morning, trail ride in the afternoon, have a swim before dinner, enjoy an after-dinner drink, and square dance to your heart's content." The lake activities, including fishing, are complemented by a friendly staff and a year-round riding program. Ask the Beadnells about their beautiful fall colors; many love to ride at this time of year.

Address: Box 369, Sherman Lake, Warrensburg, New York 12885
Telephone: 518/494-2742
Website: www.ridinhy.com
Airport: Albany
Location: 65 miles north of Albany, 15 miles north of Lake George off Route 87
Memberships: New York State Tourism Association
Guest Capacity: 175
Accommodations: Rooms range from budget singles to deluxe private cottages. All are clean and comfortable, heated, with private baths, and not far from the main lodge, beach, and pool. The main lodge has a large stone fireplace that provides a warm and cozy atmosphere. It is situated on the lake with views to the Adirondacks.
Rates: $$. American Plan. Summer riding and nonriding rates. Children's rates according to age. Winter rates and various ranch packages offered. Off-season rates.
Season: Year-round, including Thanksgiving and Easter.
Activities: Horseback riding for the whole family with pony rides for the young. Fast, slow, and intermediate mountain trail rides. Rides go out for a minimum of two hours daily. A favorite ranch activity is the weekly guest "rodeo." Riding during the fall colors is breathtaking. Lessons available from experienced wranglers. Fishing for trout, pike, and small and large-mouth bass. Plenty of water sports on Sherman Lake, including paddle-boats and rowboats. Swimming in lake or heated pool, archery, two tennis courts, and whirlpool. Golf nearby. Full winter program including cross-country skiing, sleigh rides, snowshoeing, ice skating, downhill skiing with instruction, snowmobiling, indoor pool, and horseback riding.
Children's Programs: Children's activities director. Organized activities year round. Baby-sitting available. Under age 7 ride in arena.
Dining: The large country-style dining room looks out over Sherman Lake. Enjoy poolside steak barbecues and weekly smorgasbord dinners featuring ham and turkey roasts. Full weekly menu. Families eat together at assigned tables. Three meals daily from a choice of menus.
Summary: Since 1940, run by the Beadnell family, for families. One-stop, one-price family vacation. Nearby: Lake George, fort William Henry Adirondack Museum, Stone Bridge Cave Gore Mountain gondola.

Timberlock
Sabael, New York

Timberlock is one of those hidden gems! Small, rustic and magical. Timberlock is one of the oldest summer family "camps" in the Adirondacks, with a magnificent lakeside setting. Families that come year after year savor the chance to step back in time when the pace was slower, and where camaraderie and the simple life nurtured the inner spirit. The Catlin family has owned and operated Timberlock since 1964. Today it is run by second-generation Bruce, his wife Holly, and their three children. Bruce's father Dick had gone to Timberlock as a boy back in the 1940's. As the Catlins say, "We are informal, friendly, rustic and woodsy, unprogrammed and relaxed. Over the years, we have attracted second and third generations who appreciate our nice and easy way of life — just the way it used to be." And so it is. Timberlock is a slice of heaven and a piece of paradise.

Address: P.O. Box 1052, Sabael, NY 12864 (summer) 1735 Quaker St. Lincoln, VT 05443 (winter)
Telephone: (518) 648-5494 (summer), (802) 453-2540
Website: www.timberlock.com
Airport: Albany, NY (100 miles) Burlington, VT (105 miles) 250 miles northwest of New York City, 10 miles south of Indian Lake Harnlet on Route 30.
Location: 250 miles north of New York City, 10 miles south of Indian Lake on Route 30.
Guest Capacity: 70
Accommodations: Cabins with and without baths. The only electricity is in the main kitchen. If you cannot live without your hair dryer, Timberlock is not for you. Gas lamps provide light, and propane provides hot water. Wood stoves heat cabins when necessary. The Catlin's 24-page brochure is excellent and has a map that locates all the cabins.
Rates: $. American Plan.
Season: Late June to late September
Activities: "Everything on the place is on a take it or leave it basis. There are no pre-planned programs other than meals. Do what you want when you want." Sleep, read, cool off in the lake, canoe, sail, ride, water ski, play tennis on clay courts, or enjoy archery or golf on 9-hole courses 10 miles away. Many enjoy the nature walks and birding, guided hikes and lake cruises offered each week. Be sure to ask about the fully staffed woodshop where you can make your own paddle.
Children's Programs: No organized programs, children join parents in activities and meals. Separate Teen Adventure Program called Timberlock Voyageurs for ages 12 to 16.
Dining: Family-style. Hearty, home made meals.
Summary: An Adirondack family resort since 1899. One of Kilgore's very special places! The wonderful Catlin family. Timberlock is a rustic lakeside paradise located in the heart of the Adirondacks and on fifteen mile Indian Lake. The 24-page brochure tells you everything you could possibly want to know. Ask about special foliage weekends and family reunions.

NORTH CAROLINA

Clear Creek Ranch
Burnsville, North Carolina

Located in the Blue Ridge Mountains north of Asheville, the ranch was built in 1995. The Pisgah National Forest provides 80,000 acres of riding and hiking trails. While horseback riding is the most popular activity, tubing down the South Toe River is a close second! There is also a stocked trout pond, a heated pool, hot tub, and a high-quality mountain golf course within one mile of the ranch. The warm, friendly, relaxed atmosphere is a ranch trademark.

Address: 100 Clear Creek Drive, Highway 80 South, Burnsville, North Carolina 28714

Telephone: 800/651-4510, 828/675-4510

Website: www.clearcreekranch.com

Airport: Asheville; pickup available at small additional charge

Location: 45 miles north of Asheville, North Carolina; three hours northeast of Knoxville, Tennessee; four hours north of Atlanta, Georgia

Memberships: Associate Member of The Dude Ranchers' Association, North Carolina Travel & Tourism

Guest Capacity: 64

Accommodations: Guest quarters are located in four separate buildings, all adjacent to the main lodge. There are cozy one, two, and three-bedroom units, all with lodgepole pine beds, air-conditioning, heating, and carpeting. Big covered porches with an ample supply of rocking chairs provide beautiful views of the mountains. The main lodge offers a big porch and huge deck, dining room, and living room with a Carolina fieldstone fireplace, where guests gather to play cards or tell stories about their day.

Rates: $$$ American Plan.

Season: April to December

Activities: Horseback riding is available morning and afternoon. The Buncombe Horse Trail in the Pisgah National Forest is a favorite: wonderful rides through the spectacular, lush North Carolina forests and across the crystal clear South Toe River. Tubing down the South Toe River is popular with children. Activity trips to local crafters, gem mines, hikes to Crab Tree and Linville Waterfalls, fishing in the pond or on the South Toe River for famous North Carolina mountain trout. Nearby golf and white-water rafting are also options.

Children's Programs: Optional organized activities for ages 5-12 that vary day to day.

Dining: Three hearty meals a day.

Summary: Beautiful North Carolina scenery, the crystal-clear Toe River, and a relaxed, easygoing spirit are the hallmarks of Clear Creek Ranch! Completely surrounded by the Pisgah National Forest. Breathtaking fall colors, superb 18-hole mountain golf course (minutes away), and local arts and crafts famous to this part of the country. Near Biltmore Estate, Grandfather Mountain, and the charming town of Blowing Rock.

PENNSYLVANIA

— ★ —

Malibu Dude Ranch
Milford, Pennsylvania

Founded originally back in the 1920's, Malibu Dude Ranch is located in North Eastern Pennsylvania in the scenic Pocono Mountains just 75 miles from New York City. The 800-acre ranch is one of the oldest authentic working dude rances east of the Mississippi River. Over the years, it drew people from neighboring states who were looking for the Old West cowboy experience and horseback riding on woodland trails. As in years gone by, today families, couples, singles, groups, and wedding parties come to enjoy a western cowboy-style vacation away from the computers and the fast-paced workplace. In 2010, Dr. Allan "Doc" Detweiler and his wife Phyllis purchased the ranch after learning it was to be sold and replaced with a townhouse style residential community. Since then, the ranch has undergone extensive renovations. As Doc says, "We want guests to enjoy a cowboy's vacation and savor the goodness we all share here. This is a beautiful setting that helps men, women and children reconnect and get back to nature. We've got so much to offer and we all love sharing this way of life."

Address: 351 Foster Hill Road, Milford, Pennsylvania 18337
Telephone: 800/862-5428
Website: www.malibududeranch.com
Airport: 1 1/2 hours from Newark, New Jersey, 2 hours from La Guardia or JFK, New York. 1 hour from Stewart Airport, Nework, 1 1/2 hours from Scranton/Wilkes Barre, Pennsylvania.
Location: Pocono Mountains — 75 miles Northwest of New York City.
Memberships: Pike County Chamber of Commerce, American Professional Rodeo Association, Pocono Mountain Visitor's Bureau.
Guest Capacity: 100-150
Accommodations: Guests can choose from accommodations in the main lodge with 12 spacious rooms on the 2nd floor, quad cabins which have four separate rooms that feature a private entrance, private baths, and two double beds, or lakeside and private cabins each featuring king size beds. All have private baths, air conditioning/heat, and are furnished with western decor.
Rates: $$$ American Plan.
Season: Year round.
Activities: Year-round horseback riding through beautiful forest and open meadow; mostly trail riding. Riding lessons available. Saturday night rodeos from late June to Labor day. Daily cattle drives. Spa packages. Spring/Summer/Fall ATV packages. Year-round swimming in indoor heated pool, lake activities including fishing, paddle and row boats, rifle range and skeet shooting. Miniature golf.
Children's Programs: Children of all ages welcome. Lots of activities.
Dining: American/Western cuisine, family friendly western saloon with country music, line dancing. Weather permitting, some meals served lakeside.
Summary: Malibu Dude Ranch offers an East Coast guest ranch experience with horseback riding through pristine forest and endless trails. Day, weekend and week-long stays available. Lots of fun, lots of beautiful countryside and lots of hospitality.

UTAH

—★—

Reid Ranch
Salt Lake City, Utah

The Reid Ranch sits at 7,800 feet on the slopes of the Uinta Mountains, once home to the Uinta Ouray Indians. Homesteaded in the late 1800's, the property is abundant with Western folklore and history, from Chief Tabby to Butch Cassidy and the Sundance Kid. Today the ranch is owned by Mervin and Ethna Reid, and managed by their son, Gardner. Only two hours east of Salt Lake City, the ranch owns 400 acres and is surrounded by state and federal forest land. The ranch offers lodge facilities for seminars, family reunions, and large youth group retreats.

Address: 3310 South 2700 East, Salt Lake City, Utah 84109
Telephone: 800/468-3274, 801/848-5776 (summer), 801/486-5083 (winter)
Website: www.reidranch.com
Airports: Salt Lake City, 100 miles
Location: 50 miles east of Heber City off I-40, 100 miles east of Salt Lake City
Memberships: International Reading Association
Guest Capacity: 110 - 300
Accommodations: : Two modern lodges and two guest homes. One lodge, The Bunkhouse, has two rooms that sleep 26 each in bunk beds and a 2,000 square foot dining/ meeting room. Second lodge is a three-story lodge has several large bedrooms that sleep up to seven adults each. The 24-foot cathedral ceilings, spacious entry, library with adults' and children's books, large dining area and decks provide a wonderful atmosphere. The third lodge has 20 bedrooms and sleeps 116 people. Two conference rooms areas. Large front and back deck areas. All three lodges have their own swimming pool area. Camping area can accommodate up to 500 people with its own camping bathroom facilities. Camping area has its own conference center for gathering. It can seat 300 people.
Rates: $$-$$$$. American Plan.
Season: June through August
Activities: Adults and children can participate in activities such as horseback riding. Lake activities include fishing, canoeing, and paddle boating. Hiking; fossil-hunting; swimming in three of the heated pools and whirlpool spa; sauna; one lighted sports court for tennis, lighted volleyball, sand volleyball court, and basketball. Soccer field, archery, miniature golf, campfires, square dancing, and 9-hole Frisbee golf. 4 fire pits – one firepit with stage and lights, and amphitheater seats 300 people.
Children's Programs: Excellent setting for family reunions. Kids are the complete responsibility of their parents. Reading Camp program each summer with teachers and counselors for 2 weeks.
Dining: Buffet breakfast, lunch, and dinner.
Summary: Tucked away high on the slopes of the Unita Mountains on the Red River creek, the Reid Ranch is secluded in one of the most magnificent scenic and wildlife regions in Utah. Excellent group/conference ranch facility. Great for large business groups, large family reunions, and church retreats. Special seminars for teachers on teaching methods and leadership workshops for administrators. Largest pinon and juniper forest in the world, Dinosaur National Monument. Spanish spoken.

WASHINGTON

— ✷ —

Bull Hill Guest Ranch
Kettle Falls, Washington

Bull Hill Guest Ranch is part of a working cattle ranch encompassing more than 50,000 acres of lush mountain landscapes. Founded in 1903, the ranch sits on the mountains of the Pacific Northwest not far from the Canadian Border. Bull Hill combiness all the untouched and wild beauty of the mountain meadows and forests with all the comfortable amenities of home. With panoramic views and the varied riding program, Bull Hill is a shining star in the great Northwest!

Address: 3738 Bull Hill Road, Kettle Falls, Washington 99141
Telephone: 509/732-1171, 877/285-5445
Website: www.bullhill.com
Airports: Spokane International.
Location: Two hours north of Spokane, Washington.
Memberships:
Guest Capacity: 40
Accommodations: : The seven ranch cabins are strategically situated in private settings against a back-drop of cedar, cottonwood and aspen trees. Cabins are decorated in a rustic western theme, ask about Lonestar and Bullagio. Two fully furnished tent cabins named Lakota and Laredo for those who want to rough it in comfort.
Rates: $$-$$$$. American Plan.
Season: May - November
Activities: A diversity of horseback riding adventures. Ride along the mountain tops, along the Columbia River Valley, through meadows and forests. Ask about the day ride to Lake Roosevelt and the western town. Hiking, fly-fishing on ranch lake, sporting clays, wagon rides and wildlife viewing. Winter offers cross country skiing, snowmobiling and snow shoeing. Winery tours nearby.
Children's Programs: Kids are encouraged to take part in all ranch activities. No formal program.
Dining: Excellent ranch cuisine served family style. Complimentary beer, wine and spirits.
Summary: One of the greats in the Pacific Northwest! Fourth generation ranching family. May repeat guests come to savor breathtaking mountain top views and family ranching experiences. Guests and working cattle ranch, encompassing 50,000 acres. Weekly cattle drive. Wait till you see the Columbia River and the stars at night!

WYOMING

Allen's Diamond 4 Ranch
Lander, Wyoming

Since 1973, Jim and Mary have owned and operated the Diamond 4 ranch. Jim's grandfather was also a dude rancher and ran pack trips in the Wind River Mountains during the 1920s and 30's. Over the years this remarkable family has hosted guests from around the world, showing them one of the most scenic alpine back country wilderness adventures that anyone could ask for – pristine nature at its very best. Those that come relish the remoteness and truly want to get away from it all. The Diamond 4 is without a question a once in a lifetime journey back in time, and one that you will cherish forever. Completely customized for families and couples.

Address: P.O. Box 243, Lander, Wyoming 82520
Telephone: 307/332-2995
Website: www.diamond4ranch.com
Airport: Jackson Hole or Riverton
Location: 35 miles west of Lander, Wyoming
Memberships: Wyoming Dude Ranchers Association, Wyoming outfitter and guide association
Guest Capacity: 16
Accommodations: 4 cozy handcrafted log cabins sleeping 4 to 6 family members, Each cabin has a porch with a view. Since The Ranch Is Wyoming's highest and most remote dude ranch it is off the grid. Guests enjoy propane lights, heat and a shower house nearby
Rates: $$$ American plan.
Season: Mid-June through mid-September
Activities: Spectacular mountain horseback riding, hiking and fly-fishing in crystal clear alpine lakes and streams. Activities are completely tailored and customized for each family.
Children's Programs: Kids participate with parents. Best for older children of over six years old.
Dining: Hearty ranch style meals. BYOB.
Summary: One of the most incredible wilderness dude ranch experiences in North America. Off the grid, it is Wyoming's most remote ranch at 9,200 feet. Spectacular scenery, high sparkling mountain lakes and riding that will take your breath away. Famous for high Mountain pack trips. Remotely located in the Wind River Mountains. Truly a diamond in the rough! Ask about the spectacular drive to the ranch, and be sure to have a full tank of gas when you leave Lander.

Bitterroot Ranch
Dubois, Wyoming

The Bitterroot Ranch offers one of the premier riding experiences in North America for advanced and intermediate riders, as well as novices who are motivated to learn how to ride. Owned and operated by the Fox Family (Bayard, Mel, Richard & Hadley) for the last 40 years, it is bordered by the Shoshone National Forest to the north, the Wind River Indian Reservation to the east, and a 50,000 acre game habitat area to the south and west. The riding terrain is extremely varied. Sagebrush plains, grassy meadows, and colorful rocky gorges give way to forested meadows and Alpine clearings, where the ranch cattle graze on forest permitted land during the summer. Guests are provided with several horses to help keep the horses fresh throughout the season, and riders are split into small groups according to ability. They have both English (for experienced riders) and Western tack, offer a jumping course for advanced riders, and give lessons up to intermediate level by CHA certified instructors twice a week. Several well known clinicians come to teach at the ranch during the summer including Linda Tellington-Jones, Centered Riding Clinicians, and Anna Twinney with Reach Out To Horses. The ranch raises and trains purebred Arabians and many guests enjoy spending time with the friendly broodmares and playful foals as well as riding these captivating horses. The ranch was featured in the best selling book "1,000 Places to See Before You Die."

Address: Box 807, Dubois, Wyoming 82513
Telephone: 800/545-0019, 307/455-2778
Website: www.bitterrootranch.com
Airports: Riverton or Jackson
Location: 26 miles northeast of Dubois; 80 miles west of Riverton; 105 miles east of Jackson, off routes 26 and 287
Memberships: Wyoming Dude Rancher's Association and the British Horse Society
Guest Capacity: 30
Accommodations: 12 cabins; many are old-time, rustic log cabins with modern day conveniences. Many have wood-burning stoves; all have electric heat and full bathrooms. Laundry facilities.
Rates: $$$ American Plan.
Season: Last full week of May through the last week of September
Activities: Riders are divided by ability. Cattle drives in July and September. Overnight pack trips offered (extra). Bayard is a keen fly fisherman and there is good catch and release fly-fishing in the stream running through the ranch and other excellent fishing opportunities nearby.
Children's Programs: Really best for older teens that really ride. No formal program.
Dining: Delicious Ranch cuisine; wine served with dinner.
Summary: One of Kilgore's top riding ranches in the world. Bitterroot is the rider's ranch offering excellent programs with both English and Western tack. Riding groups are kept small. Certified instructors. Riding program approved by the Certified Horsemanship Association. Ranch-raised horses. Many guests are experienced riders. Great fly-fishing, seasonal cattle work, and weekly team sorting. Unstructured and remote (16 miles from highway). Its sister company, Equitours, (also owned and managed by the Fox Family), organizes exciting riding holidays in 30 countries for riders of almost all abilities.

Brush Creek Ranch
Saratoga, Wyoming

In the world of ultra-guest ranching, the lodge and spa at Brush Creek Ranch is a leader. Brush Creek was acquired in 2008 By Bruce White, Chairman and CEO of White Lodging, one of the most respected names in the hotel industry award winning premium hotel brands across the country. The ranch is the culmination of the White family's extensive hospitality experience and unabashed passion for the sustainability of authentic western heritage preserving the western way of life. Welcome to the one and only Lodge and Spa at Brush Creek Ranch.

Address: 66 Brush Creek Ranch Road, Saratoga, Wyoming 82331
Telephone: 307/327-5284
Website: www.brushcreekranch.com
Airport: Saratoga for private aircraft, Laramie Wyoming and Denver International, Colorado.
Location: 3.5 hours northwest of Denver.
Memberships: Preferred boutique hotels. Orvis endorsed fly-fishing and wing shooting
Guest Capacity: 150
Accommodations: Magnificent executive lodge with daily housekeeping and nightly turn-down service. Cabin residences, cabin suites, and the Magee homestead, a separate ranch within a ranch. Total of 40 units, including 10 elegant two and three bedroom cabins, 13 spacious trailhead lodge rooms, and nine fully refurbished cabin rooms and suites. Wireless high speed Internet access.
Rates: $$$$$$ American plan.
Season: June through mid-October
Activities: The sky's the limit. Trail rides, arena activities and riding instruction. Orvis endorsed fly-fishing and wing-shooting programs, fly-fishing private waters, and the North Platte and Encampment Rivers. Shooting sports including sporting clays. Over 50 miles of groomed trails for mountain biking, hiking, trail running and guided ranger tours. Paintball, zip-line and full indoor sports court. Full service spa and fitness center with yoga.
Children's Programs: Little wrangler program for kids 4 to 8.
Dining: Superb Rocky mountain cuisine prepared by executive chef. Fully licensed saloon.
Summary: One of Kilgore's truly ultra luxury five star ranches in the world. Magnificent in every way! Outstanding cuisine, luxury accommodations, activities, and hospitality. Superb fly-fishing and wing-shooting. Excellent for family reunions, weddings and the executive conference groups. An ultra-private guest ranch on 30,000 acres with 20 miles of private waters. 2015 Conde Nast Traveler #1 Resort in the U.S., #1 Resort in the West, #2 Hotel and Resort in the world.

CM Ranch
Dubois, Wyoming

The CM Ranch has been a favorite dude ranch for decades and is listed with the National Historic Registry. The area features an exceptional variety of country for riding and pack trips. Children 5 and older may ride and fully participate in ranch activities. Well-cared for horses are matched to the rider's ability. The CM has 4 miles of stream for private fly-fishing and many other excellent fisheries within a few miles of the ranch. There is a heated pool on the premises. At the CM Ranch, children enjoy great freedom and will engage with other children in a variety of lawn games. Evening activities include square dancing, cookouts, cowboy music, bonfires, slide show and more. Good hiking trails on and near the ranch. Pack trips into the Fitzpatrick Wilderness may be combined with a ranch vacation, or taken separately. Accommodations are clean, comfortable with different layouts to fit different sized groups. The CM is located 1 hour from the south entrance of Yellowstone Park.

Address: PO Box 217, 167 Fish Hatchery Road, Dubois WY 82513
Telephone: 800/455-0721, 307/455-2331
Website: www.cmranch.com
Airports: Jackson Hole, Riverton, Wyoming, Salt Lake City
Location: Six miles east of Dubois Wyoming. 85 miles east of Jackson Hole, Wyoming. 60 miles from south entrance of Yellowstone National Park
Memberships: Dude Ranchers Association, Wyoming Dude Ranches Association **Guest Capacity:** 50
Accommodations: Delightful log cabins with private baths, wood-burning stoves, log furniture, large porches, tremendous views. Three log houses with full amenities can sleep up to 10 people. Daily maid service. Wireless internet available; cell service is generally good.
Rates: $$$ American Plan.
Season: Early-June to mid-September
Activities: Guests may ride, fish, hike, swim in the heated outdoor pool, go sight-seeing, or relax with a book. Horseback riding every day except Sunday. Morning and afternoon rides, breakfast ride, all-day ride, team penning, and kid's gymkhana. Fishing guide available, and a tackle shop on the ranch. Excellent hiking opportunities. Pack trips and fishing trips into the Wind River Mountains are available. 6 miles from Dubois with shops, 2 excellent museums and a 9-hole golf course.
Children's Programs: Children age 5 and older may ride and fully participate in the family program. Babysitting is available for younger children.
Dining: Three meals a day are prepared with care and consideration and are served in the main dining room. All ages eat together. Vegetarians and special diets can be accommodated.
Summary: The CM Ranch has tremendous warmth and personality where second, third and fourth generations have visted for decades. One of the old time Wyoming Dude Ranches, great location for family reunions and weddings. The 7,000 altitude offers a predominately dry and sunny summer climate. Fishing both on and near ranch. There are log cabins and private homes to suit all group sizes. Summer pack trips to base camp, or progressive trips into the wilderness.

Crossed Sabres Ranch
Cody, Wyoming

Holm Lodge was established in 1898 as a stagecoach stop by Tex Holm who is credited with the first guided and extended camping trips into Yellowstone National Park. The original stagecoach barn for housing the teams of horses still stands today at the ranch. The original lodge building burned in 1914, it was built by Mary Shawyer, and it was renamed Crossed Sabres Ranch for their livestock brand. In 2004, the second lodge building burned and has been replaced by a large two story log lodge with all the necessary amenities for a great family vacation, including a setting room, a western saloon with fireplace, telephones, gift shop, dining room, and restrooms. Located 8 miles from the East Entrance of Yellowstone National Park in the Shoshone National Forest and 43 miles from Cody, Wyoming. "Buffalo Bill's Home in the Rockies." As you step out onto the porch of your cabin and smell the clear mountain air, you will understand why Wyoming still is today what America was yesterday. Make your dream of being a cowboy for an hour, day or week come true. Crossed Sabres Ranch is a family oriented ranch where horseback riding is the primary activity. Dedicated to Wyoming hospitality at its finest, creating memories and new friends. All buildings, horseback rides and fishing are smoke free. As they say, "We will keep the latch string out for you." And so they will.

Address: 829 North Fork Hwy, Cody, WY 82414, 7000 feet above sea level
Telephone: 307/587-3750
Website: www.crossedsabresranch.com
Airports: Cody, Wyoming, Billings Montana 2 1/2 hours.
Location: 43 miles west of Cody, Wyoming on Hwy 14/16/20, 8 miles from the East Entrance of Yellowstone National Park
Memberships: The Dude Ranch Association, Wyoming Dude Ranchers Assocociation.
Guest Capacity: 35
Accommodations: 19 stand-alone one and two-bedroom authentic log cabins are modern, clean and comfortable, carpeted, with log beds and new pillow-top mattresses. Updated modern bathrooms and country décor. Small refrigerator and coffee pot. Not only views of spectacular scenery and majestic Absaroka Mountain, but beautiful Libby Creek also runs through the ranch. All cabins have been remodeled and upgraded, each has electric baseboard heat, and some have stone fireplaces. Smoke and pet free. Laundry facilities available on the premises. Daily maid service.
Rates: $$$ American Plan.
Season: May to October.
Activities: Horseback riding beginning at age 6; many diverse trails for all riding abilities. For cowboys and cowgirls 3-5 years, pony leads available. Morning and afternoon rides, 1 hour, 2 hour, half day and all day rides in the Shoshone National Forest. Guided fly fishing instruction on the Shoshone River, wildlife interpretive program, cookout, live music, campfires with smores, guided day-trip through Yellowstone National Park, Cody Night Rodeo. Photography and hiking workshops in the fall, live music at cookout, game room, and rodeo.
Activities: Full children's program.
Dining: Hearty Western ranch cuisine.
Summary: Crossed Sabres Ranch is one of the oldest Wyoming dude ranches and offers wonderful Western hospitality and trail riding. Many travel here on their way to Yellowstone National Park! Families, family reunions, corporate retreats and meetings are welcome. Cabins are all remodeled. Near East entrance of Yellowstone National Park, and famous Buffalo Bill Historical Museum in Cody.

Eatons' Ranch
Wolf, Wyoming

Eatons' Ranch is the granddaddy of dude ranches. Started in 1879 in North Dakota by three brothers, Howard, Willis, and Alden, the ranch relocated to its present site, 18 miles west of Sheridan, in 1904 to provide "more suitable and varied riding." Now run by the fourth and fifth generations, this 7,000-acre ranch has over 200 head of horses for every type of rider. There is no end to the varied riding terrain. You can hike or ride through open rangeland and wildflower studded trails that traverse the intricate Bighorn Mountains just west of the ranch. One guest said, "What makes Eatons' Ranch such a success is that is has just enough structure to draw a family together, but enough beautiful wide-open spaces to give us our reins."

Address: 270 Eatons Ranch Road, Wolf, WY 82844.
Telephone: 800/210-1049 or 307/655-9552
Website: www.eatonsranch.com
Airports: Billings, Montana - 2 hours. Sheridan, Wyoming - 30 mins.
Location: 18 Miles West of Sheridan.
Memberships: Dude Ranchers' Association, Wyoming Dude Ranchers' Association, America Outdoors.
Guest Capacity: 125
Accommodations: Guests stay in one, two and three-bedroom cabins suitable for large and small families, couples and singles. Rooms are furnished simply and comfortably in a western motif. Most have twin beds and all have private baths. The majority of the 51 cabins have living rooms and porches, and some also have fireplaces. All cabins have refrigerators and coffee makers. Most of the original cabins were built by and named after many of the early guests. Maid service is provided and laundry facilities are available.
Rates: $$$ American Plan.
Season: June to October
Activities: Eatons' Ranch is one of the few ranches that allow you to ride on your own (if you wish) only after the corral boss is confident that you are ready. Daily rides go out twice a day except Sundays. Pack trips, picnics and riding instruction available. Fishing, hiking, bird-watching, soaking in the hot tub and swimming in the heated outdoor pool are available on the ranch. Golfers will enjoy the area golf courses.
Children's Programs: Recreational staff on duty during scheduled riding times. Kids go to Howard Hall for daily activities which include crafts, games, and treasure hunts to name a few. Children must be 6 years old to trail ride.
Dining: Huge dining room. Hearty western fare, barbecues, noon cookouts, breakfast and dinner rides. At your first meal look for your personalized wooden napkin ring marking your place.
Summary: One of Kilgore's all time great guest ranches, second to none! First official American dude ranch. The ranch exudes history and intrigue. Many multi-generation families return the same week each summer, year after year. Wonderful ranch store and gift shop.

Equitours Worldwide Horseback Riding
Dubois, Wyoming

Equitours Worldwide Horseback Riding tours got their start at the Bitterroot Ranch over 30 years ago when Bayard and Mel Fox began guiding some of their summer ranch guests on winter riding tours in Kenya where Mel was raised. These exciting trips, in some of Africa's best big game country, became extremely popular, and they began to branch out by selling other rides in different places around the world. Mel, Bayard, son Richard and wife Hadley, and the Equitours staff have tested and visited the best rides in the most beautiful and interesting places they could find around the world. Slowly and carefully they have built up a broad range of the world's best riding adventures from gallops with wildebeest in Africa to dressage lessons from top instructors in Portugal; from cattle drives in Wyoming to rides through dramatic buttes of Monument Valley. Equitours is now the oldest and largest riding tour company in America.

Address: P.O. Box 807, Dubois, WY 82513
Telephone: 800/545-0019, 307/455-3363
Website: www.ridingtours.com
Airports: International.
Location: Worldwide.
Guest Capacity: Average 8 to 10 guests per riding tour.
Accommodations: Vary between palaces in India, quaint country inns in Ireland and luxury tents in Kenya.
Rates: $$$$ Broad range of prices, call for details.
Season: Year round.
Activities: Equitours riding trips cover many levels of horsemanship as well as having a great variety geographically. Many guests try riding first at the Bitterroot Ranch, where they can get expert instruction and a critique of their riding ability before they head out on an overseas adventure. They take care to be sure that all the riders on a given trip have the necessary skills so that timid or unskilled riders will not hold up the others when the pace of the ride quickens to a fast canter or gallop. Many less aggressive rides are available for those seeking a slower pace. Groups are kept small with an average of 8 or 10 riders. Riders have a chance to experience the country in great depth as well as to be active and enjoy the challenge of adapting to different horses and styles of riding around the world.
Dining: Meals are generally excellent, but vary according to the culture and their special cuisine and wine. Travelers must be willing to adapt somewhat to local customs. Special diets can be accommodated on most trips.
Summary: The finest international riding company in the world. Equitours offers a broad range of carefully tested and proven horseback riding trips worldwide. An experience staff of ride consultants is at your service for advice on the best choice of trips to meet your particular needs. The owners of the Bitterroot Ranch began branching out in 1979 to establish the world's best riding adventures in 30 countries. See also Bitterroot Ranch in Wyoming.

Flat Creek Ranch
Jackson Hole, Wyoming

A visit to the historic Flat Creek Ranch is a remarkable journey into what the pristine mountain West used to be. Guests are driven from town up a rugged dirt track to a magnificent lakeside hideaway. For decades, this ranch has carried a mystique inspired by its remoteness and its epic wild beauty. Nestled in the Bridger-Teton National Forest at 7,400 feet, the ranch centers on a legendary trout stream and lake at the base of the Sleeping Indian Mountain. Built by a countess and a cowboy in the 1920s, the ranch is listed on the National Register of Historic Places. It is owned and operated by two retired news correspondents: Joe Albright, a descendant of the countess; and his wife, Marcia Kunstel. After a complete renovation in the late 1990s, the classic log cabins opened for guests to enjoy this private wilderness—in luxury and style. Whether you hike, fish, or experience the backcountry on horseback, chances are you will see an array of wildlife from bald eagles to moose and big-horned sheep. At day's end, dine graciously and settle into your cabin's rustic elegance. Welcome to Flat Creek Ranch.

Address: Upper Flat Creek Road, P.O. Box 9760, Jackson, Wyoming 83002
Telephone: 307/733-0603, 866/522-3344
Website: www.flatcreekranch.com
Airport: Jackson Hole, 25 miles
Location: 15 miles northeast of Jackson, Wyoming
Guest Capacity: 10-15
Accommodations: The focus is on rustic luxury. Five log cabins —creekside or lakeview—feature antique claw-foot bathtubs and wood-burning stoves. Each cabin has a bedroom, full bath, living room with convertible couch or futon, and sitting porch. Cozy flannel sheets and down comforters, unusual art, and pristine views make each renovated cabin a singular experience. For a truly awesome indulgence, try the Finnish sauna that sits in the stream.
Rates: $$$$$ American Plan.
Season: Late May through late September
Activities: This private lakeside setting offers spectacular mountain views and a host of outdoor recreation opportunities. Guests come to hike the high country, fly-fish, and take scheduled wilderness trail rides. Lake and stream fly-fishing are enhanced by a free fishing clinic. Fishing equipment provided. Cruise the lake in a canoe, rowboat, or raft (hardy souls can swim).
Children's Programs: No organized children's programs. Children are welcome, but the responsibility of parents. Better for children 11 and older who can hike, swim, fish, and ride.
Dining: Joe and Marcia have traveled the world and appreciate fine cuisine, and the ranch reflects it.
Summary: One of the truly spectacular mountain lakeside hideaways in North America. It is one of the most remote ranches I've ever visited. Breathtaking scenery, superb cuisine, fly-fishing, lakeside setting and hiking, make this one of a kind. Best for those seeking complete privacy, beauty, and remoteness. Ask about the drive into the ranch. Near Jackson Hole.

Goosewing Ranch
Jackson Hole, Wyoming

Remote, small, magnificent views to the Tetons 45 miles away, and international cooking. Welcome to Goosewing Ranch, located deep in the Gros Ventre River Valley, the Goosewing marks the entry point to the Gros Ventre Wilderness Area in the Bridger Teton National Forest. At 7,400 feet, the ranch offers guests spectacular scenery, remoteness with cozy comforts. Proximity to Teton National Park, Yellowstone National Park, and the Snake River Valley allows guests to view abundant wild game including bison, elk, moose, mountain sheep, antelope, bear, eagles, geese, and cranes. The Gros Ventre River, home to native cutthroat trout, runs through the meadows of this historic ranch, providing fishing for children and adults. Fly-fishing instruction and guiding can be arranged upon request.

Address: P.O. Box 4084, Jackson, Wyoming 83001
Telephone: 888/733-5251, 307/733-5251
Website: www.goosewingranch.com
Airport: Jackson Hole, 30 miles
Location: 38 miles northeast of Jackson on Gros Ventre Road
Memberships: Jackson Hole Chamber of Commerce.
Guest Capacity: 25
Accommodations: The Goosewing has eight private one-bedroom, one-bath guest cabins, each with heating stoves, and covered porches. There is a large, family-style log home for large groups. With its large stone fireplace, the main lodge serves as a central gathering place for dinning and relaxing. A loft bar with a pool table and television overlooks the main room.
Rates: $$$-$$$$$ American Plan
Season: Summer: June through October
Activities: Summer activities include horseback riding, hiking, biking, fly-fishing, and nature walks. Hands-on horse care available. Swimming in the heated pool or relaxing in the hot tub. Winter provides an incredible trip into the ranch by snowmobile. Once there, more snowmobiling, cross-country skiing, snowshoeing, and sharing the day's activities with other guests while warming up in the hot tub.
Children's Programs: No formal program. Most parents come to be on vacation with their kids.
Dining: International cuisine.
Summary: A slice of heaven and a piece of paradise that looks out to the distant Tetons in the magnificent Gros Ventre Wilderness. International host and cuisine. Fluent French and German spoken. Activities are offered for summer, fall, and winter seasons. Summer rides and raft trips, trip to Jackson weekly.   Be sure to ask about the incredible trip into the ranch in the winter. Nearby: The town of Jackson, the Snake River, Teton and Yellowstone National Parks.

Gros Ventre River Ranch
Moose, Wyoming

At 7,000 feet, Gros Ventre River Ranch is a great place to savor the mighty Tetons, take quiet walks, fish, ride, explore, or just relax and enjoy this year-round paradise. The Ranch has been in the guest-ranching business since the early 1950s. It was bought by Karl and Tina Weber in 1987, and since then they have run one of the top guest ranches in the country! Guests enjoy the lodge, with views that capture the splendor of the Tetons, magnificent wilderness scenery, and the rushing Gros Ventre River. While preserving the past, the Webers and their daughter and son-in-law, Tori and Sean McGough, have made it possible for people from around the world to settle in and enjoy rustic elegance and nature at its best.

Address: P.O. Box 151, Moose, Wyoming 83012
Telephone: 307/733-4138
Website: www.grosventreriverranch.com
Airport: Jackson, 18 miles
Location: 18 miles northeast of Jackson; you'll be sent a map with your confirmation
Memberships: The Dude Ranchers' Association, Wyoming Dude Rancher's Association
Guest Capacity: 34
Accommodations: Nine log cabins, all winterized. Four cabins have 10-foot ceilings, fireplaces, sliding glass doors that open to decks with magnificent views of the Tetons, and kitchenettes. Beds are turned down each evening. Laundry facilities available. The handsome lodge could well be on the cover of Architectural Digest—it features original art; two decks overlooking the Gros Ventre River, with views of the distant Tetons; and a lovely dining room, living room, and bar area. On the lower level is a rec/conference room that opens out to a landscaped area overlooking the river.
Rates: $$$$-$$$$$ American Plan.
Season: May through October
Activities: Summer: Mountain horseback riding with breakfast, lunch, and all-day rides, weekly team penning and sorting. Fly-fishing in the legendary Snake River, Crystal Creek, or Gros Ventre River, which runs through the ranch (fishing gear available). The stocked beaver ponds provide a sure catch for anglers and are enjoyed by all. Ranch swimming hole, canoeing in Slide Lake, hiking, mountain biking at ranch. (Bikes available.) Golf and tennis 10 miles away.
Children's Programs: Children welcome. No formal program.
Dining: Excellent cuisine.
Summary: A charming world-class guest ranch with million dollar views of the Tetons and Gros Ventre River. Emphasis on horseback riding, fly-fishing, and relaxation. Excellent for families, couples, singles, and small corporate groups. Ask Karl to give you a ride in one of his vintage cars! Be sure to visit Yellowstone National Park, 40 miles away! Near the National Elk Refuge and the town of Jackson. Bordered by Grand Teton National Park.

H F Bar Ranch
Saddlestring, Wyoming

The H F Bar Ranch, one of the great old dude ranches in America, has preserved that old-ranch feeling. Since the late 1920s, this 10,000-acre ranch has received distinguished guests from around the world. The ranch is owned and run today by Margi Schroth and her children, Lily, Cara, Turner, Gus and Avery. The H F Bar's horse corrals, barns, and ranch head-quarters haven't changed much over the years, nor have the surrounding pastures, with native grasses rising to meet the timbered hills leading into the Big Horn Mountains. Margi has kept things as they always have been, and guests keep returning. As Margi says, "I've made a tremendous effort to maintain our Old Western traditions and keep things very, very simple and family-oriented here." H F Bar is the perfect ranch for multi-generation gatherings.

Address: 1301 Rock Creek Road, Saddlestring, Wyoming 82840
Telephone: 307/684-2487
Website: www.hfbar.com
Airports: Sheridan, 35 miles; Billings, Montana, 160 miles
Location: 12 miles northwest of Buffalo; 35 miles southwest of Sheridan; 160 miles south of Billings, Montana
Guest Capacity: 120
Accommodations: Twenty-eight older, rustic cabins built from local timber. Each has its own charm, with names like Brookside, Meadowlark, and Round Up. Each has a living room, fireplace, one to seven bedrooms, and one to two full bathrooms. Several are heated with propane or electricity. Most have that days-gone-by feeling. The ranch stream sings outside many of the cabins. Early each morning, a New York Times fax is delivered to your front porch. A horse-drawn wagon delivers old-fashioned blocks of ice to your cabin, as well as any items you request from town or the ranch general store—an old H F Bar tradition.
Rates: $$$$ American Plan.
Season: June to October
Activities: It's a relaxed atmosphere, and guests can do as they please. Many come for the riding, fly-fishing, and hiking opportunities. With 200 horses and 10,000 acres, the ranch has plenty of riding for beginners, as well as experienced riders who can ride unsupervised only after their ability has been checked out by the wranglers. Half-day and all-day rides, pack trips, and riding instruction available. All rides customized to families or individuals. Excellent catch-and-release fly-fishing in the North and South Forks of Rock Creek, which runs through the ranch. Orvis-endorsed fishing guides and day trips to private waters leased by the ranch, or to the Big Horn River. Swimming in heated pool, hiking, and sport-clay shooting. Guns available (extra).
Children's Programs: Kids of all ages welcome—very active and extensive children's programs for infants through teens.
Dining: Each family is assigned its own table. Children may eat earlier and have their own menu. Hearty country fare.
Summary: One of Kilgore's great old-time historic ranches celebrating over 100 years. A wonderful ranch for the entire family and children of all ages. Lots of family time here. Many second- and third-generation families return year after year. First-time families receive a hearty welcome. Staff of 60 college students. Fascinating geology; Indian sites on ranch. Excellent riding and Fly Fishing!

The Hideout Lodge and Guest Ranch
Shell, Wyoming

The Hideout Lodge and Guest Ranch is an upscale working guest ranch in Shell, Wyoming, and easy driving distance from Cody, Wyoming and the East entrance of Yellowstone National Park. The Hideout shares approximately 300,000 acres and 1,300 head of cattle with the 100-year old Flitner Cattle Ranch. In addition to cattle work and scenic trail rides, additional activities like trapshooting, an excellent fly-fishing program and overnight mountain horseback riding trips make The Hideout unique as a working cattle ranch-resort. The Hideout strives for excellence in all departments, yet they really excel in a professional and authentic staff and their natural horsemanship initiatives. While the guests live the cowboy life during the day, they are sure to be pampered with a selection of upscale lodging accommodations and a gourmet culinary experience throughout their stay. Open year-round The Hideout Guest Lodge and Guest Ranch aims at redefining the traditional definition of a Guest or Dude Ranch.

Address: P.O. Box 206, Shell, Wyoming 82441
Telephone: 800/354-8637, 307/765-2080
Website: www.thehideout.com
Airports: Cody, WY, 70 miles; Billings, MT, 140 miles; private planes can fly into Greybull, WY, 15 miles
Location: 70 miles East Cody, Wyoming, off Highway 14.
Memberships: The Dude Rancher's Association, Wyoming Dude Rancher's Association
Guest Capacity: 30
Accommodations: The Hideout sits on a beautiful oasis overlooking the Bighorn Mountains. There is a selection of lodging accommodations: cabins, casitas (1 bedroom style apartments with full kitchen and in-unit washer/dryer), and private homes. All lodging units have private porches, modern bathrooms with showers, Pendleton bedding, wireless internet, satellite TV, mini-fridge, and spectacular views of the Shell Canyon. Overnight trips can be organized to an upper mountain home, situated at 8,000 feet above sea-level and set up with the comfortable cabins and breathtaking views over the valley.
Rates: $$$-$$$$$ American plan.
Season: Year Round.
Activities: The Hideout offers all-inclusive packages with as much or as little riding, at all riding levels, as you desire, and with at least 3 days cattle work per week available. Additional activities include skeet shooting, hiking, culinary classes (seasonal) and private photography weeks (seasonal), Cody Night Rodeo, guided tours of Yellowstone National Park. The Hideout offers packages for fly-fisherman with professionally guided fly-fishing packages or packages allowing for a combination of fly-fishing and horseback riding. Natural horsemanship is stressed at the ranch and guests can participate in Natural Horsemanship weeks. In addition The Hideout offers colt-starting and troubleshooting sessions, please contact the Hideout directly for more information on Natural Horsemanship weeks, colt starting and horse troubleshooting sessions.
Children's Programs: Recommended for children ages 10 and older
Dining: Hearty gourmet ranch cuisine prepared by culinary schooled chefs.
Summary: One of Wyoming's best. This luxury working guest ranch offers guests the opportunity to experience the life of a cowboy with the amenities of a four-star resort. Guests will appreciate the breathtaking views, excellence in matching horse to rider, the opportunity to work alongside real cowboys, gourmet meals, and a passionate and dedicated staff.

Lazy L & B Ranch
Dubois, Wyoming

The Lazy L & B has been in the guest-ranching business since the 1920s. Today it's owned and operated today by Jason and Deb Halmay and their three children. As the Halmay's say, "Our pleasure comes from sharing our unspoiled part of the Old West with guests from around the world." Located in a secluded river valley of cottonwoods with contrasting red-clay cliffs, the ranch adjoins the Wind River Indian Reservation. With the 50,000 acre elk refuge, Wind River for fishing, rolling prairie, badlands, Alpine meadows, river gorges, and high mountain forests, the Lazy L & B offers incredible riding diversity and fun for all!

Address: 1072 East Fork Road, Dubois, Wyoming 82513
Telephone: 800/453-9488, 307/455-2839
Website: www.lazylb.com
Airports: Jackson or Riverton; private planes may land on 5,000-foot lighted and paved airstrip in Dubois.
Location: 70 miles east of Jackson; 22 miles northeast of Dubois
Memberships: The Dude Ranchers' Association, Wyoming Dude Rancher's Association.
Guest Capacity: 35
Accommodations: Parts of the lodge, cabins, and corrals are the original 1890s sheep-and-cattle-ranch buildings. The lodge provides a cozy fireplace, library, game tables, and a wonderful, large deck that looks up to the East Fork Valley where guests can enjoy the morning sun and evening cocktails. Comfortable log cabins are arranged around a central courtyard. Two are located along the river. All have private baths or showers, electric heat, and small refrigerators. Some porches have views of the distant Absaroka and Wind River Ranges.
Rates: $$$ American Plan.
Season: End of May through August; adults-only in September
Activities: Most guests come here to ride, hike, and fly-fish. Riding groups consist of no more than six, divided by skill level; 2.5 - 3.5 hour rides in the morning and afternoon, and all-day rides. Other activities include hiking, rifle range, fly-fishing and roping clinics. Anglers enjoy fishing in the East Fork River, or neighboring Wiggins Fork, Bear Creek, and Wind River. Guided fishing available. Swim in the solar-heated pool, or relax in the whirlpool by the river.
Children's Programs: Supervised riding program for children age five years and older, with riding and safety instruction.
Dining: Fresh, delicious, and high quality casual gourmet food.
Summary: One of Wyoming's most colorful guest ranches, steeped in history amidst striking red-rock formations. Beautiful setting and family-oriented riding ranch with varied riding country and wonderful fly-fishing opportunities. Excellent for families, couples, and singles. Surrounded by 50,000 acre elk refuge, Indian reservation, and national forest. Spectacular variety of riding terrain. September is adults only.

Lost Creek
Moose, Wyoming

Lost Creek is a magnificent ranch and spa with breathtaking, million-dollar views of the mighty Tetons. Located on the eastern slope of the Jackson Hole Valley at 7,000 feet, the ranch is situated on a rise with commanding views of the entire Teton Mountain Range and the valley. This privately owned ranch is bordered by Grand Teton National Park and Bridger-Teton National Forest. The beautiful lodge and lovely cabins are furnished with western decor, featuring custom-made furniture and original artwork. The cabin amenities and tremendous outdoor opportunities make Lost Creek ideal for families, individuals, and corporate groups. Ride horses, float the Snake River, hike, enjoy a dutch-oven cookout on Shadow Mountain, or relax on the expansive lodge deck and watch the sun set behind the Tetons. You can do it all at Lost Creek.

Address: 1 Lost Creek Ranch Road, Moose, Wyoming 83012
Telephone: 307/733-3435
Website: www.lostcreek.com
Airport: Jackson via Denver or Salt Lake City
Location: 20 miles north of Jackson
Conference Capacity: 20
Guest Capacity: 55
Accommodations: Two-bedroom, two-bath (with tub and shower) cabins and one-bedroom cabins, with queen and single beds in all bedrooms and a king suite. All cabins have refrigerators with icemakers, microwaves, coffee and hot chocolate, and electric heat. The living-room cabins have queen sleeper sofas and freestanding gas log fireplaces. Maid service daily. Courtesy laundry service. High-speed wireless Internet access in each cabin.
Rates: $$$$$$ Full American Plan.
Season: Late May through late September
Activities: Full riding program with instruction. Very flexible and personalized. Beginner, intermediate, and scenic rides. Ask about Chips Bluff, Snake River, and Cunningham's Overlook. The Spa at Lost Creek (a luxurious full-service spa) offers customized treatments. Heated swimming pool and giant hot tub, tennis court, Snake River scenic float trips, cookouts, guided hiking. Skeet shooting on request. Many guests enjoy the Yellowstone and Grand Teton National Parks tours. Guided fishing and golf nearby (extra).
Children's Programs: Supervised kids' program (ages 6-13).
Dining: Outstanding cuisine, with two entrées served nightly.
Summary: A wonderful luxury dude ranch with million-dollar views of the Tetons and spa/massage amenities. Excellent for family vacations, weddings, and small corporate retreats. Ask about ranch, spa and wedding packages. Afternoon and evening children's program. Near historic western town of Jackson (art galleries, shopping, white-water rafting, and western events such as rodeos, shoot-outs, theater groups, stagecoach rides). Near Yellowstone, Grand Teton National Parks and National Elk Refuge.

Moose Head Ranch
Moose, Wyoming

Moose Head Ranch is a gem nestled completely within the boundaries of Grand Teton National Park. It offers guests a wonderful panoramic view of the majestic, spectacular Teton Range. Centrally located in the Jackson Hole Valley, Moose Head provides a feeling of seclusion and solitude, yet abundant activities on and off the ranch are easily accessible. While the ranch was originally homesteaded in 1923, the Mettler family has owned it since 1967. Louise Mettler Davenport and her husband Kit run the ranch with a personal approach. Louise sits down with every family on their first day to tell them about hikes and side trips that many guests have enjoyed. A trip to Yellowstone, white-water rafting, and scenic drives fill any time when you don't feel like being in the saddle. The college-age Moose Head staff is equally friendly, with polite manners and Southern charm—what great role models for your children! Guests leave feeling like a part of the Moose Head family, usually return, and always tell their friends.

Address: P.O. Box 214, Moose, Wyoming 83012
Telephone: 307/733-3141, 850/878-7577 (winter)
Website: www.mooseheadranch.com
Airport: Jackson, 18 miles.
Location: 26 miles north of Jackson.
Memberships: The Dude Ranchers' Association, Wyoming Dude Rancher's Association.
Guest Capacity: 45
Accommodations: Log cabins scattered among the aspen, cottonwoods, spruce, and pine, by trout ponds or along streams. Each of the 14 cabins offers privacy and comfort for couples and families (eight with adjoining living rooms). All have private baths with shower and tub, electric heating, coffeemakers, refrigerators, and porches. Daily maid service. Ice is brought to your cabin each day. The spacious lodge has an incredible deck with comfortable chairs and planters overflowing with perennials—a great way to relax after a ride or before a meal. Half a dozen hummingbird feeders on the lodge deck entertain children and adults.
Rates: $$$$ American Plan.
Season: Early June to mid-August
Activities: Small, supervised horseback rides twice daily, usually one family per wrangler. Weekly all-day rides. The Davenports believe in promoting family togetherness, so you ride and eat with your children. Don't come here to do a lot of fast riding, but do come if you want to see lots of wildlife (elk, buffalo, mule deer, antelope, moose, coyotes). There is dry fly-fishing (catch-and-release) in several excellent, well-stocked trout ponds. Kit Davenport loves to teach the art of fly-casting, making converts and enthusiasts of all ages. Many fish off the property on the Snake River and other streams. Fishing flies and equipment available. Tennis and golf can be arranged at local clubs, as can scenic and white-water float trips on the Snake River.
Children's Programs: Children of all ages welcome. Lots of activities, but no organized children's program.
Dining: Louise feels that good food is just as important as good riding. Outstanding gourmet chefs.
Summary: One of the great family ranches in Wyoming, with incredible views of the Tetons! A superb Southern college staff and outstanding food. Children of all ages welcome. Near grand teton national park.

Paradise Guest Ranch
Buffalo, Wyoming

Paradise Guest Ranch is one of the leading family guest ranches in North America, offering traditional dude-ranch activities with lots of riding and fishing. As hosts and managers Clay and Leah Miller say, "We bring families together, allowing them to do as much together or apart as they like." Once the prized hunting ground for the Sioux, Crow, and Cheyenne Indians, the ranch rests in a mountain valley next to French and Three Rivers Creeks, surrounded by tall forests of evergreens. The peace and tranquility are only occasionally interrupted by the calls of wildlife or the exuberant sounds of families having fun. It's little wonder that the ranch brand is FUN. It lives up to the name "Paradise" for good reason, as it offers the rustic flavor of the Old West, along with many modern conveniences.

Address: 282 Hunter Creek Road, Buffalo, Wyoming 82834
Telephone: 307/684-7876
Website: www.paradiseranch.com
Airports: Sheridan; or Buffalo for private planes or jets
Location: 46 miles south of Sheridan, off Hunter Creek Road; 110 miles north of Casper; 176 miles south of Billings
Memberships: The Dude Ranchers' Association, Wyoming Dude Rancher's Association
Guest Capacity: 70
Accommodations: Eighteen upscale one, two, and three-bedroom log homes, each with living room, kitchenette, fireplace, central heat, and outdoor porches with mountain-meadow views. Washers/dryers in all two-bedroom or larger cabins. Each day, your hot chocolate, tea, and coffee basket will be filled. WiFi available.
Rates: $$$$ American Plan.
Season: Late May to October
Activities: Riding is the main activity, with one wrangler to a maximum of seven guests. An average of 9-12 separate rides each day. Guests can choose walking, trotting, or loping rides. Beginners can learn all three if they wish and are able. Adults and children may ride together or separately. Also offered are bag-lunch rides and occasional special cooked-on-the-trail lunch rides. Mules pack all the grub, and the wranglers do all the cookin'. Ask about rides to Seven Brothers and Sherd Lakes, and the cattle-ranch-country ride through spectacular Cougar, Red, and Sales Canyons. Weekly team penning. Instruction available on one of 130 horses. Extensive fly-fishing program for kids and adults, with instruction. Naturalist-guided hiking, heated outdoor swimming pool, indoor whirlpool spa, and massage.
Children's Programs: Excellent full-day children's program, activities counselor for kids, toddlers to teens.
Dining: Three hearty meals a day with a gourmet flair, served family-style.
Summary: Paradise Ranch is one of the very best family-oriented guest ranches in the business! Traditional dude ranch values. Excellent children's program, infants to teens - one of the best! Fly-fishing, and legendary horseback riding with optional barrel racing and riding lessons. Ask about the weekly 4 day 3 night pack trips to Frying pan lake - fantastic! Near cloud peak wilderness with excellent fishing, and inspiring mountain views. Lots of family reunions. Sam Pope Memorial Wedding Chapel. September is adults only, featuring even more riding program flexibility, as well as Ladies' Week, fly-fishing, horse training, and executive retreats and conferences. Video available.

Red Reflet Guest Ranch
Ten Sleep, Wyoming

The Red Reflet Guest Ranch is an incredible ranch, limited to 20 guests, so the extensive facilities and many activities can be enjoyed on each guests own schedule. This is one of the most spectacular ranches I have seen in all my travels. The Lodge and chalets all have stunning, sweeping views, and bring inside the natural beauty of the Big Horn Mountains. The diversity of landscapes (elevations from 4200' to 8500') is impressive and always dramatic, varied from desert, red rock cliffs, to limestone canyons, to forests of aspen. Ponderosa and lodge pole pine is the back drop for riding and the many other activities, plus experiencing a 25,000 acre working Wyoming cattle ranch. The ranch is remote enough to be a very quiet place, and while there are strong seasons, the local climate affords 310 sunny days.

Address: 10 Lodge Road, Ten Sleep, WY 82442
Telephone: 866/766-2340 or 307/366-2340
Website: www.red-reflet-ranch.net
Airports: Cody, WY is a 2 hour drive; Billings, MT is a 3 hour drive. Ranch has paved airstrip. (WY00).
Location: Ten miles South of Ten Sleep, WY (26 miles East of Worland, 63 miles West of Buffalo)
Memberships: Dude Ranch Association; Wyoming Dude Ranch Association
Guest Capacity: 20
Accommodations: Four modern chalets: 1, 2, 3, & 5 bedrooms are large, with lovely views & large decks, all have a hot tub, steam shower, full stocked kitchen, washer dryer, fireplace(s), WIFI, Direct HD TV, private phone line, air conditioned, and more.
Rates: $$$$$$ American Plan
Season: Open all year
Activities: Horseback riding is the most popular activity in both indoor and outdoor arenas, miles of ranch trails & riding with the cattle. Rides are in small groups and can do fast rides. There is usually an ATV for every guest, dirt bikes and mountain bikes, a lighted tennis court, a large heated pool, shooting range with skeet, pistols & archery, a gym, two climbing walls, basketball court, beach volleyball, trampoline, pond for fly fishing lessons, private stream fly fishing, hikes to caves, a lion's den, scenic lookouts. Abundant wildlife on the ranch. Chef offers cooking classes. Massages and plane tours are available, and are the only activities NOT included in the rate.
Children's Programs: Excellent full-day children's program, activities counselor for kids, toddlers to teens.
Dining: Chef prepares exquisite meals. All dietary and allergy requirements met. All spirits, beers (20+), and wines (120+) are included in the rate.
Summary: A stunning ranch with exceptional scenery, wonderful cuisine, extensive wine selection and vistas hard to describe. Could well be on the cover of Architectural Digest. Owners Bob & Laurence Kaplan (who reside permanently on the Ranch) have created an environment that re-defines the western ranch experience with all the comforts of home. Here they will share the beauty, expanse, and quiet of this unique lifestyle. As a guest on their ranch, at their table, and in their home on the range as they say, "It is our mission to assure your stay exceeds all expectations and you have the experiences that are special, delightfully surprising, and yours to keep forever." You will discover the special qualities of this Wyoming life. At Red Reflet, the sky is the only limit, and wait till you see the stars!

R Lazy S Ranch
Teton Village, Wyoming

Magnificent Teton scenery, a friendly staff, and Western hospitality make the R Lazy S one of America's great guest ranches. At the foot of the majestic Tetons and bordering Grand Teton National Park, the R Lazy S has hosted families from all over the country since 1947. Today, it is owned and run by Kelly and Nancy Stirn and is managed by Cathy Fonatsch. While it's close to Jackson and the world-class ski resort at Teton Village, the ranch still maintains its privacy and solitude. Being so close and yet so far gives guests many options for activities and excursions. By the end of one week, you'll only have just begun. It's difficult to enjoy all of the Jackson Hole area's activities during a typical weeklong stay, which is why the ranch enjoys a high repeat clientele. Regardless of how long you stay, you'll enjoy the friendly spirit and the magnificent mountain scenery.

Address: Box 308, Teton Village, Wyoming 83025
Telephone: 307/733-2655
Website: www.rlazys.com
Airport: Jackson, 13 miles
Location: 13 miles northwest of the town of Jackson; one mile north of Teton Village.
Memberships: The Dude Ranchers' Association, Wyoming Dude Rancher's Association.
Guest Capacity: 45
Accommodations: Fourteen beautifully modernized one, two, and three-bedroom log cabins, all with electric blankets and fabulous views, scattered around the ranch property among the aspen trees. All have one or two bathrooms, depending on size; some have living or sitting rooms; all have electric heaters, fireplaces, or wood-burning stoves, and lovely hanging baskets with colorful flowers. The main lodge is a favorite gathering place at day's end. Laundry facilities available.
Rates: $$$$ American Plan.
Season: Mid-June through September; late August through September is adults-only.
Activities: The ranch has one of the most incredible locations in the world for riding, and the fly-fishing on the Snake River, which borders the ranch, is outstanding. Half-day and all-day rides with picnic lunches. Riding instruction. Fishing in the Snake, South Fork, Green, and North Fork Rivers, and streams, lakes, and stocked ranch pond. Weekly nature walks. Hiking, swimming in ranch swimming hole, or tubing. Water-skiing or scenic boat rides once a week on Jackson Lake. River rafting, tennis, and golf can be arranged nearby. Weekly cattle drives and team penning.
Children's Programs: Extensive program for children age seven and older. Teens and children have their own wranglers and riding program.
Dining: The superb cuisine is surpassed only by the incredible views of the Tetons.
Summary: One of the great dude ranches—with up-close, million-dollar views of the Tetons and located in the Jackson Hole Valley. Wonderful riding and fly-fishing opportunities. Superb cuisine and excellent children's program for kids age seven and older. Late August and September is adults only month. Near town of Jackson, Grand Tetons and Yellowstone National Parks.

Red Rock Ranch
Kelly, Wyoming

At 7,200 feet, Red Rock Ranch is nestled in a high, secluded valley on the eastern slop of Jackson Hole's spectacular mountain country. Homesteaded in 1890, it is named for the crimson colored cliffs and rock formations nearby. Owned and operated by the MacKenzie family since 1972, Red Rock offers some of the finest amenities in the guest ranching business. On a first-rate string of saddle horses, wranglers will take you through spectacular mountain country. Fly-fishers will enjoy the stocked ranch pond and Crystal Creek, a 2.5 mile long barbless catch-and-release fly-fishing stream that runs through the ranch. With its recent restoration, the creek can proudly offer superb fishing. RRR is very private, very beautiful, and one of the best in the guest ranching business.

Address: 17760 Gros Ventre Road, Kelly, Wyoming 83011
Telephone: 307/733-6288
Website: www.theredrockranch.com
Airport: Jackson Hole, 30 miles.
Location: 30 miles northeast of Jackson Hole.
Memberships: The Dude Ranchers' Association, Wyoming Dude Ranch-er's Association.
Guest Capacity: 28
Accommodations: Ten authentic log cabins named after Native American tribes such as Apache, Navajo, Sioux and Cheyenne. Built in the early 1950's, all have been recently remodeled. The cabins are one and two-bedrooms with private baths. All have twin, queen-size, or king-size beds, adjoining living rooms, electric heat, wood stoves, small refrigerators, coffee makers, and carpeting, and are tastefully decorated in western style. Each cabin has a large pergola covered porch with chairs or a bench and an un-brella. A comfortable lodge, dining room and deck with wonderful views, and adult pool hall/bar are available. Activities room for square dancing, western swing, and a children's recreation room. Guest laundry and ranch gift shop.
Rates: $$$$ American Plan.
Season: June through September.
Activities: Here you can enjoy some of the most beautiful riding in the country. Morning, afternoon,a nd all-day rides offered. Monday morning ori-entation rides (mandatory) in the arena acquaint guests with their horse for the week. Ask about the Skyline and Grizzly Lake rides. Weekly opportunity to work with cattle, as well as a complete hiking program with experienced guides for the casual hiker to the more challenging mountain peaks. Fly-fishing gear available, along with optional weekly clinics. Swimming in a heated pool that looks out on the incredible Gros Ventre Mountain Valley, an 8 person hot tub, suana, hiking, and plenty of relaxing. Scenic white-water rafting trips can be arranged down the Snake River — a must!
Children's Programs: Hands-on learning experience for children six years of age and older. Wranglers will assist them in learning the basics of horsemanship.
Dining: Professionally trained chefs serve up a variety of superb Western ranch cooking.
Summary: One of the greats! Very private, with spectacular high-country rides that look off to the Tetons. A fun family-oriented guest ranch with lots of camaraderie, Old West sprirt, and charm! Unspoiled wilderness. Moun-tain stream fishing. Guests rarely venture off the ranch once they arrive.

7D Ranch
Cody, Wyoming

One of the old-time greats, the 7D Ranch is a cozy haven in the midst of a magnificent wilderness. Bought in the late 1950s by Dewey and Lee Dominick, a surgeon and his wife, the ranch continues its family tradition. 7D is in the remote and beautiful Sunlight Basin, deep within the Shoshone National Forest. Surrounded by the Absaroka Mountains, it has pastures where the horses are turned out each night to graze, and where you'll find a small herd of registered Black Angus cattle. The 7D appeals to all ages. For those who wish to relax, the ranch offers the peace of a mountain hideaway. The more energetic may want to take a leisurely morning or afternoon ride, cast for trout, or hike into the Absaroka Wilderness. And folks with even more get-up-and-go may enjoy a full day of riding or fishing, or a wilderness pack trip into Yellowstone Park. Most of all, there's a wonderful atmosphere of history, camaraderie, laughter, and energetic participation. If you've ever wondered where Marlboro Country is, many of the ad photographs were taken right here at the 7D.

Address: P.O. Box 100, Cody, Wyoming 82414
Telephone: 888/587-9885, 307/587-9885
Website: www.7dranch.com
Airports: Cody, Wyoming; Billings, Montana
Location: 115 miles southwest of Billings, Montana; 50 miles northwest of Cody, Wyoming, via Chief Joseph Scenic Highway (Highway 296) and Sunlight Basin Road
Memberships: The Dude Ranchers' Association, Wyoming Dude Rancher's Association
Guest Capacity: 32
Accommodations: A clear mountain-spring creek winds near 11 rustic log cabins that are nestled in a beautiful aspen grove; they have names like Trapper, Aspen, Big Buffalo, Waldorf, and The Fireplace. Cabins vary from one to four bedrooms each, with private baths, woodstoves, and fresh wildflowers. Guests enjoy using the woodstoves during delightfully cool summer evenings. Daily maid service. Laundry facilities available.
Rates: $$$$ American Plan.
Season: Mid-June through mid-September
Activities: Rides every day except Sunday. Your choice of scenic, half-day, or all-day rides. Experienced wranglers accompany riders on beautiful and varied trails. Five to eight riders go out per ride. Ask about Big Skyline, Memorial, and the "Holy Cow" rides with views into Montana. Instruction available and encouraged. Ask about the 7D's 3-10 day horse pack trips into the North Absaroka Wilderness and Yellowstone Park for groups of six or less. This has been the trip of a lifetime for many. Superb fishing on and off the property. The 7D hosts a full-time fly-fishing guide and owns a private mile-long stretch of the Sunlight River. Limited fishing gear available. Many fishing opportunities for the young and the young-at-heart. Mountain biking, hiking, mountaineering, wildflower walks, soccer, and softball. Float trips and rodeos available in Cody.
Children's Programs: Counselors for children ages 6-12 during adult daytime activities.
Dining: Excellent food! Beautiful old ranch dining room.
Summary: The 7D is one of Kilgore's old all-time greats! Because of the authentic beauty, the 7D was featured years ago in numerous "Marlboro Country" photo shoots. Lots of family reunions. Excellent wilderness pack trips. Adults only weeks in September. Featured in Town and Country magazine.

T-Cross Ranch
Dubois, Wyoming

When you pass through the gates of the T-Cross Ranch, the outside world is all but forgotten. This old-time, authentic dude ranch has been in business since the 1920's. Today, as in years gone by, the spirit, informality, and relaxed Western atmosphere offers guests the experience of a lifetime. Located 15 miles north of the small Western town of Dubois, the ranch is situated in a private valley surrounded by the Shoshone National Forest. The remote T-Cross Ranch in every way captures old-time guest ranching at its best.

Address: P.O. Box 638, Dubois, Wyoming 82513
Telephone: 877/827-6770, 307/455-2206
Website: www.tcross.com
Airports: Jackson or Riverton; surfaced airstrip three miles west of Dubois for private jets and planes; free pickup from Dubois
Location: 15 miles north of Dubois, off Highway 26/287; 85 miles east of Jackson Airport
Memberships: The Dude Rancher's Association, Wyoming Dude Rancher's Association,
Guest Capacity: 24
Accommodations: Eight wonderful, cozy log cabins tucked in the pine trees truly capture the old spirit of the West, with Indian rugs, incredible handcrafted log furniture, down quilts, woodstoves or fireplaces, hot showers, and individual porches. The main lodge is filled with Western memorabilia and charm. Laundry facilities available.
Rates: $$$ American Plan.
Season: Mid-June to Mid September.
Activities: The main activities are riding, hiking, fly-fishing, and relaxing. Guests are assigned a horse for the duration of their stay. Morning and afternoon rides go out daily except Sunday. All-day rides go out at least twice a week, with a pack mule carrying lunch and fishing gear. Ask about rides to Five Pockets, Ramshorn Basin, Deacon Lake, and Twilight Falls. Depending on ability, guests take walking, trotting , and loping rides, or Ken's rugged ride. Weekly pack-trips available. Fly-fishers enjoy Horse Creek, which runs through the ranch. Another favorite is the Wiggins Fork of the Wind River. There are also high-mountain lakes, climbing opportunities, bird-watching, wildflowers, relaxing on the porch, or soaking in the hot tub at the end of the day. Artists should bring their art supplies along.
Children's Programs: Unstructured program.
Dining: Hearty ranch cuisine.
Summary: One of the really old-time greats begun in the 1920's. Here the spirit is rich in old west tradition. Scenic horseback riding, fly-fishing, hiking, and relaxing. Perfect for small family reunions. Adults only in September. Featured in National Geographic Traveler, The New York Times, The Boston Globe, The London Financial Times, and Town & Country.

Trail Creek Ranch
Wilson, Wyoming

Trail Creek Ranch is a very special to me-it's the ranch where my parents took me as a young child. It's here that a seed was planted, which blossomed into my love for this incredible way of life. I'm proud to say that Trail Creek Ranch is largely responsible for this guidebook. Back in the 1940's, a young Olympic skier named Elizabeth Woolsey bought a run-down ranch at the foot of Teton pass, 10 miles from Jackson. With her tenacity and tremendous spirit, Betty transformed the ranch into one of the prettiest family-oriented ranches in the country, offering sincere Western hospitality. To the east, there are lush green hay meadows, the rest is timbered with many bridle trails and Trail Creek, which runs through the ranch. Trail Creek Ranch is a working ranch, raising hay to support a small horse herd. Because of the ranch's tremendous location, there are myriad activities for guests to choose from and enjoy. Betty touched many lives over the years. In 1997, Betty passed on and left the ranch to her longtime friend and colleague, Muggs Schultz (who has worked at Trail Creek since the 1950's) and the Jackson Hole Land Trust. Today, Muggs and Alex continue to greet guests and welcome them to their ranch.

Address: P.O. Box 10, Wilson, Wyoming 83014
Telephone: 307/733-2610
Website: www.jacksonholetrailcreekranch.com
Airport: Jackson via Salt Lake City or Denver
Location: Two miles west of Wilson; 10 miles west of Jackson
Memberships: Jackson Hole Chamber of Commerce
Accommodations: Two family cabins and five rooms in various multi-bedroom cabins with private baths comfortably house the guests. Cabins and rooms overlook the hay meadows and beyond to the Sleeping Indian, a beautiful mountain the Gros Ventre mountain range.
Rates: $$$-$$$$
Season: June to October
Activities: Swimming in the outdoor heated swimming pool. No organized activities. You are on your own to enjoy the many activities in Jackson Hole. World class hiking, fly fishing and mountain biking, Horseback riding, white water rafting and scenic floats (one of the most beautiful in America) with local outfitters. You'll find there is not enough time to do all you want to do!
Children's Programs: No formal program. All ages welcome.
Dining: No dining on ranch. Ktichens in two cabins. Local restaurants and general store two minutes away in downtown Wilson, WY, and tremendous variety of dining all around valley.
Summary: My first dude ranch! As wonderful today as it was when I first visited in 1960! A very special guest ranch with a long history hosting guests. Now it is operated as a B&B for independent travelers. Lovely setting in world-famous Jackson Hole Valley. Tremendous variety of off ranch activities. Great base camp for all kinds of outdoors enthusiasts. Nearby: Teton and Yellowstone National Parks, Jackson, National Elk Refuge, Snake River.

Triangle X Ranch
Moose, Wyoming

Known for its beauty, hospitality, and caring spirit, Triangle X has just about everything one could ask for, including a million-dollar view. Just outside Moose, Triangle X has panoramic views of the awesome Teton Range and Snake River valley. The ranch was established in 1926 by John Turner, Sr. as a cattle and hunting ranch. The Turner family runs a first-rate operation. Their repeat business (some guests have been returning for over 40 years) proves it. Among the ranch's unique features are its location, the river rafting program, and its well-supervised Little Wrangler riding program for kids 5 through 12. This program makes the Triangle X a perfect family stay.

Address: Star Route Box 120, Moose, Wyoming 83012
Telephone: 307/733-2183
Website: www.trianglex.com
Airport: Jackson Hole airport.
Location: 25 miles north of Jackson.
Memberships: The Dude Ranchers' Association, Wyoming Outfitters Association
Guest Capacity: 75
Accommodations: Guests stay in one, two, or three-bedroom log cabins with private baths, warm wool blankets, and covered porches. Cabins are very clean, with polished wood floors. Comfortable and ranch-cozy. Laundry facilities available. Small ranch gift shop with hats, shirts, nature books, Indian Jewelry, and river rafting reception area.
Rates: $$$$ American Plan.
Season: May to November; January to April.
Activities: Triangle X is predominantly a riding ranch. Riders enjoy a variety of trails to the tops of timbered mountains, through wildflower meadows, over sagebrush, and along the Snake River, always with the magnificent Teton Mountain Range as a backdrop. Breakfast fides and weekly dutch-oven suppers. Scenic, medium, and faster rides. Weekly nature ride by Forest Service personnel. Hiking and Triangle X Snake River rafting program. Trout fishing on the famous Snake River for either the expert or the well-versed on fly or spin-fishing. Triangle X offers the ultimate willderness experience in the form of 4-day to 2-week pack-trips into the Teton Wilderness and southern Yellowstone areas. Here, the finest of scenery, wildlife, relaxing, and fishing can be experienced. In addition, fall hunting trips for elk, moose, and deer are conducted. In winter, cross-country skiing across the vast parklands and snowmobiling on adjacent National Forest lands.
Children's Programs: Kiddie wrangler with riding lessons throughout the day.
Dining: Meals are hearty and delicious, served family-style.
Summary: Triangle X and the Turner family are old-time greats in the dude ranch business. Besides its location, million-dollar views of the Tetons, and Old West atmosphere, Triangle X is known for its riding, river rafting, and superb 4-day to 2-week pack-trips. Winter snowmobiling. Near Grand Teton and Yellowstone National parks.

Vee Bar Ranch
Laramie, Wyoming

Listed on the National Register of Historic Places, the Vee Bar Guest Ranch is located in the Centennial Valley. The nearby 12,000-foot Snowy Range Mountains, part of the magnificent Medicine Bow National Forest, are Wyoming's answer to the Tetons, only without the crowds. A showplace of Western charm, this old cattle ranch was once a stopover for stagecoaches traveling west on the Overland Trail. Since 1912, the ranch has had a colorful history taking in guests and running cattle and buffalo. What makes the Vee Bar special, over and above the hospitality, are the varied riding program and the Little Laramie River that traverses the ranch's 800 acres. Guests may ride in the wide-open meadows surrounding the ranch, or explore the owner's other beautiful 5,000-acre cattle ranch just up the valley, bordering the national forest. The Cole family serves up one of the greatest guest-ranch experiences in the country!

Address: 38 Vee Bar Ranch Road, Laramie, Wyoming 82070
Telephone: 800/483-3227, 307/745-7036
Website: www.veebar.com
Airport: Laramie; courtesy shuttle available.
Location: 20 miles west of Laramie, off Highway 130 .
Memberships: National Register of Historic Places, The Dude Ranchers' Association, Wyoming Stock Growers' Association, Wyoming Dude Rancher's Association.
Guest Capacity: 30
Accommodations: The lodge and cabins reflect the quality and charm that characterize the Vee Bar. Charming and well-appointed two- or three-bedroom cabins and duplex suites along the little Laramie River. All have sitting areas with gas fireplaces, refrigerators, and amenities such as coffee, tea, and hot chocolate. Most of the cabins have the added convenience of built-in washers (soap provided) and dryers, as well as daily housekeeping service. High-speed wireless Internet access available.
Rates: $$$-$$$$ Summer: American Plan.
Season: Year-round; guest ranch mid-June through early September; bed-and-breakfast, conferences, and special groups remainder of the year
Activities: Varied riding and terrain for all levels and ages include wide-open meadow and mountain riding, cattle work, and Deerwood Ranch overnight campout. Fishing on the Little Laramie, guided hiking, river tubing (for the brave), and trapshooting are offered. Massage on request.
Children's Programs: A great vacation place for kids. Special activities for kids 8 and younger. The terrain is gentle and safe, with plenty of room to run and play.
Dining: Buffet-style dining with a gourmet touch. Special diets accommodated.
Summary: One of Wyoming's best! Wonderful service, fantastic spirit, great hospitality, excellent wide-open riding, and a riverside setting. Tremendous for families, couples, and singles. Riverside setting with private fishing. Cattle drives and overnight campouts on owner's nearby 5,000-acre cattle ranch. Wide open spaces with side-by-side riding.

ARGENTINA

— ✦ —

Estancia Los Potreros
Cordoba, Argentina

Estancia Los Potreros is set at the top of the Cordoba hills in the center of Argentina. The estancia dates from 1574 when breeding mules for the silver mines in Peru was the principal activity. Today it is an idyllic retreat for horsemen and nature lovers. It has been in the same Anglo Argentina family for four generations and set high standards of accommodation, combining the pleasures of estancia life with exceptional riding. The owners have a passion for conservation and the preservation of the environment. They cherish the farms "spring water" and use wind and solar energy. The Begg family delight in welcoming guests to share their home and lifestyle, providing a unique and unforgettable vacation with first hand contact of the rural traditions of Argentina, whilst not abandoning creature comforts. The estancia prides itself on setting a high standard of professionalism in accommodation and hospitality, taking care of guests with unrivalled personal attention to detail. Every day on the estancia is different, so whether your passion be outstanding horses, beautiful scenery, walking, photography, bird-watching, wild flowers, soaking up the local culture, or simply enjoying good company in a truly unique setting, Estancia Los Potreros has something for everyone.

Address: Casilla de Correo 64 -5111 Rio Ceballos – Cordoba, Argentina
Telephone: +54 (0) 11 6091 2692
Website: www.estancialospotreros.com
Airport: Pajas Blancas, Cordoba, Argentina
Location: Located in the Sierras Chicas, north-west of Cordoba city, approximately one hour's drive from Cordoba (Pajas Blancas) international airport
Guest Capacity: 12
Accommodations: Comfortable rooms, traditionally furnished with plenty of antiques, all individual and with private bathrooms. Rooms are heated with wood-burning stoves or fireplaces.
Rates: $$$$
Season: Year-round.
Activities: Estancia life is usually centered around riding, but other activities available on the estancia include walking, bird watching and Polo. Within the surrounding areas can be found: Golf (3 excellent golf courses within an hour), international paragliding site, mountain biking, world class dove-hunting, the university town of Cordoba (1.5 hours), a range of Jesuit churches and buildings of interest in the area
Children's Programs: The estancia welcomes children. No formal program.
Dining: Traditional Argentine Cuisine hosted by the Begg family.
Summary: One of the great Estancias in Argentina. Wonderful English – Argentine family. Estancia Los Potreros is an exclusive working cattle farm in the Cordoba hills. Fabulous horses, charm, wonderful Argentine spirit and hospitality. One of the best ways to experience the real Argentina.

MEXICO

—★—

Rancho Las Cascadas
San Francisco Soyanilquilpan, Mexico

With the beautiful backdrop of traditional Mexican countryside, nestled between gently sloping mountains and overlooking stunning natural waterfalls, Rancho Las Cascadas offers serious equestrians, beginners, and non-riders a destination that makes dreams come true. Mexican hospitality combined with Swiss management has defined itself as one of Mexico's best kept secrets. The owner and manager, Uschi, takes pride in every aspect and detail of her guest's stay. She says, "our vision is to offer food for the body, mind and soul, provide a service second to none, and the best horses to take you on the journey of a lifetime." Welcome to Rancho las Cascadas.

Address: San Agustin Buenavista, San Francisco Soyanilquilpan, 54280, State of Mexico, Mexico
Telephone: 0052 155 10702080, 0052 155 30696670,
Website: www.ranchomex.com
Airport: Mexico City International Benito Juarez (MEX), private planes use Toluca International.
Location: 90 minutes North of Mexico City Intl. Airport.
Guest Capacity: 24
Accommodations: The accommodation is located in the Main House, in Casitas and in the Pueblito. All rooms are generously sized with en-suite facilities and either King Size or Twin beds. The casitas can accommodate up to 5 people and have a private terrace. There is a sun terrace overlooking the natural waterfalls that gave the ranch its name with loungers and parasols. Also in the terrace is a hot tub with wonderful views of the waterfalls and surrounding landscape. Laundry service available. Meeting room facilities available.
Rates: $$$ American Plan.
Season: Year-round
Activities: Rides go out every day up to 8 hours (program is tailored to suit group) and the landscape is wide open and unfenced. The rides are either half days or full days with many surprises on the way. Cater to riders of every level from complete novice to expert and groups are split according to ability. Also able to cater to mixed level groups with two wranglers so that people can ride together but also split up to enjoy faster paces. Mountain biking, river fishing (own equipment necessary) and hiking are also available. Deep-tissue or hot stone massage, Mexican cooking courses in our wonderful kitchen, private riding tuition, and a great program of excursions to historical and cultural places of interest and excellent shopping.
Children's Programs: Children welcome; no formal program.
Dining: Local chefs create the perfect blend of traditional Mexican cuisine and European fine-dining.
Summary: Rancho Las Cascadas is a hidden gem of Mexico, just 90 minutes from the airport, offering the perfect mix of adventure, luxury and genuine hospitality for the more discerning traveler. The riding horses and the scenery are wonderful, no fences, no gates, no limits, just panoramic vistas, endless space and a wide variety of terrain! Special events include Christmas, New Years, the Day of the Dead, Local Fiestas, Mexican Cooking Weeks, Singles Weeks, and Ladies Only Weeks. This is also the perfect location for special events such as weddings, honeymoons, or family celebrations. The whole ranch can be booked exclusively.

Rancho los Banos
Sonora, Mexico

Owned and operated by the english speaking Valenzuela Family since the early 1950's, Rancho los Banos is located 2 1/2 hours south of the Arizona border in the Mexican Sonoran high desert. As one guest wrote so well, " The Ranch is located in a mesmerizing high Sonoran desert setting and features dramatic landscapes characterized by narrow winding canyons, rugged mountains and typical Sonoran flora and fauna, what makes it even more special is its authenticity. This is a remote and serene working ranch. You go off the grid, literally, and back in time to a simpler, rugged way of life. The horseback rides and canyon hikes are truly world class. The people are down to earth and care about the land." Indeed , there is something very unique and special about los Banos. If you savor privacy, remoteness, and magnificent outdoor beauty give Manuel a call. Bienvenidos (Welcome) to Mexico's one and only Rancho los Banos.

Address: 2809 East Elm St. Tucson, Az. 85716
Telephone: 520/955 2577
Website: www.tierrachamahuaecoadventures.com
Airport: Tucson International.
Location: 55 miles South East of Douglas, Arizona. Northeast Sonora Mexico, 175 south of Tuscon.
Guest Capacity: 14
Accommodations: The Ranch House is your home away from home. Three simple private single and double occupancy rooms with solar energy, hot showers and 2 baths. Two separate, one and two bedroom cabins with bathrooms, electricity and hot water.
Rates: $$-$$$ American Plan.
Season: August to May
Activities: With 30,000 unspoiled and private acres of wilderness back country riding, offers almost unlimited hours of thrilling, challenging, yot fun filled adventure, riding in remote, rugged, secluded isolation surrounded by mountains, hills, canyons and unspoiled nature. In addition to riding, there is canyon hiking, bird watching, and nearby lake activities. Jeep tours, mountain biking, wildlife viewing and fishing in Lake Angostura about an hour from the ranch.
Children's Programs: No formal kids program per se but kids four and older welcome.
Dining: Lupita and Julia prepare wonderful Mexican cuisine. BYOB
Summary: A once in a lifetime adventure. 30,000 acre ranch in the Mexican Sonoran Desert. Magnificent beauty and views from the main lodge/ hacienda, warm Mexican hospitality, off the grid, exciting horseback riding and hiking. Season cattle work and November roundup. A step back in time and off the grid. A representative from the Ranch will meet you in Douglas, Arizona on the Arizona/Mexican border, or upon request, you may be picked up at Tuscon International Airport, and driven to the ranch.

CANADA

— ✳ —

Echo Valley Ranch and Spa
Clinton, British Columbia, Canada

Located in the heart of British Columbia's most unique pristine wilderness, Echo Valley Ranch & Spa offers a freedom of spirit like no other. With its diverse environment, gracious hospitality, and attentive service, the Echo Valley experience is perfect for a couples' getaway, family reunions, or small corporate meetings. Echo Valley inspires relationships, reconnects guests with nature, and shares the excitement of eco adventures that explore four distinct geographic biomes — forested mountains, deep river gorges, wind-swept plateaus, and rolling grasslands. Add to this Echo Valley's pampering care and professional spa services, and it becomes a one-of-a-kind vacation.

Address: Echo Valley Ranch, P.O. Box 916 Jesmond, Clinton, British Columbia, Canada V0K 1K0
Telephone: 800/253-8831 (reservations), 250/459-2386 (ranch)
Website: www.evranch.com
Airports: Private 3,400-foot paved airstrip at ranch, call ranch for details; Kamloops and Vancouver International for scheduled flights.
Location: 270 miles north of Vancouver; 30 miles from Clinton; 100 miles from Kamloops.
Memberships: The Dude Ranchers' Association, British Columbia Guest Ranchers' Association.
Guest Capacity: 30; groups up to 40 (based on double occupancy)
Accommodations: The Dove Lodge is of log construction, with six guest bedrooms, all with private baths. Comfortable sitting areas, spacious game room, sauna. The Lookout Lodge has nine large bedrooms, each with private bath. Two cabins each have a private bedroom, bathroom, sitting area, loft, and private deck. The honeymoon cabin has a four-poster bed, fireplace, exquisitely furnished sitting area, and private deck with its own outdoor hot tub. Be sure to ask about the amazing and beautiful Baan Thai Pavilion and suite.
Rates: $$$$$ American Plan. Ask about Spa & Lifestyle and "Reserve the Ranch" packages.
Season: April to November. Ask about Christmas and New Years.
Activities: Horseback riding, hiking, white-water rafting, gold panning. Guided trout fishing in pristine mountain lakes. Occasional cattle moving, shooting and archery. Winter: Cross-country skiing, snowshoeing, sleigh rides, and ice fishing, weather permitting. Thai spa services including fitness, meditation and Thai yoga. Heated, indoor swimming pool.
Children's Programs: Adult-oriented. Family weeks July and August.
Dining: Healthy gourmet meals prepared by a professional master chef in an open kitchen; all served in a family-style setting. Licensed to serve liquor.
Summary: Echo Valley combines the very best of guest ranching with superb professional Thai spa services for a dynamic vacation. The personal care, warm and friendly hospitality, superb cuisine, and wide-ranging activities captivate and enrich the lives of guests from around the world. Norm and Nan Dove's Echo Valley Ranch is indeed unique, and one of the very best guest ranch spas in North America!

Siwash Lake Ranch
British Columbia, Canada

At Siwash Lake Ranch, eco-adventure, horses and life's little luxuries entwine in the wilds of Canada to create a truly remarkable dude ranch experience. Explore 80,000 acres of pristine, open range on your own or with a personal riding guide. Siwash features guided riding to your heart's desire, for first-time beginners to advanced riders, with the option of riding without a guide or other guests for those with proven ability. Their hands-on horsemanship program ensures your own horse for duration of stay – plus you'll groom, saddle up, and learn as much about riding and horses as you wish. Besides riding, Siwash offers fly-fishing safaris, swimming in a private lake, wilderness survival, mountain-biking, hiking, canoeing and more. This is a 4 ½ Star boutique wilderness lodge and genuine family-run ranch that features a soul-pleasing blend of the rustic and the refined. Luxurious accommodations, organic fine food, and warm, gracious hospitality combine with first-class eco-adventure and a maximum guest capacity of 16 at this private hideaway. Rated Canada's top eco-friendly destination by the Globe and Mail (Feb 2009) and Canada's top luxury ranch by Forbes Traveler (May 2007).

Address: Box 39, 70 Mile House, BC , Canada, V0K 2K0
Telephone: 1-250-395-6541
Website: www.siawashlakeranch.com
Airport: Vancouver or Calgary International; Kamloops Regional; float plane base at the ranch.
Location: A 5-hour drive from Vancouver, 2-hour drive from Kamloops, and at the midpoint on BC's touring route between Whistler, Lake Louise, and Baniff in the Rocky Mountains.
Memberships: Five Green Keys (Hotel Association of Canada eco-rating); BC Guest Ranchers' Association; BC Wilderness Tourism Association; Tourism BC Approved Accommodation; 4 ½ Stars Canada Select
Guest Capacity: 16
Accommodations: Luxury accommodations in lodge and private cabin.
Rates: $$$$$$ All-inclusive Packages
Season: June 1 through September 30
Activities: Something for everyone with up to six-hours of guided eco-adventure each day for all ages and fitness levels. Riding can be as little or as much as you wish, from one-hour rides to all day picnic adventures on horseback, with no nose-to-tail trail rides! Plus fishing; wilderness survival; interpretive nature walks; hiking trails; mountain bikes; river and lake swimming; boating; sustainability seminars, "Free-Range Kids" children's program; campfires; outdoor games; entertainment and more.
Children's Programs: This is an adult-oriented ranch and welcomes adults and youths aged 16 and above.
Dining: Enjoy gourmet, country cuisine that rivals fine city food – ranch grown, organic and locally produced.
Summary: One of Canada's best! This luxury adult oriented ranch is well off the beaten path and very private. A safe adventure haven for families and a romantic destination for couples. The horses are well-loved. Everything about this operation is designed to be in harmony with the wilds around it, without sacrificing the luxuries and comforts. Siwash offers the discerning traveler a world of goodness.

Three Bars Cattle and Guest Ranch
Cranbrook, British Columbia, Canada

Three Bars Ranch couples old guest and cattle ranch tradition with modern-day comforts. The Old West charm has been carefully crafted with log architecture. The hospitality is under the direction of Tyler and Jenna Beckley, who grew up in the cattle and guest ranch business. When they say the welcome mat is out, and the coffee pot is on, they mean it! Three Bars is nestled up against the mountains with the St. Mary's River on the north edge of the property and the Perry Creek Valley to the south. It truly is one of the most beautiful places in Canada.

Address: 9500 Wycliffe-Perry Creek Road, Cranbrook, British Columbia, Canada V1C7C7
Telephone: 877/426-5230, 250/426-5230
Website: www.threebarsranch.com
Airport: International airports in Calgary and Vancouver link regular scheduled flights to Cranbrook.
Location: Six miles north of Cranbrook, off Highway 95A in southeastern British Columbia; 254 miles southwest of Calgary.
Memberships: The Dude Rancher's Association and British Columbia Guest Rancher's Association.
Guest Capacity: 40
Accommodations: Ten hand-hewn log duplex cabins provide 20 units all set within a landscaped yard and connected by wooden boardwalks. In the ranch's 5,000 square foot log lodge are the dining room, fireplace lounge, library and bar, complete with pool table and conference room.
Rates: $$$$ American plan.
Season: May through September riding program; October through May conferences and groups.
Activities: Progressive trail-riding program. Morning, afternoon, and an all-day ride each week to high mountain lookouts or afternoon rides by the river. 75,000 acres to explore. Private and group riding lessons. Weekly fly-fishing guide service available on request (extra). Excellent dry fly-fishing on the St. Mary's River. Most float the river with experienced guides; weekly river float trips (July and August) on the St. Mary's River. Tennis court, indoor heated swimming pool, outdoor spa, horeshoe pit, mountain bikes, trap and skeet shooting, self-guided hiking and ATV tours. Massage available (extra).
Children's Programs: Full optional kid's program for ages 5-12. Petting zoo.
Dining: Wonderful ranch cooking and evening saloon.
Summary: One of the great guest ranches in Canada for families, singles, and couples. Spectacular Canadian Rocky Mountain scenery. Excellent riding and fly-fishing on the St. Mary's River. Beautiful lodge and indoor heated swimming pool. 11,000 square foot indoor riding arena. Near historic Fort Steele, 30 minutes away, it's a must!

Tod Mountain Ranch
British Columbia, Canada

Just four hours NE of Vancouver, hidden in the Louis Creek Valley, this ranch is small and exclusive. offering a relaxing, tranquil environment for adults to enjoy horseback riding, nature and the outdoors. Surrounded by mountains, this ranch was designed and developed by the owner, a modern day lady-pioneer who arrived in Canada in 2007 with big dreams and huge passion.

Address: 3968 Heffley-Louis Creek road, Heffley Creek, BC V0E 1Z1
Telephone: 1-877-488-8881 or 1-250-578-8881; Fax: 1-250-578-8883
Website: www.todmountainranch.com
Airport: Kamloops Airport 45 minutes; Vancouver Airport 4 hours. We offer free transfers from Kamloops Airport or bus station.
Location: Located in the Southern Interior of BC, approximately 60KM North of Kamloops, and just 15 minutes drive from Sun Peaks resort.
Memberships: BC Guest Ranchers Association; Thompson-Okanagan Tourism Association.
Guest Capacity: 16
Accommodations: Whilst the ranch dates back to the 1890's, the lodge and guest cabins were newly constructed in 2009. The cabins are nestled in small clearings amongst the trees, and each one is furnished with custom-designed, hand-constructed log furniture made by a local craftsman. Modern amenities and facilities combined with the rustic style furniture and décor provide guests with an experience that is luxuriously rustic. The lodge is the hub of activity at the ranch where guests gather for meals, activities, and socializing when they're not out on the trail. There is something for everyone. A fireside lounge for relaxing; TV lounge with DVD library boasting over 100 of the best western and horse related movies ever and a recreation room with pool table, shuffleboard and card table.
Rates: $$$ American Plan.
Season: May- October for Horseback riding; December to March for winter sports & activities
Activities: Horseback riding is the main activity and because this ranch is small, they offer complete flexibility in the riding program so that it is geared to the interest level of the guests, with rides varying from a couple of hours to all day rides. Guests are welcome to spend time at the barn getting to know the horses they'll be riding and helping out with the grooming and saddling. Experienced wranglers guide you up the mountains surrounding the ranch on an extensive network of old logging roads and cattle trails through the forest to nearby lakes and streams and up into the alpine. Riding lessons are also offered. In addition to the horseback rides, there are hiking and mountain biking trails and horseshoe pitch.
Children's Programs: This is an adult-oriented ranch and welcomes adults and youths aged 16 and above.
Dining: Dining at Tod Mountain Ranch is a special experience. The resident chef creates wholesome, home-cooked meals with an emphasis on locally sourced, fresh seasonal produce. Combining the healthy with the hearty, this is gourmet cooking with a ranch twist.
Summary: One of Canada's newest guest ranches and one of Kilgore's rising stars, this is the first and only adults only ranch in British Columbia. Whether you're traveling alone, with a partner or a group of friends, this small yet upscale ranch offers stunning views, great food, good company and a peaceful, calm environment to relax, unwind and forget about the stresses of the real world.

Glossary of Ranch Terms

ADRA (Arizona Dude Ranch Association): An association of Arizona dude ranches.

BCGRA (British Columbia Guest Ranchers' Association): An association of Canadian ranches in the province of British Columbia, formed in 1989 to market ranch vacations throughout Canada and the United States.

CDGRA (Colorado Dude and Guest Ranch Association): An association founded in 1934, made up solely of Colorado ranch and ranch resort properties dedicated to marketing and maintaining excellence in the Colorado guest-ranch industry. Members meet annually.

Cross-Country Skiing Ranch: A ranch that offers cross-country skiing opportunities. Trails are normally groomed with specialized, professional equipment. Instruction, guide service, and equipment are usually available.

DRA (The Dude Ranchers' Association): An association of Western dude ranches, founded in 1926, dedicated to maintaining the quality and high standards of Western hospitality established by early ranches.

Dude: Basically, a dude is you and me — we're all dudes in one way or another! City Slickers in Ranch Country!

Dude/Guest Ranch: Usually a family-owned and -operated ranch with the primary objective of offering its guests a Western experience. Horseback riding is usually the main activity; hiking, fishing, and swimming are often included.

Fly-Fishing Ranch: A facility offering an extensive fly-fishing program with instruction and guides. Some ranches/lodges have tackle shops on the premises.

MDRA (Montana Dude Ranch Association): An association of Montana dude ranches.

Naturalist: One who is trained in the appreciation and understanding of nature and the outdoor world.

Orvis Endorsed: Orvis, the respected fly-fishing company, realized there was a need to check out and endorse top-notch fishing lodges with first-rate guides. Today, Orvis personnel monitor Orvis-endorsed lodges. These lodges provide complete fly-fishing guide services. Each has its own fly-fishing tackle shop. Orvis-endorsed lodges in this book are designated as such.

Pack-Trip: An overnight, multiple-day, week-long, or month-long trip on horseback. All supplies, including food, tents, and equipment, are carried by horses, mules, or sometimes even llamas. Usually a magnificent wilderness experience.

PRCA (Professional Rodeo Cowboys Association): An association dedicated to setting the standards for and promoting the professional rodeo industry.

Resort Ranch: A facility that may or may not have a Western theme but does offer horseback riding. Usually the amenities are upscale, with a range of resort activities offered. Note: Some properties use "resort" in their names, but may not offer resort amenities.

Rodeo: A cowboys' tournament or competition in which men and women compete in an arena; involves livestock (horses, steers, bulls) and barrel racing.

WDRA (Wyoming Dude Rancher's Association): An association of Wyoming dude ranches.

Wilderness Lodge: In the heart of wilderness areas, these facilities offer a retreat from civilization. Generally, all supplies arrive by plane, boat, horse, or sometimes four-wheel-drive vehicle.

Wrangler: Originally, a cowboy hired on at a guest ranch to "wrangle" (herd and care for) horses and take dudes out on day and overnight rides. Today, a wrangler may be male or female, a college student or a cowboy. There is no telling what a wrangler's background might be. The important ingredient is that the wrangler is experienced with horses and patient, understanding, and friendly with dudes.

Guest Ranch Associations

Arizona Dude Ranch Association
www.arizonaranches.com

British Columbia Guest Ranchers' Association
www.bcguestranches.com

Colorado Dude and Guest Ranch Association
www.coloradoranch.com

The Dude Ranchers' Association
www.duderanch.org

Montana Dude Ranch Association
www.mtdra.com

Wyoming Dude Rancher's Association
www.wyomingdra.com

Western Museums

Amon Carter Museum
3501 Camp Bowie Boulevard
Fort Worth, TX 76107
817/738-1933
www.cartermuseum.org

Buffalo Bill Historical Center & Museum
720 Sheridan Avenue
Cody, WY 82414
307/587-4771
www.bbhc.org

C.M. Russell Museum
400 13th Street North
Great Falls, MT 59401
406/727-8787
406/727-2402 fax
www.cmrussell.org

Cody Firearms Museum
720 Sheridan Avenue
Cody, WY 82414
307/587-4771
www.bbhc.org

Cowboy Artists of America Museum
1550 Bandera Highway
P.O. Box 294300
Kerrville, TX 78028
830/896-2553
830/896-2556 fax
www.cowboyartistsofamerica.com

Desert Caballeros Western Museum
21 North Frontier Street
Wickenburg, AZ 85390
928/684-2272
928/684-5794
www.westernmuseum.org

Eiteljorg Museum of American Indians and Western Art
500 West Washington Street
Indianapolis, IN 46204
317/636-9378
www.eiteljorg.org

Frederic Remington Art Museum
303 Washington Street
Ogdensburg, NY 13669
315/393-2425
315/393-4464 fax
www.fredericremington.org

Gilcrease Museum
1400 North Gilcrease Museum Road
Tulsa, OK 74127
918/596-2725
www.gilcrease.org

The Heard Museum
2301 North Central Avenue
Phoenix, AZ 85004
602/252-8848
602/252-8840
www.heard.org

Joslyn Art Museum
2200 Dodge Street
Omaha, NE 68102
402/342-3300
402/342-2376 fax
www.joslyn.org

Lea County Cowboy Hall of Fame and Western Heritage Center
Campus of New Mexico Junior College
5317 Lovington Highway
Hobbs, NM 88240
505/392-1275
505/392-5518
505/392-5871 fax
www.nmculture.org

Montana Historical Society
225 North Roberts Street
P.O. Box 201201
Helena, MT 59620
406/444-2694
406/444-2696 fax
www.his.state.mt.us

Museum of the American West
(formerly Autry Museum of Western Heritage)
4700 Western Heritage Way
Los Angeles, CA 90027
323/667-2000
323/660-5721 fax
www.museumoftheamericanwest.org

Museum of Fine Arts
107 West Palace Street
P.O. Box 2087
Santa Fe, NM 87504-2087
505/476-5072
505/476-5076 fax
www.museumofnewmexico.org

Museum of Indian Arts and Culture
710 Camino Lejo
P.O. Box 2087
Santa Fe, NM 87504-2087
505/476-1269
505/476-1330 fax
www.museumofnewmexico.org

Museum of International Folk Art
706 Camino Lejo
P.O. Box 2087
Santa Fe, NM 87504-2087
505/476-1200
505/476-1300 fax
www.museumofnewmexico.org

National Cowboy & Western Heritage Museum
1700 N.E. 63rd Street
Oklahoma City, OK 73111
405/478-2250
405/478-4714 fax
www.nationalcowboymuseum.org

National Museum of Wildlife Art
P.O. Box 6825
Jackson, WY 83002
800/313-9553
307/733-5771
307/733-5787 fax
www.wildlifeart.org

Palace of the Governors
105 Palace Avenue
P.O. Box 2087
Santa Fe, NM 87504-2087
505/476-5100
505/476-5104 fax
www.museumofnewmexico.org

Phoenix Art Museum
1625 North Central Avenue
Phoenix, AZ 85004-1625
602/257-1880
www.phxart.org

Plains Indian Museum
720 Sheridan Street
Cody, WY 82414
307/507-4771
www.bbhc.org

Pro Rodeo Hall of Fame and Museum of the American Cowboy
101 Pro Rodeo Drive
Colorado Springs, CO 80919-2396
719/528-4761
719/548-4876 fax
www.prorodeo.com

The Rockwell Museum
111 Cedar Street
Corning, NY 14830
607/937-5386
www.stny.com/rockwellmuseum

The R.W. Norton Art Gallery
4747 Creswell Avenue
Shreveport, LA 71106
318/865-4201
318/869-0435 fax
www.softdisk.com

Sid Richardson Collection of Western Art
309 Main Street
Fort Worth, TX 76102
817/332-6554
817/332-8671 fax
www.sidrmuseum.org

Stark Museum
712 Green Avenue
P.O. Box 1897
Orange, TX 77630
409/883-6661
409/883-6361 fax
www.starkmuseum.org

Whitney Gallery of Western Art
720 Sheridan Avenue
Cody, WY 82414
307/587-4771
www.bbhc.org

Woolaroc Museum
Route 3, Box 2100
Bartlesville, OK 74003
888/966-5276
918/336-0307
918/336-0084 fax
www.woolaroc.org

Annual Western Events in the U.S. and Canada

The following is a selection of annual Western events. These events and dates are subject to change. Contact the appropriate Tourism Office to verify dates.

Date	City	Event
ALABAMA		
Late January	Town Creek	National Field Trials
Early March	Gadsden	Alabama Wagon Train
	Opp	Opp Jaycee Rattlesnake Rodeo
Late March	Montgomery	Southeastern Livestock Exposition Rodeo and Livestock Week
Mid- to Late April	Bridgeport	Indian Day
	Clayton	Little Britches Rodeo
Late April	Alexander City	Lone Eagle's Legacy
	Decatur	Annual Racking Horse Spring Celebration
Late June	Clayton	Stetson Hoedown Rodeo
Late July	Selma	Selma Jaycee's Annual Rodeo
Early August	Gadsden	Boys Club Annual Rodeo
Mid- to Late August	Alabama	Indian Powwow Festival
Mid-September	Huntsville	Ole-Time Fiddling and Bluegrass Convention
Late September	Winfield	Mule Days
	Decatur	Racking Horse World Celebration
Late September to Early October	Mobile	Greater Gulf State Fair PRCA Rodeo
Early to Mid-October	Montgomery	South Alabama State Fair
	Birmingham	Alabama State Fair
	Athens	Annual Tennessee Valley Old-Time Fiddlers' Event
Early November	Montgomery	Southern Championship Charity Horse Show
Late November	Atmore Creek	Annual Poarch Band of Indians' Thanksgiving Day
ALASKA		
Early April	Juneau	Annual Alaska Folk Festival
	Valdez	World Extreme Skiing Championships
Late April	Sutton	Annual Coal Miner's Ball
	Anchorage	Native Youth Olympics
May to September	Ketchikan	Ketchikan Frontier Revue
Late May	Delta Junction	Buffalo Wallow Statewide Square Dance Festival
Early June	Palmer	Colony Days
Late June	Juneau	Gold Rush Days
Early July	Eagle River	Bear Paw Festival
Late July		World Eskimo-Indian Olympics
Early August	Fairbanks	Tanana Valley State Fair
Late August	Palmer	Alaska State Fair
	Haines	Southeast Alaska State Fair and Rodeo

Annual Western Events in the U.S. and Canada

Date	City	Event
Early November	Fairbanks	Athabascan Old-Time Fiddling Festival
	Haines	Alaska Bald Eagle Festival
Late August	Haines	Southeast Alaska State Fair and Rodeo
Early November	Fairbanks	Athabascan Old-Time Fiddling Festival
	Haines	Alaska Bald Eagle Festival

ARIZONA

Date	City	Event
Early January	Phoenix	Arizona National Livestock
	Tucson	Wrangler Bull Rider's Main
	Scottsdale	Wild Horse & Burro Auction
	Casa Grande	Annual Arizona Old-Time Fiddlers' Jam & Country Store Bazaar & Car Show
	Scottsdale	Arizona Appaloosa Assn. -
Mid-January	Bullhead City	PRCA Turquoise Circuit Finals Rodeo
	Quartzsite	Camel Races
Late January	Mesa	High Noon's Wild West Collector's Show & Auction
	Cave Creek	County Ho Down Week
	Scottsdale	Arizona Sun Country Circuit Quarter Horse Show
	Scottsdale	Jaycees' Parada Rodeo
Early February	Tucson	American Indian Exposition
	Scottsdale	Jaycees' Parada del Sol Rodeo Week
	Scottsdale	Parada del Sol Rodeo Dance
	Buckeye	Helz-a-poppin' Sr. Pro Rodeo
	Scottsdale	U.S. Team Championships
	Sierra Vista	Annual Cochise Cowboy Poetry & Music Gathering
	Ajo	Fiddlers' Old-Time Contest
	Camp Verde	Saddlebag All Women Pony
	Safford	Old-Time Fiddlers' Contest
	Wickenburg	Gold Rush Days
	Yuma	Hospice of Yuma Roping Roundup & Barbecue
	Yuma	Yuma Jaycees Rodeo
	Yuma	Silver Spur Rodeo, Parade and Fiesta
	Phoenix	Annual Native American
Mid-February	Yuma	Annual Yuma Jaycees Silver Spur Rodeo
	Scottsdale	All Arabian Horse Show and Sale
	Wickenburg	Gold Rush Days and Rodeo
	Wellton	Annual Pioneer Day Parade & Fiesta
	Benson	Territorial Days

Annual Western Events in the U.S. and Canada

Date	City	Event
Mid-February	Buckeye	Helz-A-Poppin' Senior Pro Rodeo
	Casa Grande	O'odham Tash
	Pioneer	Pioneer Celebration Days
Late February	Goodyear	Goodyear Rodeo Days
	Scottsdale	All Arabian Horse Show
	Tucson	La Fiesta de los Vaqueros Rodeo (PRCA)
	Tucson	Tucson Rodeo Parade
	Phoenix	Annual Ranch Horse Competition/Consignment Horse Sale
	Phoenix	Pioneer Bluegrass Days
	Phoenix	Annual Colors of the Sun Consignment Horse Sale
	Quartzsite	Quartzsite Maze Days "Festival in the Desert"
March	Tucson	SAILA Open & Junior Livestock Show
Early March	Scottsdale	Annual Arizona's Touch of Class Miniature Horse Show
	Scottsdale	Equine Spectacular
	Casa Grande	Arizona State Open Chili Championship
	Winslow	Annual Baca Rough Stock Rodeo
	Scottsdale	Arizona Reining Horse Classic
Mid-March	Scottsdale	Native American Festival and Art Market
	Phoenix	Jaycees' Rodeo of Rodeos
	Scottsdale	Festival of the West
	Tucson	Annual Walk Powwow
	Tucson	Annual Wells Fargo Viva Tucson Tex-Mex Jam
	Apache Junction	Annual Dons Of Arizona Lost Dutchman Gold Mine Superstition Mountain Trek
	Scottsdale	Annual Carousel Horse Show
	Phoenix	Eight Second Thunder- American West Arena
Late March	Scottsdale	Pro Rodeo Series (PRCA)
	San Carlos	Annual Powwow
	Tombstone	Annual Territorial Days
	Duncan	Greenlee County Horse Races
	Casa Grande	Pinal County Fair
	Globe/Miami	Copper Dust Stampede Rodeo
Mid-April	Cave Creek	Fiesta Days
	Kearny	Pioneer Days
	Scottsdale	Cowboys for Kids Celebrity Rodeo & Auction

Annual Western Events in the U.S. and Canada

Date	City	Event
May	Eagar/ Springerville	Marlen Rogers Family Fun Days
	Page	Lake Powell Rodeo
	Payson	PRCA Pro Rodeo
	Safford	AJRA Rodeo
May	Sonoita	Bull-O-Ramaz
Mid-May	Phoenix	PRCA Rodeo
Early May	Sedona	Cinco de Mayo
Early May to Mid-June	Flagstaff	Trappings of the American West
	Tucson	Arizona Boys Chorus Mother's Day Concert
Late May	Prescott	George Phippen Memorial Day Western Art Show & Sale
Late May	St. Johns	High Country Stampede Rodeo
	Tombstone	Wyatt Earp Days
June to August	Flagstaff	Hopi and Navajo Craftsman Exhibitions
June	Payson	Junior Rodeo
Early to Mid-June	Flagstaff	Trappings of the American West
Mid-June	Flagstaff	Pine Country Pro Rodeo
Mid-June to Early July	Flagstaff	Festival of Native American Arts
Late June	Prescott	PRCA Rodeo
July	Prescott	Frontier Days & World's Oldest Rodeo
	Tuba City	Youth Fair
Early July	Prescott	Prescott Rodeo Photo Workshop
	Window Rock	Fourth of July Celebration Rodeo & Powwow
PRCA		
	Taylor	Fourth of July Celebration
	Eagar/ Springerville	Round Valley Western July Fourth Celebration
Mid-July	St. Johns	Pioneer Days
	Snowflake	Pioneer Days Celebration
August	Chinle	Central Navajo Fair
	Fredonia	Northern Arizona Fair
August	Payson	Rodeo Parade and Dance
	Safford	Gila Valley Pro Rodeo
	Whiteriver	White Mountain Apache Tribal Fair & Rodeo
Date	City	Event
	Winslow	West's Best Rodeo
Mid-August	Prescott	Arizona Poets Gathering
	Payson	World's Oldest Continuous PRCA Rodeo
	Tucson	Desert Thunder Rodeo (PRCA)
Late August	Taylor	Sweet Corn Festival
	Payson	PRCA Rodeo

Annual Western Events in the U.S. and Canada

Date	City	Event
Late August to Early September		Sonoita Labor Day Rodeo
	Springerville	5K Cowboy & Indian Art Show
	Springerville	Valle Redondo Days
September	Dilcon	Southwestern Navajo Nation Fair
	Douglas	Chochise Country Fair
	Ft. Huachuca	Huachuca Mountain Open Rodeo
	Payson	State Championship Old-Time Fiddlers' Contest
	Safford/Thatcher	Gila Valley Cowboy Poet Roundup
	Scottsdale	Arizona State Firefighters Benefit Rodeo
Early September	Window Rock	Navajo Nation Fair
Mid-September	Holbrook	Navajo County Fair
Late September	Holbrook	All Indian Rodeo Cowboy Association Powwow
October	Benson	Butterfield Overland Stage Days
	Kingman	Andy Devine Days & PRCA Rodeo
	Marana	Founder's Day Parade & Rodeo
	Phoenix	Original Coors Rodeo Show down
	Phoenix	Arizona State Fair
	Scottsdale	Allied Signal Cliff Garrett Memorial Rodeo & Dance
	Tuba City	Western Navajo Fair
	Tucson	John Walker Memorial Rodeo
	Vail	Rincon Valley Festival-Old Spanish Trail
Early October	Phoenix	PRCA Rodeo
	Willcox	Rex Allen Days-PRCA Rodeo
Mid-October	Tombstone	Helldorado Days
Mid-October to Late November	Phoenix	Cowboy Artists of America
	San Carlos	Veteran's Memorial Fair, Pageant & Rodeo
Early November	Sells	Sells All-Indian Rodeo
Late December to Early January	Phoenix	Arizona National Livestock Show

ARKANSAS

Date	City	Event
Year-round	Toltec Mounds	Native American Events
Mid-April	Cabot	Old West Daze
Late May	Fort Smith	Old Fort Days Barrel Racing Futurity
	Crossett	Arkansas High School Rodeo Regionals

Annual Western Events in the U.S. and Canada

Date	City	Event
Late May to Early June	Shirley	Homecoming and Rodeo
Early June	Booneville	National Trails Day Equestrian Ride
	Huntsville	Hawgfest Pig Race, Rodeo, Music
	Newport	Riverboat Days and State Catfish Cooking Contest (Rodeo)
Mid-June	Mountain View	Western Music Weekend
	Calico Rock	IRA Championship Rodeo
	Dardanelle	PRCA Rodeo
	Siloam Springs	Rodeo and Parade
Early July	Springdale	Rodeo of the Ozarks
Mid-July	Clarksville	Roundup Club Rodeo
Late July	Fort Smith	Commissary Charity Hunter-Jumper Show
Early August	Mena	Polk County Rodeo
	Crossett	Rodeo Roundup Day
	Clinton	Bull Riding Spectacular
Late August to Early September	Clinton	National Championship Chuck Wagon Races
September	Clarksville	Roundup Club Junior Rodeo
Mid-September	Fort Smith	Arkansas/Oklahoma State Fair
	Harrison	Northwest Arkansas District Fair and PRCA Rodeo
Mid-September	Mountain View	Arkansas Old-Time Fiddlers' Association State Championship Competition
	DeQueen	Sevier County Fair and Rodeo
	Jonesboro	Northeast Arkansas District Fair Rodeo
	Marshall	Searcy County Fair and Rodeo
Late September	Pine Bluff	Southeast Arkansas Live stock Show and Rodeo
Late September to Early October	Texarkana	Four States Fair and Rodeo
Early October	Little Rock	Arkansas State Fair and Livestock Show

CALIFORNIA

Date	City	Event
Early January	Rancho Murietta	PRCA Rodeo
Late January	Red Bluff	Red Bluff Bull Sale/Ranch Rodeo
Mid-February	Kernville	Whiskey Flat Days
	Indio	Riverside County Fair and National Date Festival
Late February	Palm Springs	Mounted Police Rodeo and Parade
Mid-March	Red Bluff	Red Bluff Winter Roundup

Annual Western Events in the U.S. and Canada

Date	City	Event
Late March	Alturas	Livestock Market Spring Ranch Horse and Range Bull Sale
Late March to Early April	San Francisco	Junior Grand National Livestock Exposition and Rodeo
	San Jose	World's Toughest Rodeo
April	Chowchilla	Western Stampede
	King City	King City Riding Club Junior Rodeo
Date	City	Event
Early April	Oakdale	PRCA Rodeo
Mid-April	Bakersfield	Kern County Horse Show Classic on the Green
	Red Bluff	PRCA Rodeo
Late April	Auburn	Wild West Stampede (PRCA)
	Clovis	Clovis Rodeo (PRCA)
	Springville	Frontier Days
	Springville	Springville Sierra Rodeo
May	Marysville	Marysville Stampede
Early May	Borrego Springs	Cinco de Mayo Celebration
	Calexico	Cinco de Mayo Celebration
	Cottonwood	Cottonwood Rodeo Week
	Delano	Cinco de Mayo Celebration
	San Jose	Cinco de Mayo Celebration
	Santa Maria	Cinco de Mayo Celebration
	Sonoma	Cinco de Mayo Celebration
	Valley Springs	Snyder's Powwow
Mid-May	Angels Camp	Calaveras County Fair, Frog Jumping Jubilee and Rodeo
	King City	Salinas Valley Fair
	Redding	Redding Rodeo Week (PRCA)
	Sonora	Mother Lode Roundup Parade and Rodeo
Late May	Bishop	Mule Days Celebration
	Yucca Valley	Grubstake Days and PRCA Rodeo
Late May to Early June	Santa Maria	Elks Rodeo and Parade
June	Quincy	California State High School Rodeo Championships
Mid-June	Livermore	Livermore Rodeo (PRCA)
	Sonora	PRCA Rodeo
Late June	Folsom	Folsom Championship PRCA Rodeo
July	Santa Barbara	Horse and Flower Show (PRCA)
	Fortuna	Fortuna Rodeo, "Oldest, Longest, Most Westerly"
Mid-July	Merced	Merced County Fair
	Plymouth	Amador County Fair
Late July	Susanville	Doyle Days Rodeo
	Salinas	The California Rodeo

Annual Western Events in the U.S. and Canada

Date	City	Event
Early August	Paso Robles	California Mid-State Fair
	Santa Barbara	Old Spanish Days
	Grass Valley	Nevada County Fair
	Quincy	Plumas County Fair
Mid-August	Susanville	Lassen County Fair
	Truckee	Truckee Rodeo (PRCA)
	Inglewood	PRCA Rodeo
	San Juan Capistrano	PRCA Rodeo
Mid-August to Early September	Sacramento	California State Fair
Late August	Norco	PRCA Rodeo
	Ventura	PRCA Rodeo
Early September	Lancaster	Antelope Valley Fair, Alfalfa Festival and Rodeo
	Barstow	Calico Days Stampede Rodeo
Late September	Bishop	Tri-County Fair and Wild West Weekend
	Poway	PRCA Rodeo
	Bakersfield	Kern County Fair and PRCA Rodeo
Early October	Santa Rosa	PRCA Rodeo
Mid-October	City of Industry	Industry Hills Charity Pro Rodeo
Late October	San Francisco	Grand National Rodeo, Horse and Stock Exposition
Early November	Death Valley	Death Valley Encampment
Mid-November	Brawley	Cattle Call & PRCA Rodeo

COLORADO

Date	City	Event
Mid-January	Steamboat Springs	Cowboy Downhill
	Denver	National Western Stock Show and Rodeo (PRCA)
June to August	Durango	Durango Pro Rodeo Series
June to August	Steamboat Springs	Cowboys' Roundup Rodeo
Mid-June	Grand Junction	Colorado Stampede
	Colorado Springs	Pikes Peak Little Britches Rodeo
Late June to Late August	Snowmass	Snowmass Stables Rodeo
Late June	Evergreen	Rodeo Weekend
	Greeley	PRCA Rodeo
July	Canon City	Royal Gorge Rodeo
Early July	Greeley	Biggest Fourth of July Rodeo
	Greeley	Independent Stampede Greeley Rodeo
	Durango	All Girls Rodeo Classic
Mid-July	Estes Park	Rooftop Rodeo
	Gunnison	Cattlemen's Days, Rodeo and Celebration

Annual Western Events in the U.S. and Canada

Date	City	Event
Late July	Livermore	Cheyenne Frontier Days Rodeo
	Monte Vista	Ski-Hi Stampede Rodeo
Early August	Colorado Springs	Pikes Peak or Bust Rodeo
	Loveland	Larimer County Fair and Rodeo
Mid-August	Rifle	Senior Pro Rodeo
Late August	Pueblo	Colorado State Fair, Livestock Show and Rodeo
Early September	Durango	Ghost Dancer All-Indian Rodeo
Early October	Durango	Family Ranch Rodeo

DISTRICT OF COLUMBIA

Date	City	Event
Late October	U.S. Air Arena	Washington International Horse Show

FLORIDA

Date	City	Event
January to October (Last weekend each month)	Davie	5-Star Pro Rodeo Series (PRCA)
Early to Mid-February	Kissimmee	Edition Silver Spurs Rodeo
	Tampa	Florida State Fair PRCA Rodeo
	Hollywood	Seminole Tribal Fair and Rodeo
Early February	Homestead	Frontier Days Rodeo
Mid-March	Arcadia	PRCA Rodeo
July	Kissimmee	Silver Spurs Rodeo
Early July	Arcadia	PRCA Rodeo
Early September	Ocala	PRCA Rodeo
	Okeechobee	PRCA Rodeo
Late September	Tallahassee	Native American Heritage Festival
Mid-October	Orlando	Pioneer Days
Mid-October	Davies	Sunshine State Pro Rodeo Championship
Early November	Okeechobee	PRCA Rodeo

GEORGIA

Date	City	Event
Mid-April	Chatsworth	Beaulieu North American Classic
Early July	Chatsworth	Appalachian Wagon Train
Late September	Chatsworth	National Racking Horse Assocation's World Jamboree
Early October	Chatsworth	Georgia State and Red Carpet Championship Mule-Draft Horse Frolic

Annual Western Events in the U.S. and Canada

Date	City	Event
IDAHO		
Mid-March	Pocatello	Dodge National Circuit Finals Rodeo
Late April	Lewiston	Dogwood Festival
Mid-June	Weiser	National Old-Time Fiddlers' Contest
Late June to Early July	Rupert	July 4th Celebration-IMPRA Rodeo
Early July	Grangeville	Grangeville Rodeo
Early July	Hailey	4th of July Hailey Days of the Old West
	Salmon	Salmon River Days Rodeo
Mid-July	Nampa	Snake River Stampede
Late July	Caldwell	Canyon County Fair
	Glenns Ferry	Elmore County Fair, ICA Rodeo
	Montpelier	Oregon Trail Rendezvous Pageant
	Preston	That Famous Preston Night Rodeo, PRCA Rodeo
Late July to Early August, Rodeo	Grace	Caribou County Fair & Rodeo, PRCA
	Rupert	Minidoka County Fair & Rodeo
August pion- (USTRC) Northwest Finals	Caldwell	U.S. Team Roping Chamships
Early August	CascadeValley	County Fair & Rodeo
	Downey	South Bannock County Fair
	Fort Hall	Shoshone-Bannock Indian Festival
	Homedale	Owyhee County Fair
Early August	Idaho Falls	War Bonnet Roundup, PRCA Rodeo
	Jerome	Jerome County Fair & Rodeo
Early August	New Plymouth	Payette County Fair & Rodeo
Early August	Rexburg	Madison County Fair
	Rupert	Minidoka County Fair & Rodeo
Mid-August	Burley	Cassia County Fair & PRCA Rodeo
	Caldwell	Caldwell Night Rodeo
	Emmett	Gem County Fair & Rodeo
	Gooding	Gooding County Fair & Rodeo
	Montpelier	Bear Lake County Fair
	Pocatello	North Bannock County Fair
	Preston	Franklin County Fair
	Terreton	Mud Lake Fair & IMPRA Rodeo

Annual Western Events in the U.S. and Canada

Date	City	Event
Mid to Late August	Boise	Western Idaho Fair & Rodeo
Late August	Coeur d'Alene	North Idaho Fair & Rodeo
	Sandpoint	Bonner County Fair
	Spalding	Nez Perce Cultural Days
	Filer/Twin Falls	County Fair & PRCA Rodeo
Late August to Early September	Blackfoot	Eastern Idaho State Fair
Early September	Ketchum	Ketchum Wagon Days Celebration
	Lewiston	Lewiston Roundup Rodeo
Mid-September	Lewiston	Nez Perce County Fair
	Orofino	Clearwater County Fair & Lumberjack Days

ILLINOIS

Date	City	Event
Early January	Peoria	World's Toughest Rodeo
Late January	Moline	World's Toughest Rodeo
	Rockford	World's Toughest Rodeo
Mid-March	Rosemont (Chicago)	World's Toughest Rodeo
Late March	Springfield	World's Toughest Rodeo
Early September	Palestine	PRCA Rodeo

INDIANA

Date	City	Event
Mid-February	Evansville	World's Toughest Rodeo
Late October	Fort Wayne	World's Toughest Rodeo

IOWA

Date	City	Event
Early February	Cedar Rapids	World's Toughest Rodeo
Late May to Early June	Cherokee	Cherokee Rodeo
Late June	Edgewood	Edgewood Rodeo Days
Early August	Sidney	Iowa Championship Rodeo
September	Audubon	Operation T-Bone
Early September	Fort Madison	Tri-State Rodeo Festival
Mid-September	Cherokee	Cherokee Rodeo

KANSAS

Date	City	Event
Early May	Hays	Spring Rodeo, FHSU
Early June	Fort Scott	Good Ol' Days Celebration
	Garden City	Beef Empire Days
Mid-July	Pretty Prairie	PRCA Rodeo
Late July	Wichita	Mid-America Inter-Tribal Indian Powwow
Late July	Manhattan	PRCA Rodeo
Early August	Dodge City	Dodge City Days (PRCA Rodeo)
	Phillipsburg	Kansas Biggest Rodeo

Annual Western Events in the U.S. and Canada

Date	City	Event
Mid-August	Abilene	Central Kansas Free Fair and Wild Bill Hickok Rodeo
Mid-September	Hutchinson	PRCA Rodeo
Late September	Medicine Lodge	Indian Summer Days
Early October (Every three years)	Medicine Lodge	Indian Peace Treaty Pageant

KENTUCKY

Date	City	Event
Early and Mid-February	Bowling Green	Kyana Quarter Horse Show
Early February	Bowling Green	Championship Rodeo
Mid-April	Lexington	Spring Horse Affair
	Henderson	Tri-Fest
Late April	Lexington	Rolex Kentucky CCI 3-Day Event
Early May	Louisville	The Kentucky Derby
	Lexington	Kentucky Spring Classic Horse Show I
Mid-May	Lexington	Kentucky Spring Classic Horse Show II
	Lexington	High-Hope Steeplechase
Early June	Lexington	The Egyptian Event
Early July	Lexington	Lexington Junior League Horse Show
Mid-July	Grayson County	Kentucky State Fiddlin' Festival
Late July	Lexington	Wild Horse & Burro Adoption & Exposition
Mid-August	Lexington	Kentucky Hunter/Jumper Association Annual Show
	Louisville	Kentucky State Fair, Horse Show and Rodeo
	Harrodsburg	Pioneer Days Festival
Mid-September	Lexington	Annual International Rocky Mountain Horse Show
Early November	Louisville	PRCA Rodeo

KANSAS

Date	City	Event
Mid-January	Lake Charles	Calcasieu Parish Junior Livestock Show
Early February	Lake Charles	Southwest District Livestock Show and Rodeo
Late February	Covington	Dixie Trail Riders
Late March	Lake Charles	Silver Spur Riders Club
Late April	Lake Charles	Silver Spur Riders Club
Mid-May	Lake Charles	Tennessee Walking and Racking Horse Show
Late May	Lake Charles	Silver Spur Riders Club
Mid-June	Lake Charles	Silver Spur Riders Club
Early July	Lake Charles	Silver Spur Riders Club
Early August	Lake Charles	Silver Spur Riders Club
Mid-September	Lake Charles	Silver Spur Riders Club

Annual Western Events in the U.S. and Canada

Date	City	Event
October	Angola	Angola Prison Rodeo
Mid-October	Raceland	LaFourche Parish Agriculture Fair and Livestock Show
	Lake Charles	Silver Spur Riders Club
Mid-November	Lake Charles	Silver Spur Riders Club
Mid-December	Lake Charles	Silver Spur Riders Club

MAINE

January	Kingfield	White World

MARYLAND

Early May	Crownsville	Dave Martin Championship Rodeo and Anne Arundle County Fair
Early July	McHenry	American Indian Inter-Tribal Cultural Organization Powwow
Early August	Cordova	St. Joseph Jousting Tournament and Horse Show
Early September	Easton	Tuckahoe Championship Rodeo
Mid-September	Fort Meade	Southwest Fest

MICHIGAN

Mid-January	Detroit	World's Toughest Rodeo
Mid-July	Iron River	Upper Peninsula Championship Rodeo

MINNESOTA

Early February	St. Paul	World's Toughest Rodeo
Early April	Mankato	World's Toughest Rodeo
Early May	Crookston	Great Northern Horse Extravaganza
Mid-June	Granite Falls	Western Fest Rodeo
Late June	Buffalo	Buffalo Rodeo
	Park Rapids	PRCA Rodeo
Mid-July	Detroit Lake	Little Britches Rodeo
Mid-September	Shakopee	PRCA Rodeo

MISSISSIPPI

Early February	Jackson	Jackson Dixie National Livestock Show and Rodeo
and		Western Festival
Early May	Tunica	PRCA Rodeo
Late May	Natchez	Adams County Sheriff's Rodeo

Annual Western Events in the U.S. and Canada

Date	City	Event
Late July to Early August	Philadelphia	Neshoba County Fair
Mid-September	Natchez	Shriner's Pro Rodeo

MISSOURI

Date	City	Event
Late June to Early July	Kansas City	Kansas City Rodeo
Early September	Independence	Santa-Cali-Gon Days
Early August	Sikeston	Jaycee Bootheel Rodeo
Mid-August	St. Joseph	Trails West!
Early November	Kansas City	American Royal Livestock, Horse Show and Rodeo

MONTANA

Date	City	Event
Mid-January	Great Falls	PRCA Rodeo
Early February	Billings	Northern Rodeo Association Finals
Early February	Helena	Race to the Sky Sled Dog Race
Mid-February	Anaconda/Butte	Big Sky Winternational Sports Festival
Mid-March	Great Falls	C. M. Russell Auction of Original Western Art
Late March	Whitefish	North American Ski Laser Championships
Mid-May	St. Ignatius	Buffalo Feast and Powwow
	Miles City	Miles City Bucking Horse Sale
Late May	Virginia City	Spring Horseback Poker Run
	Hardin	Custer's Last Stand Re-enactment
Early June	Forsyth	Forsyth Horse Show and Rodeo
June to August	Laramie	Laramie River Rodeo
Early June to Late August	Billings	Billings Night Rodeo (nightly)
Mid-June	Bozeman	College National Finals Rodeo
Late June	Great Falls	Lewis & Clark Festival
	Hamilton	Bitterroot Festival of the American West
Early July	Red Lodge	Home of Champions Rodeo
	Butte	Butte Vigilante Rodeo Roundup
	Landers	Old-Timers' Rodeo
	Livingston	PRCA Rodeo
	Harlowton	July 4th Celebration and Rodeo
	Ennis	Fourth of July Rodeo
	Red Lodge	Home of Champions Rodeo
	Wolf Point	PRCA Rodeo

Annual Western Events in the U.S. and Canada

Date	City	Event
Mid-July	Bannack	Bannack Days
	Browning	North American Indian Days
	Deer Lodge	Western Heritage Days
	Libby	Libby Logger Days
	Polson	Kerr Country Rodeo
Late July	Lewistown	Central Montana Horse Show Fair and Rodeo
	Helena	Last Chance Stampede and Fair
	Red Lodge	Red Lodge Mountain Man Rendezvous
Late July to Early August	Great Falls	Montana State Fair and Rodeo
Early August	Missoula	Western Montana Fair & Rodeo
	Glendive	Dawson County Fair and Rodeo Red Lodge Festival of Nations
	Riverton	Fremont County Fair and Rodeo
	Buffalo	Johnson County Fair and Rodeo
	Pine Bluffs	Trail Days
Mid-August	Lewiston	Montana Cowboy Poetry Gathering
	Billings	Montana Fair
	Kalispell	PRCA Rodeo
	Plentywood	Sheridan County Fair and Rodeo
Late August	Dillon	Beaverhead County Fair & Jaycee Rodeo
	Plains	Sanders County Fair and Rodeo
	Roundup	Roundup Cattle Drive
Late August	White Sulpher Springs	Labor Day Rodeo and Parade
Early September	Reedpoint	Running of the Sheep-Sheep Drive
	Dillon	PRCA Rodeo
Late September	Libby	Nordicfest
October	Billings	Northern International Livestock Exposition and Rodeo
Early October to November		West Yellowstone Cross-Country Fall Camp
Mid-October	Billings	PRCA Rodeo

NEBRASKA

Date	City	Event
Mid-February	Lincoln	World's Toughest Rodeo
Mid-June	North Platte	Celebration and Buffalo Bill Rodeo
Late July	Burwell	Nebraska's Big Rodeo
Early July	Crawford	Crawford Rodeo
	Chadron	Fur Trade Days and Buckskin Rendezvous

Annual Western Events in the U.S. and Canada

Date	City	Event
Late July	Winnebago	Indian Powwow
Mid-August	Ogallala	Ogallala Roundup Rodeo
Late August	Sidney	Cheyenne County Fair
	Gordon	Sheridan County Fair and Rodeo
September	Bayard	Chimney Rock Pioneer Days
Mid-September	Ogallala	Indian Summer Rendezvous
Late September	Omaha	River City Roundup and World Championship Rodeo
Early October	Valentine	Cowboy Poetry Gathering

NEVADA

Date	City	Event
Every other weekend except in August	Mesquite	Peppermill Year-Round Roping Competition
Late January	Elko	Cowboy Poetry Gathering
	Reno	Biggest Little Cutting Horse in the World Competition
March	Dayton	Dayton Cowboy Poetry & Western Art Show
Early March	Carson City	Cowboy Jubilee & Poetry
	Reno	Reno Ranch Rodeo
Late March	Laughlin	USPA Invitational Rodeo
	Minden	Cowboy Culture Weekend
	Reno	Beefmaster and Romagnola Cattle Show/Sale
Early April	Logandale	Clark County Fair
Late April	Reno	Western National Angus Futurity
Early May	Reno	HN Spanish Rodeo
	Las Vegas	PRCA Rodeo
Mid-May	Reno	Nevada Junior Livestock State Show
	Las Vegas	Helldorado Days and Rodeo
	Wells	Buckaroo Rodeo
Late May	Mesquite	Mesquite Days
	Reno	Showcase of the West Horse Show
June	Pahrump Valley	Over the Hill Stampede Rodeo
Early June	Carson City	Kit Carson Rendezvous & Wagon Train
	Las Vegas	PRCA Rodeo
Mid-June	Reno	BLM Horse Event
	Reno	Wild Horse and Burro Show
Late June	Reno	Reno Rodeo (PRCA)
July	Ely	Lund Rodeo
	Virginia City	Way It Was Rodeo
Early July	Fallon	Silver State International Rodeo
	Fallon	International Invitational High School Rodeo
	McDermitt	Twin States Ranch Hand Rodeo

Annual Western Events in the U.S. and Canada

Date	City	Event
Early July	Reno	Region III Arabian Horse Show
Mid-July	Fallon	All Indian Stampede and Pioneer Days
	Reno	Convention Rodeo and Barbecue
	Reno	Dressage in the Sierra
	Elko	Silver State Stampede Rodeo (PRCA)
Late July	Elko	Native American Festival
August	Elko	Western Folklife Roundup
	Lovelock	World Fast Draw Championship
Early August	Reno	Limousin Cattle Show
	Reno	Appahann Appaloosa Horse Show
Mid-August	Reno	Nevada and Zone II Paint Horse Show
	Ely	White Pine Country Days Fair and Pony Express Days and Horse Races
Late August	Reno	Nevada State Fair
	Yerington	Spirit of Wovoka Days Powwow
Late August to Early September	Elko	Elko County Fair and Horse Races
	Winnemucca	Buckaroo Heritage Western Art Roundup
September	Lund	Duckwater Classic Roping
	Virginia City	Virginia City Camel Races
Early September	Fallon	Nevada Cutting Horse Spectacular
(Labor Day)	Winnemucca	Nevada's Oldest Rodeo & Western Art Roundup Show and Sale and Tri-County Fair
Early September	Reno	Silver Sire Breeders Horse Show/Sale
	Reno	NSHA Horse Show
Mid-September	Pahrump Valley	Harvest Festival, Parade & Rodeo
	Reno	National Reining Cowhorse Association Snaffle Bit Futurity Competition
	Winnemucca	Pari-Mutuel Thoroughbred, Quarter Horse and Mule Racing Events
Late September	Ely	Whitepine High School Rodeo
	Reno	Bullnanza
	Elko	Spring Creek Ranch Hand Rodeo
Late October	Beatty	Great Beatty Burro Races
	Carson City	Nevada Day Celebration

Annual Western Events in the U.S. and Canada

Date	City	Event
Late October	Nixon	Pyramid Lake Nevada Day Open Rodeo
	Reno	Western States Celebration
	Reno	ACTRA Team Roping
Early November	Minden	Rhymer's Rodeer Cowboy Poetry
	Reno	National Senior Pro Rodeo Finals
Early December	Las Vegas	National PRCA Finals Rodeo
	Las Vegas	NFR Bucking Horse and Bull Sale
Mid-December	Reno	Hereford Cattle Show and Sale
	Reno	American Shorthorn Cattle Show and Sale
Late December	Reno	Buck 'n' Ball New Years Eve Rodeo

NEW JERSEY

Date	City	Event
Late May to Late September	Woodstown	Cowtown Rodeo, PRCA (Weekly)
Late May to Mid-October	Netcong	Wild West City-Replica of Dodge City

NEW MEXICO

Date	City	Event
Early January	Red River	Red River Winterfest
Late February	Chama	High Country Winter Carnival
	Angel Fire	Angel Fire Winter Carnival Festival Weekend
Late March	Shakespeare	New Mexico Renegade Ride
Mid-April	Truth or Consequences	Ralph Edwards Fiesta and Rodeo
Mid-May	Deming	Fiddlers' Contest
Late May	Silver City	Endurance Horse Ride
	Cloudcroft	Mayfair Hayrides and Rodeo
Early June	Clovis	Pioneer Days Celebration and PRCA Rodeo
	Fort Sumner	Old Fort Days
	Mescalero	Apache Indian Maidens' Puberty Rites and Rodeo
	Las Vegas	Rails and Trails Days
	Farmington	Sheriff Posse Rodeo
Mid-June	Cloudcroft	Western Roundup
	Dulce	All-Indian Rodeo
	Taos	San Antonio Corn Dance
	Gallup	Lions Club Western Jubilee Week and Rodeo
Late June	Taos	Rodeo de Taos
	Tucumcari	PisRodeo de Taos Jubilee Week and Rodeo

Annual Western Events in the U.S. and Canada

Date	City	Event
Late June to Early July	Clayton	Rabbit Ear Roundup Rodeo
Early July	Cimarron	Cimarron Rodeo
	Eunice	Eunice Fourth of July Celebration and Junior Rodeo
	Santa Fe	Rodeo de Santa Fe
	Taos	Taos Pueblo Powwow
Mid-July	Carlsbad	Western Days and AJRA Rodeo
	Dulce	Little Beaver Roundup Rodeo
	Galisteo	Galisteo Rodeo
	Ruidoso	Billy The Kid-Pat Garrett Historical Days
Late July	Las Vegas	Fort Union's Santa Fe Trail Days
	Taos	Fiesta de Santiago y Santa Ana
August	Lovington	Lea County Fair and PRCA Rodeo
	Gallup	Inter-Tribal Indian Ceremonial and Rodeo
Early August	Los Alamos	Los Alamos County Fair and Rodeo
Mid-August	Capitan	Lincoln County Fair
	Santa Fe	Indian Market
Mid-August	Albuquerque	Bernalillo County 4-H Fair and Rodeo
September	Albuquerque	New Mexico State Fair and Rodeo
	Santa Fe	Fiesta de Santa Fe
Early September	Socorro	Socorro County Fair and Rodeo
	Ruidoso Downs	All American Futurity
	Clayton	Hayden Rodeo
Late September	Lovington	Days of Old West Ranch Rodeo
	Las Cruces	Southern New Mexico State Fair and Rodeo
	Roswell	Eastern New Mexico State Fair and Rodeo
Late September	Deming	Southwestern New Mexico State Fair
	Taos	The Old Taos Trade Fair
	Taos	San Geronimo Day Trade Fair
Early October	Ruidoso	Cowboy Symposium
Mid-October	Carlsbad	Alfalfa Fest (Mule Races, Largest Parade, and Hayride)
Late October	Truth or Consequences	Old-Time Fiddlers' Contest

Annual Western Events in the U.S. and Canada

Date	City	Event
Mid-November	Hobbs	Llano Estacado Party and Cowboy Hall of Fame and Western Heritage Center Introduction Banquet
Late November	Albuquerque	Indian National Finals Rodeo
Late December	Taos	The Matachines Dances at Taos Pueblo

NEW YORK

Date	City	Event
Late May	Saratoga Springs	Dressage at Saratoga
Early June	Apalachin	Otsiningo Powwow and Indian Craft Fair
	Elmont	The Belmont Stakes
	Kinderhook	Columbia County Carriage Days
Late June	Lake Placid	Lake Placid Horse Show
Early July	Sandy Creek	Oswego County Fair & Horse Show
	Lake Placid	I Love New York Horse Show
Mid-July	Brookfield	Madison County Fair
	Lowville	Lewis County Fair
	Pulaski	Cowboy Roundup
Late July	Cazenovia	Horse Driving Competition
	Queen	Thunderbird American Indian Mid-Summer Powwow
Early August	Attica	Attica Rodeo
Early August	Gerry	Rodeo
Late August	Bridgehampton	Hampton Classic Horse Show
	Howes Cave	Iroquois Indian Festival
	Rhinebeck	Dutchess County Fair
	Syracuse	The Great New York State Fair
Early September	Ballston Spa	All American Professional Rodeo
Late October	Manhattan	National Horse Show

NORTH CAROLINA

Date	City	Event
Mid-January	Raleigh	Midwinter Quarter Horse Show
Early February	Raleigh	Southern National Draft Horse Pull
Late March	Raleigh	North Carolina Quarter Horse Association Spring Show Championship Rodeo
	Pinehurst	Kiwanis Charity Horse Show
	Raleigh	Great Smokies Pro Rodeo
	Oak Ridge	Oak Ridge Easter Horse Show & Fiddlers' Convention
	Fayetteville	Shrine Club Rodeo

Annual Western Events in the U.S. and Canada

Date	City	Event
Early April	Blowing Rock	Opening Day Trout Fishing Derby
	Southern Pines	Moore County Pleasure Horse Drive Show
	Pembroke	Spring Racking Horse Show
	Pinehurst	Harness Horse Racing Matinee
	Raleigh	Appaloosa Horse Show
Mid-April	Raleigh	Easter Bunny Quarter Horse Circuit
Mid-April	Tryon	Tryon Thermal Belt Chamber of Commerce Horse Show
Late April	Asheville	Carolina Mountains Arabian Show
Early May	Statesville	Tarheel Classic Horse Show
	Asheville	Southern Horse Fair (PRCA)
Mid-May	Burnsville	Jaycees Championship Rodeo
	Monroe	Mid-Atlantic Championship Rodeo
	Raleigh	NC All Arabian Horse Show
	Southern Pines	Sandhills Combined Driving Event
Late May	Union Grove	Old-Time Fiddlers' and Bluegrass Festival
Late May	Raleigh	Southern States Morgan Horse Show
	Tryon	Tryon Horse Show
Early June	Raleigh	Capitol Dressage Classic
	Wilmington	Sudan Horse Patrol Coastal Plains Horse Show
Mid-June	Love Valley	Junior Showdown
	Raleigh	Appaloosa Horse Show
Late June	Love Valley	Frontier Week Rodeo
	Andrews	Wagon Train
	Raleigh	NC Hunter Jumper Association Show
	Pembroke	Racking Horse Show
Early July	Hayesville	Clay County Rodeo
	Sparta	Lions Club Horse Show
Mid-July	Love Valley	Junior Showdown
	Raleigh	NC State 4-H Horse Show
	Waynesville	Waynesville Lions Club Horse Show
Late July	Waynesville	Trail Riders Horse Show
	Raleigh	NC All Amateur Arabian Horse Show
	Raleigh	Raleigh Summer Hunter Jumper Show
	Asheville	Carolina Mountains Summer All Arabian Horse Show
	Blowing Rock	Blowing Rock Charity Horse Show

Annual Western Events in the U.S. and Canada

Date	City	Event
Late July	Tryon	Tryon Thermal Belt Chamber of Commerce Horse Show
Early August	Robbins	Farmer's Day & Wagon Train
	Waynesville	Fraternal Order of Police Horse Show
Early September	Mocksville	Lake Myers Rodeo
Mid-September	Monroe	Mid-Atlantic Championship Rodeo
	Raleigh	NC State Championship Charity Horse Show
Late September	Asheville	Carolina Mountains Fall All Arabian Horse Show
Early November	Pinehurst	Fall Horse Carriage Drive
Late November	Raleigh	Eastern Quarter Horse of NC Show & Futurity

NORTH DAKOTA

Date	City	Event
Early March	Valley City	North Dakota Winter Show and Rodeo
Mid-April	Grand Forks	Native American Days
Mid-May	Beach	Beaver Creek Ranch Roundup & Branding
Late May	Medora	Dakota Cowboy Poetry Gathering
Early June	Bottineau	Old-Time Fiddlers' Contest
Mid-June	Fessenden	Parimutuel Horse Racing
Mid-June	Williston	Fort Union Trading Post Rendezvous
Late June	Jamestown	Fort Seward Wagon Train
Early July	Dickinson	Rough Rider Days
	Mandan	Rodeo Days
Late July	Taylor	Taylor Horsefest
	Devil's Lake	Fort Totten Days
Early August	Sentinel Butte	Champions Ride Rodeo, Home on the Range for Boys
Mid-August	West Fargo	Pioneer Days
September	Bismarck	United Tribes International Powwow
Early September	Dickinson	NDRA Rodeo
Late September	Jamestown	Buffalo Days
Late October	Bismarck	Badlands Circuit Finals Rodeo

OHIO

Date	City	Event
Mid-January	Dayton	World's Toughest Rodeo
Early March	Cleveland	World's Toughest Rodeo
Mid-March	Toledo	World's Toughest Rodeo
October	Columbus	All-American Quarter Horse Congress

Annual Western Events in the U.S. and Canada

Date	City	Event
OKLAHOMA		
January to December	Sallisaw	Parimutuel Mixed Breed Horse Racing
Mid-January	Tulsa	Longhorn World Championship Rodeo
Late January	Oklahoma City	International Finals Rodeo
February to May	Oklahoma City	Parimutuel Thoroughbred Horse Racing
Early February	Oklahoma City	Wild Horse Adoption
Early March	Guthrie	Timed Event Championship of the World
	Tulsa	Super Bull Tour
Mid-March	Oklahoma City	Western Heritage Awards
Mid-April	Guthrie	'89er Days and PRCA Rodeo
	Oklahoma City	Centennial Horse Show
Late April	Checotah	Duvall Jackpot Steer Wrestling
May to July	Oklahoma City	Parimutuel Quarter Horse Racing
Early May	Oklahoma City	Non Pro Cutting Horse Show
Early May	Guymon	Pioneer Days and PRCA Rodeo
Mid-May	Guthrie	Ben Johnson Pro Celebrity Rodeo
Late May	Boley	Boley Rodeo and BBQ Festival
Late May	Guthrie	OCA Range Roundup
	Henryetta	Bullchallenge
	Hugo	PRCA Rodeo
	Idabel	Oklahoma Championship Chuck Wagon Races
	Oklahoma City	Chuck Wagon Festival
June to August	Pawnee	Pawnee Bill Wild West Show
Early June	Boise City	Santa Fe Trail Daze
	Yukon	Chisholm Trail Festival
Mid-June	Claremore	Will Rogers Stampede Rodeo
	Oklahoma City	National Appalo

Annual Western Events in the U.S. and Canada

Date	City	Event
ALBERTA, CANADA		
Late April	Red Deer	Silver Buckle Rodeo
Early May	Red Deer	Marching Band Festival
Late May	Alder Flats	Annual Alder Flats Rodeo & Race Meet
	Calgary	The Nationals at Spruce Meadows
Early July	Calgary	The North American: Spruce Meadows
	Calgary	Calgary Exhibition & Stampede
Late July	Red Deer	Westerner Days
	Edmonton	Edmonton Klondike Days
	Medicine Hat	Medicine Hat Exhibition & Stampede
Mid August	Jasper	Jasper Lions Indoor Professional Rodeo
Early November	Edmonton	Canadian Finals Rodeo
BRITISH COLUMBIA, CANADA		
Early June	Hazelton	Kispiox Valley Rodeo
Late June	Prince Rupert	National Aboriginal Day
Mid August	Dawson Creek	Professional Stampede & Chuck Wagon Races
	Tumbler Ridge	Grizzly Valley Days

Notes:

Notes:

Notes:

Notes:

Gene Kilgore Ranch Vacations
The leading Guide to Dude, Guest, Resort, Flyfishing, Working Cattle
Ranches & Pack Trips
2016

Ranchweb Travel Publishing
809 Broadway, Suite 1
Sonoma, CA 95476

Send all suggestions to:
Gene Kilgore Ranch Vacations
809 Broadway, Suite 1
Sonoma, CA 95476
707/939-3801
info@ranchweb.com
www.ranchweb.com

Graphics Director / Production Coordinator: Stephanie Long
Cover Designer: Stephanie Long

Printing History
1st Edition—1989
9th Edition—January 2016
5 4 3 2 1

ISBN: 978-0-692-03180-3

Front Cover Photo: David Stoecklein
© Copyright

Inside Cover Photo: Robert Holmgren
© Copyright